# PRACTICE RESURRECTION

# Practice Resurrection

## A Conversation
## on Growing Up in Christ

Eugene H. Peterson

WILLIAM B. EERDMANS PUBLISHING COMPANY

GRAND RAPIDS, MICHIGAN / CAMBRIDGE, U.K.

Published 2010 by
Wm. B. Eerdmans Publishing Co.
2140 Oak Industrial Drive N.E., Grand Rapids, Michigan 49505 /
P.O. Box 163, Cambridge CB3 9PU U.K.
www.eerdmans.com

Published in association with the literary agency of
Alive Communications, Inc.,
7680 Goddard St., Suite 200, Colorado Springs, CO 80920
www.alivecommunications.com

Printed in the United States of America

16 15 14 13 12 11 10        7 6 5 4 3 2 1

**Library of Congress Cataloging-in-Publication Data**

Peterson, Eugene H., 1932-
Practice resurrection: a conversation on growing up in Christ /
Eugene H. Peterson.
p.        cm.
ISBN 978-0-8028-2955-9 (cloth: alk. paper)
1. Bible. N.T. Ephesians — Commentaries.    I. Title.

BS2695.53.P47    2010
227′.5077 — dc22

2009037051

"Looking for Mt. Monadnock," reprinted from Robert Siegel, *The Waters Under the Earth* (Moscow: 2005), 70, by permission of Canon Press.

Excerpt from Part I of "Choruses from 'The Rock'" in COLLECTED POEMS 1909-1963 by T. S. Eliot, copyright 1936 by Houghton Mifflin Harcourt Publishing Company and renewed 1964 by T. S. Eliot, reprinted by permission of the publisher. Also reprinted by permission of Faber and Faber, Ltd.

Unless otherwise noted, Bible quotations in this publication are taken from the New Revised Standard Version Bible, copyright © 1989, by the Division of Christian Education of the National Council of the Churches of Christ in the United States of America.

*For Jan—*

*yoked together in love for fifty years*

*in the practice of resurrection*

# Contents

# CONTENTS

# Acknowledgments

I first taught Ephesians in 1965 to an adult class in my newly formed congregation in Bel Air, Maryland. The class had three members: Catherine Crouch, Betty Croasdale, and Lucille McCann. I was thirty-three; they were all in their fifties. Catherine and Betty had no schooling past high school; Lucille, a farmer's widow, never got past the eighth grade. Many scholars hold that Ephesians is Paul's most difficult letter. I set out to prove them mistaken. It doesn't take a college degree to learn how to mature in the resurrection life; it doesn't take a life of accomplishment in the professional world to grow up in Christ. I spent a year with these three women in the text of Ephesians and when the year was over realized that I had discovered the text that would comprehensively form my identity as a pastor working in a congregation in which the Holy Spirit was developing a community of saints — men and women growing up to the "full measure of the stature of Christ." Over the next twenty-six years I taught Ephesians many times over in my church. Then I was invited to be Professor of Spiritual Theology at Regent College in Vancouver, B.C. The first course I designed was formed on the text of Ephesians. I called it "Soulcraft: The Formation of a Mature Life in Christ." I taught that course every year for six years. Those thirty-two years of conversations in Ephesians (twenty-six years with my congregation, another six years in my classroom) have come together now in this book. I didn't write it by myself. Those three named women — Catherine, Betty, and Lucille — started it, but they have been followed by the comments and questions, the writing and praying of literally hundreds of unnamed Christians in congregations and classrooms, the "good soil" in which the pages of *Practice Resurrection* grew.

There are also significant others to be named: Jonathan Stine, a steady conversational partner throughout; my editors Jon Pott and Jennifer Hoffman at Eerdmans Publishing; my agent Rick Christian, president of Alive Communications; Dr. Joyce Peasgood, teaching assistant (Regent College); Dr. Steven Trotter, teaching assistant (Fuller Seminary); and pastors Michael Crowe, Miles Finch, Linda Nepsted, Eric Peterson, Ken Peterson, Wayne Pris, and David Woods.

# Introduction

This is a conversation on becoming a mature Christian, Christian formation, growing up to the stature of Christ.

All of us are born. No exceptions. Birth brought us alive, kicking and crying, into a world that is vast, complex, damaged, demanding ... and beautiful. In increments, day-by-day, we begin to get the hang of it. We drink from our mother's breast, go to sleep, and wake up. One day on waking up we stand upright and amaze everyone with our pedestrian acrobatics. It isn't long before we're old hands at language, using nouns and verbs with the best of them. We are growing up.

Jesus used the birth event as a metaphor for another kind of birth: becoming alive to God. Alive to God-alive. Life vast, complex, damaged, demanding ... and beautiful. Alive to God's holiness, God's will, God's kingdom, power, and glory. There is more to life after birth than mother's milk, sleeping and waking, walking and talking. There is God.

Jesus introduced the birth metaphor in a conversation with rabbi Nicodemus one night in Jerusalem, telling him, "You must be born from above" (John 3:7). The metaphor can also be translated "born anew" (RSV) and "born again" (KJV). Nicodemus didn't understand the metaphor, didn't get it. Literalists, maybe especially religious literalists, have a difficult time with metaphors. A metaphor is a word that makes an organic connection from what you can see to what you can't see. In any conversation involving God, whom we can't see, metaphors are invaluable for keeping language vivid and immediate. Without metaphors we are left with colorless abstractions and vague generalities.

Jesus liked metaphors and used them a lot. "Born from above" is one of his most memorable. But as Jesus elaborated on his born-from-above metaphor (John 3:5-21), we can be fairly certain that Nicodemus did eventually get it, for the next time he is mentioned, playing a major role along with Joseph of Arimathea in the burial of the crucified body of Jesus (John 19:38-40), it looks very much as if he had decided to participate in the way of Jesus. Despite, or more likely because of, the metaphor, Nicodemus was born from above. And not only born, but growing. His presence at the burial is evidence that ever since that conversation with Jesus he had been growing, growing in understanding and participation, on his way to maturity in the world of God alive.

So, birth. Then growth. The most significant growing up that any person does is to grow as a Christian. All other growing up is a preparation for or ancillary to this growing up. Biological and social, mental and emotional growing is all ultimately absorbed into growing up in Christ. Or not. The human task is to become mature, not only in our bodies and emotions and minds within ourselves, but also in our relationship with God and other persons.

Growing up involves the work of the Holy Spirit forming our born-again spirits into the likeness of Christ. It is the work anticipated by St. Luke's sentence on John the Baptist. After the story of his birth we read: "the child grew and became strong in spirit, and he was in the wilderness until the day he appeared publicly" (Luke 1:80). That is followed a page or so later by this sentence on Jesus, following the story of his birth: "and Jesus increased in wisdom and in stature, and in divine and human favor" (Luke 2:52).[1] St. Paul uses a similar vocabulary in describing the agenda he sets out for Christians in the Ephesian letter: that we "come . . . to maturity, to the measure of the full stature of

---

1. Luke adapts his summary sentence on both John and Jesus from 1 Samuel 2:26: "Now the boy Samuel continued to grow both in stature and in favor with the LORD and with the people."

2

Christ . . . grow up in every way into him who is the head, into Christ" (Eph. 4:13, 15). Or, as I have translated it: "God wants us to grow up, to know the whole truth and tell it in love — like Christ in everything . . . so that we will grow up healthy in God, robust in love" *(The Message)*.

John grew up.

Jesus grew up.

Paul tells us, "Grow up."

*     *     *

First birth and then growth. Neither metaphor stands alone. Birth presupposes growth, but growth proceeds from birth. Is it an exaggeration to say that birth has received far more attention in the American church than growth? I don't think so. It is true that the metaphor of growth is used frequently, as in "church growth" and "growing churches." But it is also obvious that the metaphor has been torn out of its origin in biology and emasculated into an abstract and soulless item of arithmetic, a usage as remote from the biblical soil as is imaginable — an outrageous perversion of the metaphor and responsible for an enormous distortion in the Christian imagination of what is involved in living in the kingdom of God.

For parents, birth is marked by joy and wonder and accompanied by birth announcements and gifts. The details, sparse as they are — weight: 6 pounds 10 ounces; length: 21 inches; name: Veronica Ann; date of birth: May 6 — are received with awed reverence. The euphoria of birth lasts a few weeks, considerably longer than the orgasm that accompanied its inception, but hardly indefinitely. For these same recently euphoric parents, growth is marked by fatigue, anxiety, panicked late-night calls to the doctor, confused decisions regarding discipline, worried conferences with teachers, puzzling over adolescent behavior and misbehavior. Birth is quick and easy (at least it seems that way to fathers — mothers have a different slant on it); growth is endless and complex.

*     *     *

I have a good friend who, shortly after I met her — she was about forty years old at the time — told me that she grew up in Arkansas poverty in a harsh fundamentalist atmosphere in abusive circumstances. She escaped family and town for California, and when she was eighteen she became pregnant. She told me how she felt: absolutely ecstatic, this life growing within her. She had never felt more "herself." She had meaning, she had joy, carrying in her womb this new, innocent, un-spoiled life — this mystery. She was no longer religious in any conven-tional sense, but she was absolutely convinced, not a shadow of a doubt, that God had created and given her this life that was within her.

She gave birth to the baby. Sheer ecstasy, beauty, goodness. She had never felt so much alive, so uniquely herself. And then, after a few weeks, she fell apart. She knew nothing about life. She didn't know what to do, was confused, bewildered, without bearings. She had no idea what to do with a baby. She started drinking and became an alco-holic. She went on to using cocaine and became an addict. It wasn't long before she was a prostitute. She spent the next twenty years on the streets of San Francisco trying to keep herself and this baby alive.

And then one day she wandered into a church. The church was empty. She became a Christian. She didn't know exactly how it hap-pened, but she knew that it *had* happened. Another pregnancy. It was an act almost as casual and unintentional as when she had become pregnant with her baby boy. She didn't yet know what it meant, but she knew that *that* was what she was. She was a Christian.

This time around she knew that she knew nothing about living, but she also knew that there wasn't going to be any more hand-to-mouth living on drugs and alcohol and sex. After poking around a bit she discovered and embraced the Christian way and gave herself to growing up into Christ, which she has been doing ever since.

But do you know what she found most difficult? American churches. Not that she wasn't welcomed. She was. She was something of a prize, a "brand plucked from the burning" — a Christian! But she also found that these American churches seemed to know everything about being born in Jesus' name but seemed neither interested nor competent in matters of growing into the "measure of the full stature of Christ."

She looked around her and saw that her new friends were doing the same thing she had done earlier, only not so obviously. These churches seemed to her to be full of ideas and projects that they used as she had once used alcohol, drugs, and sex — to avoid God, to avoid being present to life, being present to neighbor. They were doing everything religious except following Jesus. They were feeding their most childish and adolescent impulses and refusing to take up the cross of Jesus. They were not growing up in Christ. Lots of doctrine, lots of Bible study, lots of moral and ethical concern, lots of projects. But it struck her as pretty thin soup. She was alarmed by the parallels to her former life and determined to live more sanely as a Christian than she had as a pagan.

It took her a while, but eventually she found a few friends, a teacher, a pastor. She now had companions to a life of growing up to the full stature of Christ, becoming mature.

*       *       *

So — growing up "healthy in God, robust in love." That is my subject: finding and living into the form of what one psalm translation terms "the beauty of holiness" (Ps. 29:2 KJV). The formation of our minds and spirits, our souls, our lives — our lives transformed, growing up strong in God, growing to maturity, to the stature of Christ.

We cannot overemphasize bringing men and women to new birth in Christ. Evangelism is essential, critically essential. But is it not obvious that growth in Christ is equally essential? Yet the American church has not treated it with an equivalent urgency. The American church runs on the euphoria and adrenaline of new birth — getting people into the church, into the kingdom, into causes, into crusades, into programs. We turn matters of growing up over to Sunday school teachers, specialists in Christian education, committees to revise curricula, retreat centers, and deeper life conferences, farming it out to parachurch groups for remedial assistance. I don't find pastors and professors, for the most part, very interested in matters of formation in holiness. They have higher profile things to tend to.

Americans in general have little tolerance for a centering way of life that is submissive to the conditions in which growth takes place: quiet, obscure, patient, not subject to human control and management. The American church is uneasy in these conditions. Typically, in the name of "relevance," it adapts itself to the prevailing American culture and is soon indistinguishable from that culture: talkative, noisy, busy, controlling, image-conscious.

Meanwhile, what has in previous centuries and other cultures been a major preoccupation of the Christian community, becoming men and women who live to "the praise of God's glory," has become a mere footnote within a church that has taken on the agenda of the secular society — its educational goals, its activity goals, its psychological goals. By delegating character formation, the life of prayer, the beauty of holiness — growing up in Christ — to specialized ministries or groups, we remove it from the center of the church's life. We disconnect growth from birth and, in effect, place it on a bench at the margins of the church's life. Wendell Berry, one of our most perceptive prophets of contemporary culture and spirituality, wrote, "We think it ordinary to spend twelve or sixteen or twenty years of a person's life and many thousands of public dollars on 'education' — and not one dime or a thought on character."[2]

Plato formulated what he named the "universals" as the True, the Good, and the Beautiful. He held that if we are to live a whole and mature life, the three had to work together harmoniously in us. The American church has deleted Beauty from that triad. We are vigorous in contending for the True, thinking rightly about God. We are energetic in insisting on the Good, behaving rightly before God. But Beauty, the forms by which the True and the Good take shape in human life, we pretty much ignore. We delegate Beauty to flower arrangers and interior decorators. Plato, and many of our wisest teachers who have followed him, insisted that all three — Truth, Goodness, Beauty — are organically connected. Without Beauty, Truth and Goodness

---

2. Wendell Berry, *What Are People For?* (San Francisco: North Point Press, 1990), p. 26.

have no container, no form, no way of coming to expression in human life. Truth divorced from Beauty becomes abstract and bloodless. Goodness divorced from Beauty becomes loveless and graceless.

If we need a formal term for this, "theological aesthetics" will do as well as any.

\* \* \*

For most of my adult life I have protested this marginalization of matters of maturity, of spiritual formation, of theological aesthetics, of growing up in Christ "healthy in God, robust in love." I have attempted to give witness to all that is involved in its practice. Without, I must say, much success.

I have not exactly been ignored, in fact I have been treated with much appreciation; but more often than not it feels like kindly condescension. Pastors tell me that they cannot make it with an agenda like this — theological *aesthetics*? People won't put up with it, congregations will not put up with it. Not long ago a pastor who has made an art form of pole vaulting from church to church told me that I was wasting my time on this, there was no challenge to it, it was about as exciting as standing around watching paint dry.

I suggested to him that most of our ancestors in both Israel and church have spent most of their time watching the paint dry, that the persevering, patient, unhurried work of growing up in Christ has occupied the center of the church's life for centuries, and that this American marginalization is, well, American. He dismissed me. He needed, he said, a challenge. I took it from his tone and manner that a challenge was by definition something that could be met and accomplished in forty days. That's all the time, after all, that it took Jesus.

\* \* \*

For far too long now, with full backing from our culture, we have let the vagaries of our emotional needs call the shots. For too long we have let ecclesiastical market analysts set the church's agenda. For too long we have stood by unprotesting as self-appointed experts on the Christian life have replaced the "full stature of Christ" with desiccated stick figures.

So what I want to do here is engage in an extended and serious conversation with my brother and sister Christians around the phrase "growing up in Christ." And I want to bring an old and wise and trusted voice into the conversation, the voice of St. Paul, the man who coined the "growing up" metaphor. The words he wrote in a letter to a congregation of Christians in Ephesus two thousand years ago is as up-to-date as anything we are likely to hear these days, and strategically crucial for what faces us. I want him to have a major voice in the conversation.[3]

*    *    *

The resurrection of Jesus establishes the conditions in which we live and mature in the Christian life and carry on this conversation: Jesus alive and present. A lively sense of Jesus' resurrection, which took place without any help or comment from us, keeps us from attempting to take charge of our own development and growth. Frequent meditation on Jesus' resurrection — the huge mystery of it, the unprecedented energies flowing from it — prevents us from reducing the language of our conversation to what we can define or control. "Practice resurrection," a phrase I got from Wendell Berry,[4] strikes just the right note. We live our lives in the practice of what we do not originate and cannot anticipate. When we practice resurrection, we continuously enter into what is more than we are. When we practice resurrection, we keep company with Jesus, alive and present, who knows where we are going better than we do, which is always "from glory unto glory."

---

3. Not all agree that Paul is the author of Ephesians, and I don't insist on it. But to avoid the clutter of qualifications I will use the traditional "Paul" when referring to the author. A thorough and even-handed survey of all the considerations involved is in Ernest Best, *A Critical and Exegetical Commentary on Ephesians* (Edinburgh: T. & T. Clark, 1998), pp. 6-35.

4. Wendell Berry, "Manifesto: The Mad Farmer Liberation Front," in *Collected Poems* (San Francisco: North Point Press, 1985), pp. 151-52.

# I

# EPHESUS AND THE EPHESIANS

*Anyone who reads this book*
*risks losing forever any belonging that*
*he thought defined himself.*

MARGARET AVISON, *Always Now*

## CHAPTER 1

# The Church of Ephesus: Ephesians 1:1-2

*Paul, an apostle of Christ Jesus by the will of God, To the saints who are in Ephesus and are faithful in Christ Jesus: Grace to you and peace from God our Father and the Lord Jesus Christ.*

EPHESIANS 1:1-2

*[T]he church is not an ideal to be striven for; she exists and they're within her.*

GEORGES BERNANOS, *Diary of a Country Priest*

Church is the textured context in which we grow up in Christ to maturity. But church is difficult. Sooner or later, though, if we are serious about growing up in Christ, we have to deal with church. I say sooner. I want to begin with church. Many Christians find church to be the most difficult aspect of being a Christian. And many drop out — there may be more Christians who don't go to church or go only occasionally than who embrace it, warts and all. And there are certainly plenty of warts. It is no easier for pastors. The attrition rate among pastors leaving their congregations is alarming.

So, why church? The short answer is because the Holy Spirit

formed it to be a colony of heaven in the country of death, the country William Blake named, in his comprehensive reimagining of the spiritual life, "land of Ulro." Church is the core element in the strategy of the Holy Spirit for providing human witness and physical presence to the Jesus-inaugurated kingdom of God in this world. It is not that kingdom complete, but it is a witness to that kingdom.

But it takes both sustained effort and a determined imagination to understand and embrace church in its entirety. Casual and superficial experience with church often leaves us with an impression of bloody fights, acrimonious arguments, and warring factions. These are more than regrettable; they are scandalous. But they don't define church. There are deep continuities that sustain church at all times and everywhere (*ubique et ab omnibus*, as the Latin tag has it) as primarily and fundamentally God's work, however Christians and others may desecrate and abuse it. C. S. Lewis introduced the term "deep church" to convey the ocean fathoms of tradition that are continuously re-experienced "at all times and everywhere."[1] I like that: deep church.

Church is an appointed gathering of named people in particular places who practice a life of resurrection in a world in which death gets the biggest headlines: death of nations, death of civilization, death of marriage, death of careers, obituaries without end. Death by war, death by murder, death by accident, death by starvation. Death by electric chair, lethal injection, and hanging. The practice of resurrection is an intentional, deliberate decision to believe and participate in resurrection *life*, life out of death, life that trumps death, life that is the last word, Jesus life. This practice is not a vague wish upwards but comprises a number of discrete but interlocking acts that maintain a credible and faithful way of life, Real Life, in a world preoccupied with death and the devil.

These practices include the worship of God in all the operations of the Trinity; the acceptance of a resurrection, born-from-above identity (in baptism); the embrace of resurrection formation by eating and drinking Christ's resurrection body and blood (at the Lord's Table); at-

---

1. Lewis's phrase first appeared in a letter he wrote to the *Church Times* 135 (February 8, 1952): 95.

tentive reading of and obedience to the revelation of God in the Scriptures; prayer that cultivates an intimacy with realities that are inaccessible to our senses; confession and forgiveness of sins; welcoming the stranger and outcast; working and speaking for peace and justice, healing and truth, sanctity and beauty; care for all the stuff of creation. The practice of resurrection encourages improvisation on the basic resurrection story as given in our Scriptures and revealed in Jesus. Thousands of derivative unanticipated resurrection details proliferate across the landscape. The company of people who practice resurrection replicates the way of Jesus on the highways and byways named and numbered on all the maps of the world.

This is the church.

The practice of resurrection is not an attack on the world of death; it is a nonviolent embrace of life in the country of death. It is an open invitation to live eternity in time.

But the practice of resurrection, by its very nature, is not something any of us are very good at. Outsiders (and plenty of insiders too!) look at us and see how badly we do it. They observe how hit-and-miss so much of our practice is.

It is easy to dismiss the church as ineffective and irrelevant. And many do dismiss it. It is easy to be condescending to the church because so many of its members are unimpressive nonentities. Condescension is widespread. It is common to become disillusioned with the church because expectations formed in the country of death and by the lies of the devil are disappointments. Disillusionment is, as a matter of course, common.

In the face of all the easy dismissals, the widespread condescension, and the epidemic disillusionment, how are we going to maintain the practice of resurrection in the company of the men and women in the church?

This requires serious conversation, for if the church is intended as God's advertisement to the world, a utopian community put on display so that people will flock to it clamoring to get in, it has obviously become a piece of failed strategy. And if the church is intended to be a disciplined company of men and women charged to get rid of corruption in government, to clean up the world's morals, to convince people to live chastely and honestly, to teach them to treat the forests, rivers, and air with reverence, and children, the elderly, the poor, and the hungry with dignity and compassion, it hasn't happened. We've been at this for two thousand years now, and people are not clamoring to join us. We've been at this for two thousand years, and we have just been through the bloodiest and most violent century in recent history, and the present century hard at its heels seems to be hell-bent on surpassing it. Obviously, the church is not an ideal community that everyone takes one look at and asks, "How do I get in?" Clearly, the church is not making much headway in eliminating what is wrong in the world and making everything right. So what's left?

What's left is this: we look at what has been given to us in our Scriptures and in Jesus and try to understand why we have a church in the first place, what the church, as it is given to us, is. We are not a utopian community. We are not God's avenging angels. I want to look at what we have, what the church is right now, and ask, Do you think that maybe this is exactly what God intended when he created the church? Maybe the church as we have it provides the very conditions and proper company congenial for growing up in Christ, for becoming mature, for arriving at the measure of the stature of Christ. Maybe God knows what he is doing, giving us church, this church.

## The Church We Never See

Ephesians is a revelation of the church we never see. It shows us the healthy soil and root system of all the operations of the Trinity out of which the church that we *do* see grows. It does not describe the various expressions of what grows from that soil into cathedrals and catacombs, storefront missions and revival tents, tabernacles and chapels. Nor does it deal with the various ways in which church takes form in liturgy and mission and polity. Rather, it is an inside look at what is beneath and behind and within the church that we do see wherever and whenever it becomes visible.

\*     \*     \*

The Ephesus church was a missionary church established by the eloquent and learned Jewish preacher Apollos (Acts 18:24). Paul stopped by to visit this fledgling Christian community in the course of his second missionary journey, met with the tiny congregation (there were only twelve of them), and guided them into receiving the Holy Spirit. The year was probably A.D. 52. He stayed on for three months, using the local synagogue as his center for preaching and teaching "the kingdom of God" (Acts 19:8). That three-month visit, following the dramatic encounters with the seven sons of Sceva and the mob scene incited by Demetrius over the matter of the goddess Artemis (Diana), extended to three years. Paul was in Ephesus three years, pastor to this Christian congregation in formation (Acts 20:31).

Later, the name Ephesus was attached to a letter that provides our best access to what is involved in the formation of church, not so much the way the church appears in our towns and cities, but the essence that is behind the appearances: God's will, Christ's presence, the Holy Spirit's work. This, not what we do or do not do in belief and doubt, in faithfulness or betrayal, in obedience or disobedience, is what we simply must get through our heads if we are going to understand and participate rightly in any church that we are part of. This is the only writing in the New Testament that provides us with such a detailed and lively account of the inside and underground workings of the complex and various profusion of "churches" that we encounter and try to make sense of.

There are fifteen named churches in the New Testament.[2] All but two (Antioch and Jerusalem) had letters addressed to them. The Ephesian letter is unique in that it is the only one that is not provoked by some problem, whether of behavior or belief. Ephesians may have been a general church letter that circulated among the first-century congregations. The contrast of Ephesians with all the other New Testa-

---

2. Rome, Corinth, Thessalonica, Galatia, Philippi, Colossae, Smyrna, Pergamum, Thyatira, Sardis, Philadelphia, Laodicea, Antioch, Jerusalem, Crete.

ment letters is stark. All the others were written *ad hoc*. If something had not gone wrong or been misunderstood in these other churches, there would have been no letters written to them. Ephesians works from the other direction. It immerses us in the holy and healthy conditions out of which a mature life can develop.

In Thessalonica, some members of the church were so sure that the Lord was returning any day that they quit working. They sat around speculating about what kind of cloud would provide the chariot for Jesus' arrival and letting their less spiritual brothers and sisters provide them with meals. The Corinthians were a fractious crew, arguing and squabbling over various items of behavior having to do with diet and sex and worship. The Christians in Colossae were muddled in their esoteric thinking about Christ and needed straightening out. The Galatian Christians were regressing into some tired old legalisms and needed a thorough shaking up. The Romans, a mixed congregation of Jews and Gentiles, were having a hard time finding a common base in Christ. Philemon, one of the leaders in the Colossian church, had a runaway slave returned to him and required some firm counsel from Paul in how to treat him. Timothy and Titus were responsible for leading less than ideal churches and needed Paul's specific instruction and encouragement.

Sometimes we hear our friends talk in moony, romantic terms of the early church. "We need to get back to being just like the early church." Heaven help us. These churches were a mess, and Paul wrote his letters to them to try to clean up the mess.

But the dominant concern in this Ephesian letter is not to deal with the human problems that inevitably develop in church — no church is exempt — but to explore God's glory that gives the church its unique identity. The letter also gives us an adequate vocabulary and large enough imagination for living in the fullness of God's glory, living to "the praise of his glory" (Eph. 1:14). "Glory" is a large word in our Scriptures, radiating the many dimensions of God's grandeur, brightness, effulgence, and illuminating everything around it. The letter also makes it clear that none of us can comprehend this individually, each Christian picking out items that appeal to him or her, cafeteria style.

We do this as a *church*, a congregation of Christians who sit down at table together and receive in gratitude what is prepared and served to us by our Lord, the Spirit. It is as if Paul takes time out from his responsibilities for straightening out the problems of belief and behavior that have cropped up in the various churches and writes out, as clearly and completely as he can, what makes church *church*. And what comes clear is that church is not what we do; it is what God does, although we participate in it.

When we who follow Jesus enter a church and participate in its life, our understanding of the place and company we are in is strongly conditioned by what we observe and experience in this congregation and its local history, these people with their personal and collective virtues and faults. That means that none of us ever sees the church whole and complete. We have access only to something partial, sometimes distorted, always incomplete.

Ephesians provides us with an understanding of church from the inside, the hidden foundations and structural elements that provide grounding and form to the people, whoever they are, and the place, wherever it is. Ephesians documents the Trinitarian realities from which congregations are formed, however incomplete or fragmented the formation. We have the Ephesian letter before us so that even though we are surrounded with immature and deficient and incomplete churches, we can acquire a feel for what maturity is, what growing up in Christ consists of. By means of Ephesians we get an accurate account of what God is doing and the way the Spirit is working at the heart of every congregation. As such, it is a great gift of revelation. Without Ephesians we would be left to guesswork, making up "church" as we went along, and we'd be easy prey to every church fad that comes along. Without the clear vision of Ephesians we are left looking at the church through a cracked windshield marred by smudges and spattered bugs.

So we don't read Ephesians as a picture of a "perfect church" to which we compare our congregations and try to copy what we see. Rather, we read Ephesians as the revelation of all the operations of the Triune God that are foundational beneath what is visible among us and at work throughout each congregation. *This* is what makes us what we are, however imperfectly or neurotically we happen to be living it out.

\*     \*     \*

There are some who idealize the Ephesian church as the one New Testament church that had it all together. But there are two, maybe three, references that definitively prevent that. Some years after the time that Paul spent with the Ephesian congregation (Acts 19:20), he wrote a letter to Timothy, who had been sent to the Ephesian congregation to be their pastor. The first letter of Paul to Timothy is his counsel in how to deal with the Ephesian church. The picture we get from the letter is nothing remotely like an ideal congregation. The Ephesians come off the pages of Paul's letter as a talkative, argumentative gathering, engaged in silly speculations and "meaningless talk . . . without understanding either what they are saying or the things about which they make assertions" (1 Tim. 1:6-7). Paul goes over some very elementary things about appointing leaders. As he comments on the congregation that Timothy is now in charge of, Paul mentions the danger of "profane myths and old wives' tales" (4:7). He notes that "some have already turned away to follow Satan" (5:15). He warns of those who have a "morbid craving for controversy and for disputes about words" (6:4). In short, a squabbling congregation. This does not sound like a mature or healthy church.

Paul also makes a reference to Ephesus in his first letter to the Corinthians when he tells them, "I fought with wild animals at Ephesus" (1 Cor. 15:32). He doesn't specify whether these "wild animals" were inside or outside the church itself. Many readers understandably suspect that they may have been inside.

The other New Testament reference to the church at Ephesus comes from a time twenty or thirty years later, after Paul's time with them. It was during a time of persecution of the Christian churches by Rome. At the time the apostle John was pastor to a circuit of seven congregations that included Ephesus. In the persecution he found himself exiled to the prison island of Patmos. One Lord's Day he had a magnificent vision of what was going on at the time and what was going to come from it. As his seven churches worshiped week by week in these desperate circumstances, he was given a vision of a great war between good and evil that the churches were caught in, a cosmic conflict between the angels of heaven and apocalyptic beasts and a great dragon. Christians were being killed as Rome targeted the weak and impoverished churches with the raw power of swords and horses. Christians within the congregations were wavering, trying to survive by adapting to the conditions.

But there is something far greater than the raw power of Rome here. There is worship: God is on his throne, Christ is revealing his comprehensive salvation, the elders and all creation are in jubilant song and adoration, and Babylon/Rome, even while the Christians in their churches are at worship with their Scriptures and prayers, is doomed. John writes out the vision for his seven congregations. He stretches their imagination to take in everything that is going on that very day in their Lord's Day worship.

But before he lays the big picture out before them, he addresses each of his seven congregations in turn. He is a pastor and knows that each congregation has its own unique strengths and weaknesses that need to be recognized and dealt with locally, even while they are being embraced by the horizon-filling vision. Each church is first commended for what it is doing well in faithfulness to Jesus, then rebuked for what it is doing badly, and finally left with a gracious promise.[3] Ephesus is the first to be addressed. Jesus commends them for their "patient endurance" (Rev. 2:2). These are hard times, and he commends them for their magnificent stand against evil. But this is followed by a most devastating rebuke: "But I have this against you, that you have abandoned the love you had at first. Remember then from what you have fallen" (2:4-5). A congregation without love? This doesn't sound like an ideal congregation.

No, the Ephesian church is not the ideal church. A few years after

---

3. One church out of the seven, Sardis, is not commended: "you have a name for being alive, but you are dead" (Rev. 3:1).

Paul had spent his three years with them as their pastor, they had devolved into a squabbling, contentious, argumentative anarchy, and Timothy had to be sent in to bring health to their community. Thirty years or so later they showed courageous character in not caving in to the persecution, but they were conspicuously lacking in the "one thing needful." They were determined, but loveless.

\*     \*     \*

So what I want to do, for as long as it takes to read and ponder this Ephesian letter, is set aside for the time being the problems of behavior, the heresies of belief, the sillinesses of immaturity that concern us in the congregations that we belong to. These matters of bad theology and bad morals and bad manners are all addressed in other New Testament letters. I want to give Paul free rein in teaching and encouraging us as Christians-in-the-making to make the most in finding the appropriate forms for expressing who we have been created and saved to be, and to live to "the praise of his glory."

Throughout the twenty centuries in which we have been the church in various forms and conditions, Ephesians has remained the best text in the entire Bible for getting us in on what is involved behind the scenes in our congregations as we "grow up healthy in God, robust in love" (Eph. 4:16 *The Message*).

## Church Illusions and Deceptions

My understanding of church as I grew up was of a badly constructed house that had been lived in by renters who didn't keep up with repairs, were sloppy housekeepers, and let crabgrass take over the lawn. Later on, after I became a pastor, I assumed that my job was to do major repair work, renovating it from top to bottom, cleaning out decades, maybe even centuries, of accumulated debris so that we could make a fresh start.

I acquired this understanding from the pastors that served the congregation I grew up in. They never lasted long in our small Montana town.

One of my favorite sermon texts on church, preached with variations by every pastor I can remember, was from the Song of Songs: "You are beautiful as Tirzah, my love, comely as Jerusalem, terrible as an army with banners" (Song of Songs 6:4). This was a favorite text in that long-ago Montana culture to refer to church. The church was the beautiful Tirzah and the army terrible with banners. Those metaphors were filled out with glorious imagery by my pastors. For at least thirty or forty minutes our shabby fixer-upper church with its rotting front porch was transformed into something almost as good as the Second Coming itself.

Those sermons functioned like the picture on the front of a jigsaw puzzle box. Faced with a thousand disconnected pieces spread out on the table, you keep that picture propped before you. You know that if you just stay at it long enough, all those pieces will finally fit together and make a beautiful picture. But my pastors weren't that patient. Maybe they concluded that there had been some mistake in the packaging of the puzzle and many of the pieces had been accidentally left out. At any rate, it soon became obvious that there were not enough pieces in the pews of our congregation to complete the picture of Tirzah and the army terrible with banners. My pastors always left after a couple of years for another congregation, and then another, and then another. My surmise now is that they had concluded that our church was too far gone in disrepair to spend any more time on it.

Another text favored by my pastors was from Ephesians, where Christ is portrayed as cleansing the church "with the washing of water with the word" so that it might be presented to him "in splendor, without a spot or wrinkle or anything of the kind," so that it might be "holy and without blemish" (Eph. 5:26-27). But I never really took to the "spot or wrinkle" metaphor — it smacked too much of laundry day in our unglamorous dirt-floor basement with a pile of dirty laundry waiting to be loaded into our wringer washing machine, and the tedious hours my mother spent at the ironing board. Beautiful Tirzah and the army terrible with banners was the text for me, metaphors that invested church with delicious romance, this ravishing woman set alongside a fiercely fought victory over the forces of evil. The combined metaphors never failed to ignite vision and idealism in my adolescent soul. They also brought the best out of my pastors as they extravagantly embellished the metaphors.

And then I became a pastor. I found it hard to abandon my sentimentalized, romantic, crusader illusion of church. Not that I even tried. That illusion was pretty deeply embedded in my imagination. I didn't even know that it was an illusion, for by this time the illusion had developed into a delusion. I knew what the church was supposed to look like. My ordination put me in charge of the repairs, renovations, and housekeeping required to bring it up to code so that people could be inspired by the lovely Tirzah and find their disciplined place in the banner-bedecked army.

But that delusion didn't last long. I soon found that the imagery I had grown up with to form by turns either a romantic or a crusader church had changed. Sermons from the Song of Songs or Ephesians were no longer preached to eroticize or militarize the church. Bible texts were no longer sufficient for these things. New and fresh imagery was now provided by American business. While I was growing up in my out-of-the-way small town, a new generation of pastors had reimagined the church. Tirzah and Terrible-as-an-army-with-banners had been scrapped and replaced with the imagery of an ecclesiastical business with a mission to market spirituality to consumers to make them happy. Simultaneously, campaigns targeted outsiders to get them to buy whatever it was that was making us happy.

For me, these were new terms for bringing the church's mandate into focus. The church was no longer conceived as something in need of repair but as a business opportunity that would cater to the consumer tastes of spiritually minded sinners both within and without the congregation. It didn't take long for American pastors to find that this worked a lot better as a strategy for whipping the church into shape than the terrible-as-an-army-with-banners and the without-spot-or-wrinkle sermons. Here were tried-and-true methods developed in the American business world that had an impressive track record of success. Pastors, I learned, no longer preached fantasy sermons on what the church should be. We could actually do something about the shabby image we had of ourselves. We could use advertising techniques to create an image of church as a place where we and our friends could mix with successful and glamorous people. We could use media manipulation to get people to do something they were already pretty good at doing: being consumers. All we had to do was remove pictures of the God of Gomorrah and Moriah and Golgotha from the walls of our churches and shift things around a bit to make our meeting places more consumer friendly. With God depersonalized and then repackaged as a principle or formula, people could shop at their convenience for whatever sounded or looked as if it would make their lives more interesting and satisfying on their own terms. Marketing research quickly developed to show us just what people wanted in terms of God and religion. As soon as we knew what it was, we gave it to them.

\*     \*     \*

I have been a participating member of the Christian church in North America all my life (for seventy-five years at the time I am writing this). For fifty of those years I have had a position of responsibility as pastor in the church. Over the course of these fifty years I have seen both the church and my vocation as a pastor in it relentlessly diminished and corrupted by being redefined in terms of running an ecclesiastical business. The ink on my ordination papers wasn't even dry before I was being told by experts in the field of church that my main task was to run a church after the manner of my brother and sister Christians who run service stations, grocery stores, corporations, banks, hospitals, and financial services. Many of these experts wrote books and gave lectures on how to do it. I was astonished to learn in one of these best-selling books that the size of my church parking lot had far more to do with how things fared in my congregation than my choice of texts in preaching. After a few years of trying to take all of this seriously, I decided that I was being lied to.

This is the Americanization of congregation. It means turning each congregation into a market for religious consumers, an ecclesiastical business run along the lines of advertising techniques and organizational flow charts, and then energized by impressive motivational rhetoric.

\*　　\*　　\*

It turned out that I didn't have an adequate imagination to deal with either my actual experience as a participating member in a church or my vocational responsibilities as pastor. The childhood and adolescent illusions I grew up with didn't survive long as I found my way as an adult in the church, worshiping and working for the most part with decidedly unglamorous and often desultory men and women. There were always a few exceptions, but nothing that matched the lissome Tirzah or the terrible army. On the other hand, the pragmatic vocational embrace of American technology and consumerism that promised to rescue congregations from ineffective obscurity violated everything — scriptural, theological, experiential — that formed my identity as a follower of Jesus. It struck me as a terrible desecration of a way of life to which the church had ordained me, something on the order of a vocational abomination of desolation.

## The Miracle of Church

And so I set out on a search for "church" that ended me up in Ephesians. But I didn't begin with Ephesians. I began with the Acts of the Apostles in which the term "church" occurs twenty-four times, more times than in any other book in the Bible. It is also the book in which Ephesus is first mentioned.

What I noticed first of all was something that I had never taken seriously before, the exact parallel between the Holy Spirit's conception of Jesus and the Holy Spirit's conception of the church. Luke 1–2 and Acts 1–2 are parallel stories, the birth of our Savior Jesus and the birth of our salvation community, the church.

How did God bring our Savior into the world, into our history? We have the story of what he could have done but didn't. God could have sent his Son into the world to turn all the stones into bread and solve the hunger problem worldwide. He didn't do it. He could have sent Jesus on tour through Palestine, filling in turn the seven grand amphitheaters and hippodromes built by Herod and amazing everyone with supernatural circus performances, impressing the crowds with miracles of God's reality and presence among them. But he didn't do it. He could have set Jesus up to take over the work of governing the world — no more war, no more injustice, no more crime. He didn't do that either.

We also have the story of what God in fact did do. He gave us the miracle of Jesus, but a miracle in the form of a helpless infant born in poverty in a dangerous place with neither understanding nor support from the political, religious, or cultural surroundings. Jesus never left that world he had been born into, that world of vulnerability, marginality, and poverty.

How did God bring our salvation community into the world, into our history? Pretty much the same way he brought our Savior into the world. By a miracle, every bit as miraculous as the birth of Jesus, but also under the same conditions as the birth of Jesus. Celebrity was conspicuously absent. Governments seemed oblivious to what was going on.

God gave us the miracle of congregation the same way he gave us the miracle of Jesus, by the Descent of the Dove.[4] The Holy Spirit descended into the womb of Mary in the Galilean village of Nazareth. Thirty or so years later the same Holy Spirit descended into the collective spiritual womb of men and women, which included Mary, who had been followers of Jesus. It happened as they were at worship on the Jewish feast of Pentecost in the city of Jerusalem. The first conception gave us Jesus; the second conception gave us church.

It was a miracle that didn't look like a miracle, a miracle in the

4. The phrase is from Charles Williams, *The Descent of the Dove: The History of the Holy Spirit in the Church* (London: Longmans, Green and Co., 1939).

form of the powerless, the vulnerable, the unimportant — not so very different from any random congregation we might look up in the yellow pages of our telephone directories. Paul's account of the first-generation church is totally devoid of the romantic, the glamorous, the celebrity, the influential: "Consider your call, brothers and sisters: not many of you were wise by human standards, not many were powerful, not many were of noble birth. But God chose what is foolish in the world to shame the wise; God chose what is weak in the world to shame the strong; God chose what is low and despised in the world, things that are not, to reduce to nothing things that are, so that no one might boast in the presence of God" (1 Cor. 1:26-29). He still does.

Here is another way to put it: "Take a good look, friends, at who you were when you got called into this life. I don't see many of 'the brightest and the best' among you, not many influential, not many from high-society families. Isn't it obvious that God deliberately chose men and women that the culture overlooks and exploits and abuses, chose these 'nobodies' to expose the hollow pretensions of the 'somebodies'?" *(The Message).*

We talk a lot about Christ killed on a cross as a scandal, "a stumbling block to Jews and foolishness to Gentiles" (1 Cor. 1:23). I want to talk about church, this actual congregation that I attend, as stumbling block, as scandal, as absurd.

The Holy Spirit could have formed congregations out of an elite group of talented men and women who hungered for the "beauty of holiness," congregations as stunning as the curvaceous Tirzah and as terrifying to the forces of evil as the army with banners. Why didn't he? Because that is not the way the Holy Spirit works. We know that is not the way the Savior was brought into our lives. Why would the Spirit change strategies in bringing the salvation community, the church, the congregation, into our lives?

Luke is a careful writer. He writes his story of the church in Acts as a continuation of the story of Jesus in his Gospel. The way he tells the story of the church replicates the story of Jesus as it continued to be lived in Palestine, Syria, Galatia, Greece, and Rome under Roman occupation. It is the same Jesus story that is presently lived out in congregations in Norway under a democracy, in China under communism, in Zimbabwe under a dictator.

The longer I paid attention to the way Luke told the story of Jesus in his Gospel and saw the parallel to the way he told the story of the church in Acts, I was able to see the same story being lived and told in my congregation. Comprehension came slowly. Those old romantic illusions of sweet Tirzah and the terrible banners were hard to give up. And the deceptive rush of adrenaline and ego satisfaction that put me in control of a religious business were continuously seductive. Spiritual consumerism, the sin "crouching at the door" (Gen. 4:7) that did Cain in, was always there. But Luke's storytelling had its way with me, and I gradually saw my congregation on his terms. Emily Dickinson has a wonderful line in which she says that "the truth must dazzle gradually/Or every man be blind."[5]

I realized that this was my place and work in the church, to be a witness to the truth that dazzles gradually. I would be a witness to the Holy Spirit's formation of congregation out of this mixed bag of humanity that is my congregation — broken, hobbled, crippled, sexually abused and spiritually abused, emotionally unstable, passive and passive-aggressive, neurotic men and women. Men at fifty who have failed a dozen times and know that they will never amount to anything. Women who have been ignored and scorned and abused in a marriage in which they have been faithful. People living with children and spouses deep in addictions. Lepers and blind and deaf and dumb sinners. Also fresh converts, excited to be in on this new life. Spirited young people, energetic and eager to be guided into a life of love and compassion, mission and evangelism. A few seasoned saints who know how to pray and listen and endure. And a considerable number of people who pretty much just show up. I wonder why they bother. There they are. The hot, the cold, and the lukewarm, Christians, half-Christians, almost Christians. New-agers, angry ex-Catholics, sweet new converts. I didn't choose them. I don't *get* to choose them.

---

5. Emily Dickinson, *Collected Poems*, ed. Thomas H. Johnson (Boston: Little, Brown and Company, 1960), p. 506.

Any congregation is adequate for taking a long, loving look at these people. It doesn't seem at all obvious at first, but when we keep at it, persist in this long, loving look, we realize that we are, in fact, looking at the church, this Holy Spirit–created community that forms Christ in this place. But not in some rarefied "spiritual" sense, precious souls for whom Christ died. They are that, too, but it takes a while to see it, see the various parts of Christ's body right here and now: a toe here, a finger there, sagging buttocks and breasts, skinned knees and elbows. Paul's metaphor of the church as members of Christ's body is not a mere metaphor. Metaphors have teeth. They keep us grounded to what we see right before us. At the same time they keep us connected to all the operations of the Trinity that we can't see.

This is what is involved in realizing and embracing the Holy Spirit–created realities of church. We take a long and loving look at what we see right before our eyes in our chosen or assigned or last-chance congregation. And then, persisting in what we see, internalizing in our prayers as church takes form in worship and baptism and eucharist, we give witness to what we gradually but very surely know the church is in the only terms in which the Holy Spirit forms it — on this earth, this ground, this local San Diego, Wichita, Chicago ground, with these local and named saints and sinners.

Who else other than a baptized Christian has such continuous access to the story that keeps us attentive to what the Holy Spirit brings into view, into awareness — *church* as it actually is? Not a Tirzah illusion, not a "terrible as an army with banners" illusion, not the lie of a humanly managed popular provider of religious goods and services, but a congregation of embarrassingly ordinary people in and through whom God chooses to be present to the world.

This is not what the church looks like to outsiders; in fact, this is not even what it seems to be most of the time to insiders. But this is what it *is*. God does not work apart from sinful and flawed (forgiven, to be sure) men and women who are mostly without credentials.

Romantic, crusader, and consumer representations of the church get in the way of recognizing the church for what it actually is. If we permit — or worse, promote — dreamy or deceptive distortions of the

Holy Spirit creation, we interfere with participation in the real thing. The church we want becomes the enemy of the church we have.

It is significant that there is not a single instance in the biblical revelation of a congregation of God's people given to us in romantic, crusader, or consumer terms. There are no "successful" congregations in Scripture or in the history of the church.

*   *   *

But we do have Ephesians. We immerse ourselves in Ephesians to acquire a clean, uncluttered imagination of the ways and means by which the Holy Spirit forms *church* out of just such lives as ours. This is the holy soil in which we have been planted, the conditions that make it possible for us to grow up in Christ, to become mature, "healthy in God, robust in love."

## CHAPTER 2

# The Message to the Ephesians: Ephesians 4:1, 7

*I therefore, the prisoner in the Lord, beg you to lead a life worthy of the calling to which you have been called. . . . But each of us was given grace according to the measure of Christ's gift. Therefore it is said,*
  *"When he ascended on high he made captivity itself a captive;*
  *he gave gifts to his people."*

EPHESIANS 4:1, 7-8

*This letter is pure music. . . . What we read here is truth that sings, doctrine set to music . . . the most contemporary book in the Bible.*

JOHN A. MACKAY, God's Order:<br>The Ephesian Letter and the Present Time

"What we know about God and what we do for God have a way of getting broken apart in our lives. The moment the organic unity of belief and behavior is damaged in any way, we are incapable of living out the full humanity for which we were created.

"Paul's letter to the Ephesians joins together what has been torn apart in our sin-wrecked world. He begins with an exuberant exploration of what Christians believe about God, and then, like a surgeon skillfully setting a compound fracture, 'sets' this belief in God into our behavior before God so that the bones — belief and behavior — knit together and heal.

"Once our attention is called to it, we notice these fractures all over the place. There is hardly a bone in our bodies that has escaped injury, hardly a relationship in city or job, school or church, family or country, that isn't out of joint or limping in pain. There is much work to be done.

"And so Paul goes to work. He ranges widely, from heaven to earth and back again, showing how Jesus, the Messiah, is eternally and tirelessly bringing everything and everyone together. He also shows us that in addition to having this work done in and for us, we are participants in this most urgent work. Now that we know what is going on, that the energy of reconciliation is the dynamo at the heart of the universe, it is imperative that we join in vigorously and perseveringly, convinced that every detail in our lives contributes (or not) to what Paul describes as God's plan worked out by Christ, 'a long-range plan in which everything would be brought together and summed up in him, everything in deepest heaven, everything on planet earth.'"[1]

## The *Axios* Metaphor

We begin at the center, first with a metaphor and then with a text. At the center of Ephesians there is single Greek word, *axios*, on which the entire letter pivots. Translated as "worthy," the word occurs in this sentence: "I therefore, the prisoner in the Lord, beg you to live [or *walk*] a life *worthy* of the calling to which you have been called" (4:1).

*Axios* is a word with a picture in it. The Greek word *axios* in Ephesians functions as a metaphor. An *axios* is a set of balancing scales, the kind of scales formed by a crossbeam balanced on a post, with pans suspended from each end of the beam. You place a lead weight of, say,

---

1. Eugene H. Peterson, introduction to Ephesians in *The Message* (Colorado Springs: NavPress, 1993).

one pound in one pan, and then measure out flour into the other pan until the two pans are in balance. Balance means to be in equilibrium. When the flour in one pan balances the one-pound lead weight in the other, you know you have one pound of flour. The unknown weight of what is being measured in one pan is equivalent to the known weight in the other. The two items, lead and flour, are *axios* — worthy. They have the same value, or, in this case, weight. They can be as different as lead and flour, but they "fit," like a pair of shoes fits a man's feet, like a dress fits a woman's body, like a crescent wrench fits the head of a nut, like a wedding ring fits the finger of the beloved.

The items balanced in the Ephesians scales are God's calling and human living: "I beg you," writes Paul, "to *walk (peripateo)* worthy of the *calling* to which you have been *called (kaleo)*." When our walking and God's calling are in balance, we are whole; we are living maturely, living responsively to God's calling, living congruent with the way God calls us into being. *Axios,* worthy — mature, healthy, robust.

The balancing scales, the *axios,* centers the Ephesian letter. Everything in Paul's letter is designed to keep God's calling (chapters 1–3) and our walking (chapters 4–6) in equilibrium. We cannot measure ourselves by examining ourselves in terms of ourselves, by evaluating ourselves against a non-relational abstraction such as "human potential." Nor can we abstract God into an impersonal "truth" apart from our hearing and responding to the words he uses to call us into life, into holiness, into relationship. We can understand neither God nor ourselves in any living, adequate, and mature way that is an impersonal, non-relational way. When God's calling and our walking fit, we are growing up in Christ.

God calls; we walk.

*    *    *

Calling. God calls us. He doesn't hand out information to us. He doesn't explain. He neither condemns nor excuses. He calls.

Adam in the garden disobeyed God's command and broke the intimacy that had been created by God's speech. The equilibrium between God's word and Adam's walk was destroyed. God called again and placed him in the balancing scales, began the process of getting Adam back in relationship with the word that made him in the first place, setting him again in a position of responsiveness to God's calling.

Abraham in Ur was called by God to leave his country and go to Canaan. There he would initiate the formation of a people of salvation. Abraham set out, walked westward across the desert. The call and the walk combined became the dynamic responsiveness that resulted in Abraham becoming our father in the faith.

Moses tending sheep in Midian was called by name at the burning bush: "Moses! Moses!" He heard his name called and learned the name of the One who called him: "Yahweh." Moses' personal response, his "walk," to that personal call at the burning bush developed into a congregation of people walking out of Egypt through the sea into freedom.

Jesus on the shores of Galilee called four disciples by name. Jesus kept calling: the four soon became twelve. They followed him up and down the roads of Galilee, listening, obeying, questioning, observing, praying. Later, after they had become accustomed to the sound of his voice, Jesus called them again. This time the call was to take up their cross and follow him to his cross, his death in Jerusalem. They heard the call and walked with him. In the fusion of Jesus' call and their walk, they became the company that the Holy Spirit formed into the church.

A man named Saul walking on the road to Damascus to persecute Christians was stopped in his tracks by a voice that addressed him by name: "Saul! Saul!" Like Moses 1,200 years before him, he learned the name of the One who called him by name; this time the name of the One who called was "Jesus." And in that calling Saul's very name was changed. Saul was converted on the spot from chasing Jesus down to being a follower — Jesus' call and Saul's response became Paul's walk, now in an easy rhythm.

God speaks the decisive word that puts us on the way, the road, the path of life. The Hebrew word for Bible is *Miqra*, a noun formed from the verb "to call," *qara*. The Bible is not a book to carry around and read for information on God, but a voice to listen to. I like that. This word of God that we name Bible, book, is not at root a word to be read and looked at and discussed. It is a word to be listened to and obeyed, a word that gets us going. Fundamentally, it is a call: God calls us.

*       *       *

The response to calling is walking. Walk is what we do. We follow God's call. We respond with our lives. We don't start out by thinking about God. God is not an idea. We hear and respond. We obey. But the obedience is not a trained Pavlovian response to a stock stimulus: "sit," "fetch," "roll over." It takes place in a textured context and personal relationship. It is the act of following a personally addressed command or invitation. We hear our name and respond to the named One who calls us.

A call is not an impersonal cause that makes something happen in a mechanical way in obedience to the laws of physics, like a baseball that is launched by a swung bat knocking it out of the ballpark. Call comes into our ears, beckoning us into the future, bringing us into a way of life that has never been experienced in just this way before: a promise, a new thing, a blessing, our place in the new creation, a resurrection life.

When the calling and walking are in equilibrium, we are worthy. We are in the balancing scales, in sensitive and simultaneous touch with the God whose name we know and the God who knows our name. God calls; we walk.

The balancing scales do not provide a picture of something rigidly static, an achievement that once achieved is welded into place. The usefulness of the metaphor is in keeping us alert to the delicate, sensitive connection between call and walk, a relation that is never one-sided but always reciprocal. This is what it means to grow up in Christ, to live into maturity, to be *axios*, worthy, healthy.

As our language matures in these God-initiated conversations along the Christian way, they become increasingly personal. We often start out looking for information *about* God, but we soon find ourselves developing the language of intimacy *with* God, God's personal language of revelation in colloquy with our personal language of listening obedience. God's voice and our ears are in organic intimacy. We acquire a feel for the intricacies that are involved when God's speaking and our walking mesh. The *axios* metaphor prevents our language and our lives from diminishing in this constant, listening, responsive quality.

If language is reduced to information or flattened into explanation, that is, if it loses its connection with a living voice, calling and commanding and blessing, and if there are not open ears, listening and responding and believing, language goes dead. Words, lively verbs and luminous nouns, severed from the living voice soon become dead leaves blown around by the wind.

*     *     *

But as our language becomes more personal it also becomes more *inter*-personal. This is a multi-voiced conversation. It cannot be narrowed down, reduced, to a private Jesus-and-me-in-the-garden-alone exchange of words. There are, to be sure, plenty of occasions when we are by ourselves on the road, listening and speaking, hearing the "still small voice," and whispering responsively to our Lord. These are authentically precious moments, but we soon learn that we cannot have Jesus all to ourselves. If we are to get in on all that is going on in this adventure called life that we live responsively into, we must extend the conversation to include the others whom God is calling, the others who are walking in response to the call. The life into which we grow to maturity in Christ is a life formed in community.

The Ephesians letter shapes our imaginations to an awareness not only of ourselves but of all the other pilgrims on the road in simultaneous diversity and unity. This company of called fellow-travelers, all different and all one, is the church. Paul's metaphor for it is a human body to which Christ is the head, "the body of Christ" (Eph. 4:12). Everybody different, everyone organically connected. Shimmering diversity and harmonic unity — "joined and knit together by every ligament" is Paul's vivid metaphor (4:16). "Christ and the church" (5:32) is

35

the paradigmatic form for this multitudinous and yet improbably unified company.

Common worship, that is, corporate worship (worship "in common"), gives the basic form and provides the essential content for this aspect of "growing up" to the "full stature of Christ." Private worship while alone in semi-paralysis before a TV screen is not mature worship. Certainly we can worship in solitary. Some of our richest moments of worship will come while strolling on a beach or wandering in a garden or perched on a mountain peak. What we must not do is deliberately exclude others from our worship or worship selectively with like-minded friends. These are not options on offer in Ephesians. Maturity develops in worship as we develop in friendship with the friends of *God*, not just *our* preferred friends. Worship shapes us not only individually but as a community, a church. If we are going to grow up into Christ we have to do it in the company of everyone who is responding to the call of God. Whether we happen to like them or not has nothing to do with it.

\*　　\*　　\*

Here is another metaphor that provides an image for the common worship that develops out of the equilibrium of Paul's *axios*. This one comes from Wallace Stevens's poem, "Anecdote of the Jar."

> I placed a jar in Tennessee,
> And round it was, upon a hill.
> It made the slovenly wilderness
> Surround that hill.
>
> The wilderness rose up to it,
> And sprawled around, no longer wild.
> The jar was round upon the ground
> And tall and of a port in air.
>
> It took dominion everywhere.
> The jar was gray and bare.

It did not give of bird or bush,
Like nothing else in Tennessee.[2]

The jar is placed on a hill in Tennessee. Simply by sitting there it brings order to the wilderness world. There is nothing elegant about the jar. It is an artifact, something made, to the inattentive eye devoid of elegance ("gray and bare"). And yet, just by being there, it centers the weeds and underbrush, "the slovenly wilderness."

This jar is a companion metaphor to Paul's body of Christ metaphor, to affirm what happens when the church worships, when this unassuming gathering of men and women, called and following God, gathers to worship.

One of the common dismissals of worship is that it is, well, so common. It is boring, nothing happens — "I don't get anything out of it." And so well-meaning people decide to put adrenaline in it.

What I find useful in the metaphor of the jar is that it, like worship, isn't intended to make anything happen. Worship brings us into a presence in which God makes something happen.

Unpretentious common worship brings this kind of order to common life, life in common with others. Existence as we experience it is a kind of chaos. Things happen with apparent unpredictability and in a disorderly way. Life is a constant struggle against this disorder, and so we attempt to impose some kind of order upon it with our clocks and watches, our schedules and rules. The natural energies of living tend toward chaos. Physicists give it an imposing name, "The Second Law of Thermodynamics": left to themselves, things tend to fall apart. The most well-constructed and well-organized household, if lived in without housecleaning, straightening, and repair work, in a very short time becomes disorderly, slovenly, and what some people would call "unlivable." Most of us have routines that impose order upon these disorderly energies by dusting, bed-making, weeding the garden, washing the dishes, carrying out the trash.

2. Wallace Stevens, "Anecdote of the Jar," in *The Oxford Book of American Verse*, ed. F. O. Matthiessen (New York: Oxford University Press, 1950), p. 630.

Common worship functions this way in our lives in response to God's call. But it is not an imposed order. The order of worship works its way into the disorder almost imperceptibly as we sing and pray together, listen and obey and are blessed.

It is important to note the kind of order that is introduced. It is not the so-called order of creation as narrated in Genesis 1–2, finding a place for everything and putting everything in its place: the orderliness of the seven creation days, the orderliness of man and woman in the garden. Worship does not rearrange existence according to Genesis 1–2. It does not try to go back previous to human sin and clamp society into the nice clean divisions in which the cosmos was once organized.

Rather, the order is one of redemption, an order of reciprocal love rather than an imposed order of law. Worship is not first of all telling people how they must live. It calls us into the presence of the redeeming Christ and provides us with a community of appropriate response. The life of worship is comprised of prayer and praise, proclaiming and listening to the word (the voice!) of God, baptism and eucharist. None of these can be imposed by Christians on Christians. Worship is that jar, an unembellished, unobtrusive presence that without fanfare or coercion, without calling undue attention to itself, creates order by simply being there. It is the farthest thing imaginable from being a fence.

\*     \*     \*

So, here it is: St. Paul's metaphor of the balancing scales, holding the polarities of calling and walking together, with a little help from Wallace Stevens's metaphor of the jar in Tennessee, as a witness to the ordering power of Presence in a wilderness culture. Together they are two complementary metaphors of the church at work and worship.

Worship uses personal, conversational language to nurture the recognition of our essential capacity for hearing ourselves personally addressed (called) by the voice of God. It then treats us with the dignity of being able to live (walk) worthily, that is, appropriately, into the calling. It makes certain that we know that we are never isolated in this calling/walking life. We are all necessarily in relation to one another. What each of us does affects all the others. When we hear and respond to God, we usually do it alone but implicitly always in community, whether we are in the same room with others or not.

And worship is a quiet but insistent witness to the ordering presence of God in a company of people, who just by being themselves in a particular place, "a jar in Tennessee," center the landscape.

Worship is the most characteristic act of the Christian community as it makes itself at home in the conditions conducive to growing to maturity in Christ.

## The Psalm 68 Text: "You ascended the high mount . . ."

Paul's *axios* metaphor is matched in imaginative energy by his choice of a text to anchor his message in a spirituality of maturity. The text is taken from Psalm 68, a most vigorous, celebratory catalog of God's magnificent acts of salvation pulled together into an equally magnificent act of worship. Paul selects a stanza (vv. 17-20) from the center of the psalm for his text:

> With mighty chariotry, twice ten thousand,
>> thousands upon thousands, the Lord came from Sinai
>> into the holy place.
> You ascended the high mount,
>> leading captives in your train
>> and receiving gifts from people,
> even from those who rebel
>> against the LORD God's abiding there.

The psalm begins with an urgent invocation: "Let God rise up, let his enemies be scattered." God does it; he does rise up. Stanza after stanza proclaims God in action: he is sovereignly majestic ("who rides upon the clouds," vv. 1-4) as his enemies flee; he marches through a wilderness world rescuing widows and orphans, the homeless and prisoners, in a lavish display of salvation ("rain in abundance, O God," vv. 5-10); he commands a host of prophets to proclaim the great gospel reversal ("the tidings") as the arrogant powerful and the left-behind weak change places ("the women at home divide the spoil," vv. 11-14); rugged mountains, accustomed to dominating the landscape, are astonished at the throne-mountain ("the mount that God desired for his abode," vv. 15-16) that puts them in the shadows; in his triumphant ascent to the heights, laden with gifts from friend and foe, he gathers the saved around him ("daily bears us up," vv. 17-23) to share his triumph. God is on a salvation march through the country of the dead and the damned, taking captives on the way.

Abruptly this wide-ranging Psalm 68 documentary of God in saving action (vv. 1-23) shifts to a comprehensive act of worship in the sanctuary (vv. 24-35). All that God is and does — riding the clouds, transforming the wilderness, commanding the prophetic proclamation of good news, taking charge once and for all by ascending the "high mount" — is brought together in a worshiping procession of singers and musicians into the sanctuary, bringing gifts, acclaiming blessings. All of this now comes into final focus in a renewed attention to the voice, the "mighty voice," that changes the world from oppression and damnation into a salvation world and (this is the final sentence in the psalm) "gives power and strength to his people."

The sanctuary is the setting for this worship: worship begins in the sanctuary (v. 24) and ends in the sanctuary (v. 35). Sanctuary is a set-apart place consecrated for worship, paying reverent attention to who God reveals himself to be and how he reveals himself in our history. The sanctuary is also a theater in which we find our place and our part for participating in the wide-ranging salvation drama. This Psalm 68 worship is not merely watching, not a show-and-tell about God at work. Nor is it a workshop for figuring out how God goes about his work. Psalm 68 worship is a listening attentiveness to God in word and action, which develops into glad participation in that word and action.

The final, God-activated verb in the sanctuary is *give* (v. 35). God *gives* to his people. Who God is and what God does, his "power and strength," are given to us, his people. The people receive it all and run with it, singing and playing tambourines, from the least of them, Benjamin, in the lead to the high-profile princes of Judah and Zebulun following behind.

\* \* \*

My sense is that Paul has absorbed Psalm 68 whole in his meditations and prayers. He not only takes the text for his Ephesian letter from Psalm 68 but finds in the psalm a structure that gives literary and theological shape to what he writes: first in a thorough meditative immersion in the action and word of God (chapters 1–3), which then takes form in a worship-generated life of believing obedience (chapters 4–6).

The *axios* metaphor and the Psalm 68 text reinforce one another by knitting, the way a broken bone is knit together, the call of God and the walk of God's people into a living organism. This is not an arbitrary or programmatic juxtaposition of two parts. Maturity is not a patch-work affair assembled out of bits and pieces of disciplines and devotions, doctrines and causes. It is all the operations of the Trinity in the practice of resurrection.

\* \* \*

But here is something that you may have noticed. Paul does not translate his Psalm 68 text literally but condenses and adapts it to refer to Jesus. The way he condenses and adapts is heuristic, that is, it discovers meanings in the text that we might otherwise have missed. He does this in two ways.

His translation runs,

> When he ascended on high
>> he made captivity itself a captive;
> he gave gifts to his people.

His first adaptation makes Jesus the subject of the verb "ascended." The psalm text most probably refers to a great enthronement festival in which the Hebrews celebrated God's sovereign rule and victory over all enemies. But in the process of translation, Paul changes pronouns: he replaces the *"you* [God] ascended" with "when *he* [Jesus] ascended." He puts the psalmic hymn of worship of God on his throne into service as a witness to Jesus' ascension, Jesus' ascension into heaven — "to the right hand of the Father" as Scripture tells us (Acts 2:25, 33, etc.).

Following Jesus' resurrection, his followers had forty days to be present with him and listen to his voice, listen to him "speaking about the kingdom of God." They needed every single day they had with him in order to thoroughly assimilate the here-and-now, flesh-and-blood, body-and-soul, on-the-ground details and implications of resurrection, not only for Jesus but for themselves — resurrection not only as a promise of life beyond death but as a presence now.

Hallucinations can't be maintained for forty days. Dreams don't last forty days. Religious hysteria cannot be sustained for forty days. Those forty days grounded Jesus' resurrection as a life to be lived on streets, in homes, with families and neighbors — a life *they*, his followers, will live. And not as a private "spiritual" experience, but historically in the company of all of Jesus' followers in workplace and politics, in the carnage of war and the quietness of worship.

Before leaving his disciples, Jesus ordered them to stay in Jerusalem and wait for the "promise of the Father." He was explicit about the promise: "you will receive power when the Holy Spirit has come upon you; and you will be my witnesses" (Acts 1:8).

And then he left them. They watched him go. A chariot cloud took him to heaven out of their sight (Acts 1:9-11). They never saw him again. Ten days later the promise was kept. Ten days after Jesus ascended from Bethany, the Holy Spirit, as promised, descended on the assembled disciples in Jerusalem. Charles Williams described it as theological trigonometry, the "meeting of two heavenward lines, one drawn from Bethany along the Ascent of Messias, the other from Jerusalem against the Descent of the Paraclete."[3] Those lines, drawn up-

---

3. Charles Williams, *The Descent of the Dove* (London: Longmans, Green, 1939), p. 1.

ward into the bright cloud of Ascension and descending in the rushing wind of Pentecost, mark the beginning of the church at a point in place and time. The lines of ascent and descent connect the vast horizon of heaven to the church on earth, forming an immense equilateral triangle of eternity: a trigonometry measuring the profound operations of the Trinity. The Ephesian church, and ours, is a result of its actual beginning, and ending, in heaven. All that we see of the church, and the world for that matter, is always a result.

Ascension may be one of the most under-celebrated events in the church's life. Part of the reason is that Ascension Day always falls on Thursday, never on a Sunday, and so no sermon is required. Luther said that the creedal "right hand of the Father" means "everywhere." That throne relativizes and marginalizes all earthly thrones and all the world's politics. The Ascension of Jesus prevents us from reducing the rule of Jesus to my heart as his throne. It is that, too, but much, much more.

In order to keep the Ascension of Jesus in sharp focus, the church has commonly used Psalm 47 to shape our response to all that is involved. The psalm sets a scene of joyful triumph:

> God has gone up with a shout,
>   the Lord with the sound of a trumpet. . . .
> Sing praises to our King, sing praises. . . .
> God is king over all the earth;
>   God sits on his holy throne.
>
> (Ps. 47:5, 6, 8)

The same Jesus who just over forty days earlier had been crowned "King of the Jews" on his Golgotha throne is now ruling from heaven's throne. Everything he said and did in Roman-occupied Palestine is now being spoken and acted upon from "on high."

When Paul's companion Luke set out in Acts to tell us the story of the church, he began with Jesus' Ascension. Ascension is the opening scene that establishes the context for everything that follows: Jesus installed in a position of absolute rule — Christ our King. All men and women live under the rule of Jesus. This rule trumps all other thrones and principalities and powers.

Knowing this, with the knowing elaborated and deepened in worship, the church has the necessary room to live robustly under the conditions of resurrection. If we don't know this, the church, its imagination conditioned by death and the devil, will live timidly and cautiously.

Paul places the Ascension focus that Luke established at the threshold of the story of the church's birth and early development by repeating the Ascension imagery, "he *ascended* on high," as his orienting text for lives formed into a mature resurrection life: the resurrected Jesus rules church and world and every last one of us from heaven's strategic center. *That* he rules is basic belief; the *way* he rules is subjected to numerous squabbles among Christians who insist on replacing a personal Lord with an impersonal doctrine.

*    *    *

The other adaptation that Paul makes to his Psalm 68 text is a change of verbs. He changes the psalmist's *"received gifts"* to *"gave gifts."*

In Psalm 68 God the King rides in triumphant procession from Sinai to the "holy place," leading captives and receiving gifts from both friend and foe. He is showered with gifts from those who worship him. His enemies, "those who rebel," also bring tribute, acknowledging his impossible-to-dispute rule. Later in the psalm the gift theme is picked up again in the phrase "kings bear gifts to you" (v. 29), as God is enthroned in the temple, the place of worship.

This is what you do when a king is enthroned: you bring gifts. Your gifts are evidence of your joy at having such a beloved king. Or, if you are a rebel and not happy about this king, your gift is a symbolic, albeit reluctant, giving up of your self-sovereignty. In either case, gifts acknowledge the festivity of the day, a festivity in which everyone is involved, whether you are eager to be so or not.

Most of the readers (or listeners) to Paul's message to the Ephesians would be familiar with Psalm 68, especially the Jews who had grown up with the psalms as their prayerbook. Would there have been a startled, even shocked, surprise at hearing "gave" instead of "received"? I think so. It would, at the least, catch their attention. Had Paul nodded? Was his memory failing?

I think not. Paul is intentional and deliberate in his diction. Paul knows exactly what he is writing. He wants the Ephesians, and us, to read that word "gave" in such a way that we will never forget it.[4]

Yes, kings receive gifts at their coronation. Yes, worship of our glorious God and King involves bringing our gifts. Yes, reverent homage is properly and rightly observed in the presentation of our very best. Giving to God and to one another is well established as an integral part of every life. And God receives what we bring. The Magi brought gifts as an offering to the cradled king Jesus as an act of worship. Jesus received the gift of a boy's five loaves and two fish and then continued the giving by feeding the five thousand, who understood it as a coronation banquet and were about to make him king (John 6:15). Jesus received the gifts of bread and wine at the Last Supper and gave them back to his disciples as his flesh and blood.

But Paul wants us to see Jesus, the ascended king at the right hand of the Father, not as the king who receives gifts (although he does that too) but as the king who gives gifts. He changes the verb from the expected "receive" to the gospel "give."

*   *   *

Paul wants us to grow up to "the measure of the full stature of Christ" (Eph. 4:13). A primary condition for developing into maturity is that we take up responsibilities commensurate with our strength and understanding as we grow up and "no longer be children" (4:14). A precondition for exercising these responsibilities in Christ is receiving the Spirit

---

4. Not everyone agrees. Some conjecture that Paul was drawing on other translations (Aramaic Targums and Syriac Peshitta) of the Hebrew text that also make the change. Others maintain that the "give" is implicit in "receive" and so is semantically equivalent. See Markus Barth, *Ephesians*, Anchor Bible, vol. 34A (Garden City, NY: Doubleday, 1974), pp. 473-75.

of Christ. He gave us his Spirit, his gift of himself. He poured out his Spirit on the day of Pentecost, ten days after his Ascension.

Paul lays out the conditions in which we grow up, namely, in a profusion of gifts: "When he ascended on high . . . he gave gifts to his people." The ascended Jesus, Jesus at the right hand of the Father, Christ the King, launched his rule by giving gifts, gifts that turn out to be ways in which we participate in his kingly, gospel rule. This kingdom life is a life of entering more and more into a world of gifts, and then, as we are able, using them in a working relationship with our Lord.

We understand gift language well enough. We begin as gift. We don't make ourselves. We don't birth ourselves. We find our fundamental identity as a gift. And then, immediately, we are given gifts: gifts of love and food and clothing and shelter, gifts of healing and nurture and education and training. "What do you have that you did not receive? And if you did receive it, why do you boast as though you did not?" (1 Cor. 4:7 NIV). "Isn't everything you *have* and everything you *are* sheer gifts from God?" *(The Message)*. Gradually these gifts develop into the strengths and responsibilities of maturity. Infants are totally dependent on parents, but as children we gradually learn to dress and feed ourselves, make independent decisions, take initiative. Adolescence is the critical transition between childhood and adulthood. It is an awkward and often turbulent time as we learn to incorporate the gifts that we have been given into adult responsibilities. We have been given much. Now we begin exercising these gifts in community. We gradually learn to live what we have been given wisely and well. We grow up.

Paul introduces his Ascension text with the phrase: "each of us was given grace according to the measure of Christ's gift" (Eph. 4:7). Grace *(charis)* is a synonym for gift. And this gift is not given sparingly, not a token gift, but "according to the measure of Christ's gift." I take "measure," which he later expands to "that he might fill all things" (v. 10), to carry a sense of extravagance and exuberance. If we are to become mature, we must gradually but surely realize ourselves as gift from first to last. Otherwise we will misconceive our creation as self-creation and end up in some cul-de-sac or other of arrested development.

Paul enumerates five gifts: apostles, prophets, evangelists, pastors, teachers. Each gift is an invitation and provides the means to participate in the work of Jesus. These are not gifts to be placed on a mantle like a vase of flowers. These are not gifts to be used for our convenience like, say, a cell phone. These are not gifts to divert or entertain us, like a gift of tickets to the symphony. These are not gifts of appreciation like an anniversary ruby necklace or a retirement Rolex. These are gifts that equip us to work alongside of and in company with Jesus — "the work of ministry, for building up the body of Christ" (Eph. 4:12). We are being invited into a working relationship in the operations of the Trinity.

This is important to understand. Too often the gifts have been understood individually, conferred on us to be used as we have willingness and aptitude and inclination. This is wrong. The work is the work of the Trinity: Father, Son, and Holy Spirit. We may be fellow-workers with Jesus. But implicit in each gift is an assignment. And we share the work with one another. It is not as if these are job descriptions for specialized tasks. These are aspects of the work that is initiated at the Pentecostal "descent of the Dove," and *then* spills over into the world. Any one of us, at any one time, may be given any of the jobs. We are in on this together. This is not specialty work — this is the community at work.

Paul loves listing gifts. Five times he lists gifts that the ascended Christ gives ("gave gifts to his people"). In addition to the five he lists in Ephesians (apostles, prophets, evangelists, pastors, teachers), he lists nine gifts in 1 Corinthians 12:4-19: utterance of wisdom, utterance of knowledge, faith, gifts of healing, working of miracles, prophecy, discernment of spirits, various kinds of tongues, the interpretation of tongues. He lists eight in 1 Corinthians 12:28-29: apostles, prophets, teachers, deeds of power, healing, assistance, leadership, tongues. He lists five in 1 Corinthians 14:26: hymns, lessons, revelations, tongues, interpretations of tongues. In Romans 12:6-8 he lists seven: prophecy, ministry, teachers, exhorters, givers, leaders, compassion. In addition to these five lists he refers in several other places to gifts, named and unnamed. John Stott counts "at least twenty distinct gifts," noting that some are very prosaic and unsensational, such as "doing acts of mercy" (Rom. 12:8).[5] No one list is complete. Several items are repeated in the listings. Some refer to the person exercising a gift, others to the gift itself. There is a continuous concern interwoven in the listings: though there is a variety of gifts given by the Spirit, there is one Spirit. The diversity of gifts adds up to a unity of function. There can be no rivalry among either gifts or the gifted.

Considerable attention has been given to the details regarding the nature of each gift and the way it is used in the company of God's people.[6] But my concern right now is to establish the overall Ephesian context in which the gifts are given. What Paul insists on is that everything we do in the name of Jesus and by the power of the Spirit is an obedient exercise of some aspect of the work of the Trinity that we get in on as we become mature enough to do it. Each Christian participates in his or her own specific way in the context and conditions of his or her own life circumstances, but none of us do it on our own or under our own power.

We live and work and have our being in a world lavishly showered with gifts. T. S. Eliot in his great poem on the church, "The Rock," captures the essence of Paul's insight on the nature and place of the Spirit's gifts:

> There is work together
> A Church for all
> And a job for each
> Every man to his work.[7]

5. John Stott, *The Message of Ephesians: God's New Society* (Downers Grove, IL: InterVarsity, 1979), p. 159.

6. There are excellent summaries of Paul's writing on gifts in the *Dictionary of Paul and His Letters*, ed. Gerald F. Hawthorne and Ralph Martin (Downers Grove, IL: InterVarsity, 1993); *The Westminister Dictionary of Christian Spirituality*, ed. Gordon S. Wakefield (Philadelphia: Westminster, 1983); and the *Anchor Bible Dictionary*, ed. David Noel Freedman (New York: Doubleday, 1992).

7. T. S. Eliot, *The Complete Poems and Plays* (New York: Harcourt, Brace and Company, 1958), p. 98.

\* \* \*

Paul uses his Psalm 68 text to anchor his *axios* metaphor in Christ's kingly rule and Christ's generosity. Christ in his Ascension is High King. Christ exercises his rule most conspicuously by giving gifts. The nature of Christ's sovereignty is not to lord it over his people but to invite them into the exercise of his self-giving. Which is to say, to become mature, to grow up as participants in who he is and what he does.

Mature living means realizing that we are included in the workforce. We embrace the work as a gift. And what a gift! — working alongside our Lord in this great salvation enterprise. *Ascend* and *give* and *gifts* gather resonance as the Ephesian message is meditated, prayed, and lived. We become willing participants in the way that Christ is King, a life given. *Worthy* gradually and incrementally acquires texture. We grow up.

II

# THE BLESSING OF GOD

*Great theology is always a kind of giant and intricate poetry, like epic or saga.*

MARILYNNE ROBINSON, *The Death of Adam*

## CHAPTER 3

# God and His Glory: Ephesians 1:3-14

*Blessed be the God and Father of our Lord Jesus Christ, who has blessed us with every spiritual blessing in the heavenly places, just as he chose us in Christ before the foundation of the world to be holy and blameless before him in love. . . . [T]his is the pledge of our inheritance toward redemption as God's own people, to the praise of his glory.*

EPHESIANS 1:3-4, 14

*What's lost is nothing to what's found, and all the death that ever was, set next to life, would scarcely fill a cup.*

FREDERICH BUECHNER, *Godric*

The 201 words beginning with "blessed" (1:3) and ending with "glory" (v. 14) is a single sentence in Paul's Greek. One scholar, E. Nordon, called it "the most monstrous sentence conglomeration . . . I have ever met in the Greek language."[1] But the eminent scholar, notwithstanding

---

1. Markus Barth, *Ephesians 1–3*, The Anchor Bible, vol. 34 (Garden City, NY: Doubleday, 1974), p. 77.

his erudition, had a tin ear. Christians who hear or read this sentence in the company of a worshiping congregation are likely to dismiss the fussy grammarian's outrage as a whimpering whine. Who can resist this marvelous, tumbling cataract of poetry that introduces us to the vast and intricate complexities of this world in which we live? Not many. Paul is playful, extravagant, and totally engaging as he tells us what is going on in this God-created, Christ-saved, Spirit-blessed world into which we have been born and are now growing up. This is no small, cramped world in which we live from hand to mouth. The horizons are vast. The heavens are high. The oceans are deep. We have elbowroom to spare.

The sheer size, the staggering largeness, of the world into which God calls us, its multi-dimensioned spaciousness, must not be reduced to dimensions that we are cozily comfortable with. Paul does his best to prevent us from reducing it. Sin shrinks our imaginations. Paul stretches us. He counters with holy poetry. If we calculate the nature of the world by what we can manage or explain, we end up living in a very small world. If we are going to grow to the mature stature of Christ, we need conditions favorable to it. We need room. The Ephesian letter gives us room, dimensions deep and wide. Ephesians plunges us into ocean deeps, and we come up gasping for air. This is going to take some getting used to.

## Lost in the Cosmos

Walker Percy wrote six novels[2] in which he made us insiders to the spiritual disease of alienation that he found pervasive in American culture. His name for the condition is "lost in the cosmos." We don't know who we are or where we are. We don't know where we came from or where we are going.

Percy began his vocational life as a physician, intending to use

2. *The Moviegoer* (1961), *The Last Gentleman* (1966), *Love in the Ruins* (1971), *Lancelot* (1977), *The Second Coming* (1980), *The Thanatos Syndrome* (1987).

medicines and surgeries to heal sick and damaged bodies. He had hardly gotten started before he changed jobs. Sometimes we have to change jobs in order to maintain our vocation. Percy did. He became a writer so he could tend to the healing of souls, using nouns and verbs to cure what ails us. It is not insignificant that he was also a Christian. His diagnosis of the spiritual "lostness" of his American brothers and sisters was intended to wake us up to our desperate condition and set up a few signposts for finding our way home.

Predating Percy by two thousand years, Paul also knew a good deal about lostness. He provides a trenchant diagnosis of the condition in the thirteen letters he wrote to Christian congregations and friends in the middle decades, the fifties and sixties, of the first century. His diagnosis was essentially the same as Percy's "lost in the cosmos." But Paul also does something else. In contrast to the few signposts that Percy set up, Paul provides an extensive witness to the ways in which God in Christ by the Holy Spirit is at work in this cosmos.

Prominent among the contributing factors to being "lost in the cosmos" is the rampant secularizing debasement of language into depersonalized facts, with a corresponding evisceration of imagination into cardboard cutouts of roles and functions. We live in a language world in which every "you" gets neutered into an "it" and imagination is crowded to the sidelines by numbers. Paul gives us back our mother tongue, a vocabulary and syntax by which we can name and therefore recognize what is going on all around us and find our way home, no longer lost.

Paul's launch of his Ephesian letter (1:3-14) is a remarkable tour-de-force recovery of a language that reorients us in the cosmos. One of our finest scholars gives witness that this is "one of the most splendidly Jewish passages of praise and prayer in the New Testament . . . a prayer of blessing to the one God for his mighty acts in creation and redemption."[3] This single sentence — 201 nouns and verbs, adverbs and adjectives, prepositions and conjunctions cascading off Paul's pen! — comprises an extravagant pageantry: the central action of the cosmos, God

---

3. N. T. Wright, *Paul: Fresh Perspectives* (London: SPCK, 2005), p. 101.

at work in comprehensive salvation ways, on parade. We are no longer lost. We can find our way home.

## God's Verbs

God. We begin with God. That seems obvious enough. "In the beginning God" . . . "God said" . . . "God so loved the world" . . . God. God. God. God who got the cosmos going. God who sent Jesus. God in whose name we received our baptismal identity. But obvious as it is, it is mighty difficult to maintain a visceral sense of that beginning, God *begetting*, when we don't have our Bibles open before us, or are not in church.

We have short attention spans. Having been introduced to God, we soon lose interest in God and become preoccupied with ourselves. Self expands and soul atrophies. Psychology trumps theology. Our feelings and our emotions, our health and our jobs, our friends and our families muscle their way to center stage. God, of course, is not exactly sent packing or shut in a closet or closed up in the Bible. But God is consigned to the sidelines, conveniently within calling distance to help out in emergencies and be available for consultation for the times when we have run out of answers.

Our days are busy with little leisure for frills. We have work to do, interests to pursue, books to read, letters to write, the telephone to answer, errands to run, children to raise, investments to tend to, the lawn to mow, food to prepare and serve, the garbage to take out. We don't need God's help or counsel in doing any of these things. God is necessary for the big things, most obviously creation and salvation. But for the rest we can, for the most part, take care of ourselves.

That usually adds up to a workable life, at least when accompanied by a decent job and a good digestion. But — it is not the practice of resurrection, it is not growing up in Christ, it is not living in the company of the Trinity, it is not living out of our beginnings, our begettings. If we live too far removed from, or worse, disconnected from, our origins, we will never arrive at the "full stature of Christ."

\*    \*    \*

Paul gets our resurrection attention by shooting off seven verbal rockets: verbs that get things done, verbs that run the cosmos intentionally and personally. There will be plenty of opportunity later to find our place in all this, but first we must find out what keeps "all this" going: seven verbs, each one detonated by God, verbs that fill the sky and illuminate the earth with God's ways of working among us.

Seven verbs: *blessed . . . chose . . . destined . . . bestowed . . . lavished . . . made known . . . gather up. . . .*

\*    \*    \*

Verb one: God *blessed.* "Blessed be the God and Father of our Lord Jesus Christ, who has blessed us in Christ with every spiritual blessing in the heavenly places" (Eph. 1:3).

Two variations on "bless" festoon first God and then us: the adjective "blessed" characterizes God, who blesses as he himself is blessed; the noun "blessing" comprehensively designates our experience of being blessed by God. What God *does* comes out of who God *is*. And what we receive from God is who God is. The being of God is expressed in the action of God. Our experience of God is who God is.

Which is to say that there is no dividing God up into parts or attributes. God is who he is. We don't figure God out. We don't explain God. We don't define God. We worship God who is *as* he is.

And God is what he gives. We don't second-guess God. We don't Monday-morning-quarterback God. We don't evaluate God on a scale of one to ten. We don't, as Dostoevsky's character Ivan Karamazov so famously did, "return the ticket." We don't presume to tell God how to be God. When we worship God, we let God be God.

There is more to be said and prayed and sung, doubted and questioned, of course. And this "more" has been and will continue to be said and prayed and sung, doubted and questioned. But the first verb, *bless,* is map and compass for finding our way through the country.

Blessed be, blessed us, spiritual blessing. "Bless" accumulates resonance and nuance as the story of creation and salvation is told across the centuries: God blessing Abraham; David and Zechariah blessing God; Mary identified as blessed; Jesus blessing the children; children praying a blessing over a meal; the unthinking reflex *gesundheit,* "bless you," at a sneeze; parents blessing their children; pastors and priests dismissing their congregations with a blessing. Everybody says it, and many do it. The word permeates our language and experience. We can't get away from it.

*   *   *

Verb two: God *chose.* "Just as he chose us in Christ before the foundation of the world to be holy and blameless before him in love" (Eph. 1:4).

Everybody I have ever become acquainted with has a story, usually from childhood, of not being chosen: not chosen for the glee club, not chosen for the basketball team, the last chosen in a neighborhood sandlot softball team (which is worse than not being chosen at all), not chosen for a job, not chosen as a spouse. Not chosen carries the blunt message that I have no worth, that I am not useful, that I am good for nothing.

Not many of us take it lying down, at least not at first. We insist on being noticed. Sometimes we do it by borrowing a recognizable identity from others, loyally following and cheering an athletic team or embracing a political cause. Others develop the persona of a bully who breaks decorum and rules, compelling notice even though it gets us expelled from a classroom or club or saloon, and maybe even puts us in jail. And there is always hair dye. Dye your hair purple and you can be sure of being noticed in a crowd. And nobody with a well-placed tattoo is invisible.

These and a host of other compensatory strategies often work quite well, sometimes spectacularly well, but they don't have much staying power.

Against this background, common to all of us, of not being noticed, being ignored, being dismissed as of no account, being indistin-

58

guishable from the background, the verb "chose" is a breath of fresh air: God *chose* us.

And yes, *God* chose us. It wasn't a last-minute thing because he felt sorry for us and no one else would have us, like a stray mutt at the dog pound, or an orphan whom nobody adopted. He chose us "before the foundation of the world." We are in on the action, long before we have any idea that we are in on the action. We are cosmic.

*    *    *

Verb three: God *destined*. "He destined us for adoption as his children through Jesus Christ, according to the good pleasure of his will, to the praise of his glorious grace" (Eph. 1:5-6).

"Destined" has affinities with "chosen." Both words carry a sense of intention. Life is not random. Human beings cannot be lumped into impersonal and abstract categories. As difficult as it is to imagine, maybe impossible to imagine given the billions of men and women involved, we are not a swarm of bees buzzing in and out of a hive, not a colony of ants following a scent in and out of an anthill. Deep within God and deep within us there is a relational element of intentionality: God chooses us, God destines us — the verbs can be synonyms. But not quite.

"Destine" provides a slight tilt from the intentionality in God conveyed by "choose" to something that takes place in us: "destine" clarifies into "destination." God notices, identifies, and chooses us. But that generalized choice now gels into an appointment that is congruent with God's choice.

The verb "destine" (*prooridzo*) derives from the noun "boundary" (*oros*).[4] Literally, it means to set a limit, to mark a boundary. A fence line on the prairie sets a boundary, determines where the land that a farmer has been appointed to work begins and ends. Without that fence line, the farmer would be paralyzed by the ocean of prairie, the endless possibilities stretched out before him — "Where do I start? Is there any

---

4. *Theological Dictionary of the New Testament*, ed. Gerhard Friedrich, trans. Geoffrey W. Bromiley (Grand Rapids: Eerdmans, 1967), vol. 5, pp. 452-56.

end to it?" When God destines, he marks out the boundaries in which we live the purposed life to which he appoints us. We aren't set loose in the cosmos to find our place and way in it as best we can. There are lines of God's purposing appointments that intersect our chosenness. Being chosen is not an abstract category; it develops into a relationship that is mutual and reciprocal.

A few years ago my wife and I were in the airport in Athens, returning home from Israel by way of a few days in Rome. We obtained our boarding passes and went looking for our gate. I was surprised to recognize a Greek word over the gate entrance, *Proorismos Roma* — "Destination Rome." I was familiar with that word from reading my Bible. But I had assumed that *proorismos*, "destination" (or "predestination"), was a uniquely Bible word, one of Paul's special words, a word reserved exclusively for what God did.

It is a wonderful thing when a word we had thought was reserved exclusively for God's revelation and occurs only in the Bible shows up on a street in our town, or, in this case, in an airport while looking for our way home. All during that flight to Rome I mused with delight on the earthy, practical presentness of what I had always assumed referred to one of the more arcane theological dogmas.

There is more, of course, to "destine" than getting me to Rome, but I had a good time for those few hours realizing that I, among others, was "destined . . . for adoption as his children" in much the same way that having walked through the gate marked *Proorismos Roma* I was headed for Rome. Sit back and enjoy the flight.

*     *     *

That God destines, or, if you prefer, predestines, encompasses huge mysteries. The moment we recognize that virtually everything that has to do with God takes place previous to our knowing anything about it, it becomes obvious that since we are not gods ourselves, we are forever unable to totally comprehend this "everything." This has two very salutary effects on us: it absolutely demands humility — we don't know enough to either protest or approve; and adoration is spontaneous. We become aware that we are in the presence of a reality that cannot be used, cannot be packaged, cannot be grasped on any other terms than are given to us by God. We open our hands and *receive*.

That has not prevented a number of very bright, very learned men and women from decontextualizing and depersonalizing the word so that it is flattened, emptied of mystery, into a blueprint that determines the way we will live our lives in each detail. Some even go so far as to say that the blueprint actually determines the eternal fate, salvation or damnation, of each and every person who has ever lived. George Eliot's comment is both acerbic and appropriate: "The dunce who can't do sums wants to solve the problems of the universe."[5]

Since none of us has access to the blueprint, a great deal of speculation is squandered in guessing, over study Bibles in churches and over pitchers of beer in saloons, exactly what the dimensions and specifications of predestination might be. Almost inevitably this fuels an enormous amount of neurotic soul-searching on how to get inside information of the blueprint, so that "I don't miss the will of God for my life." The blueprint version of predestination wreaks havoc in too many lives. It is not a satisfactory formula for growing up in Christ.

Markus Barth, whose father Karl Barth wrote magnificently on these matters, distinguishes this Ephesian passage from any taint of determinism by noting that the tone throughout is adoring rather than calculating. This is a rescue from impersonal fate, from astrological charts, from karma and kismet, from "biology is destiny."

The God who destines/predestines cannot be depersonalized into a cosmic blueprint — even if the blueprint has "God's will" inscribed on it and a host of angels are energetically making sure its specifications are being enacted in each and every life on planet Earth.

\*     \*     \*

Verb four: God *bestowed*. ". . . grace that he freely bestowed on us in the Beloved" (Eph. 1:6).

---

5. George Eliot, *Felix Holt* (New York: The Century Co., 1911), p. 69.

Translators have a difficult time catching the unique quality of the verb used here. It occurs only twice in the New Testament and never in classical Greek writings. Luke conveyed Gabriel's greeting to Mary at the Annunciation by using this verb to address her as "favored one" (Luke 1:28). Paul uses the verb here to express God's action of bestowing grace on us. The difficulty for the translator is to find a way to carry over from Paul's Greek into English the emphatic energy, so expressive of sheer extravagance. God bestows grace, his favor, his pleasure in us, his delight in giving what we could never imagine or guess.

"Bestow" is the noun "grace" verbalized. In its verbal form it carries over the meaning of the noun, "grace," but also intensifies it. Markus Barth translates it "poured out."[6] I would prefer something more on the order of "drenched." Following analogies in English — to dream a dream, to die the death — we could attempt "begrace with grace." But that doesn't carry the punch of the text. The English language doesn't have a verb that picks up the word "grace," preserving its centuries of stored-up meaning and then activating it with a kind of take-your-breath-away energy. "Bestowed" seems too tame. Paul's verb signals an exuberant artesian-well eruption of grace, something on the order of St. John's classic reference to Jesus: "From his fullness we have all received, grace upon grace" (John 1:16).

"Grace" is one of Paul's biggest, most loaded, most comprehensive words. Variations on the word will occur twenty times in the Ephesian letter. It is not a word that we can pin down with a crisp definition. What is required is that we enter into the ways it is used, the ways it gathers meanings from the various contexts in which God acts and in which we experience his actions.

We need to make ourselves conversant with the largeness, the sheer immensity of the world in which we are growing up in Christ. Every part of the landscape, every shift in the weather, every conversation, every person we meet, every book we read provides a different and unique slant on what is involved: God's grace activated, God's

6. Barth, *Ephesians*, pp. 76 and 81.

grace in motion — in us. It isn't our business to figure this out or catalogue it or master it. Get used to abundance. God isn't a noun to be objectively defined. God is the verbing of a noun.

\*     \*     \*

Verb five: God *lavished*. "In him we have redemption through his blood,
the forgiveness of our trespasses, according to the riches of his grace
that he lavished on us" (Eph. 1:7-8).

Paul uses "bestowed" only once in Ephesians but with striking ap-
propriateness, transmuting the noun "grace" into a surprising new
verb form. Was he responsible for the coinage, or was it his companion
and friend Luke? Regardless, they are the only early church writers
who used it — and each in a strategic setting. But the word "lavish," a
near synonym for "bestow," gets our attention here because it is ubiq-
uitous. "Bestow" is rare; "lavish" is everywhere. It is one of Paul's favorite words. We might say he uses it lavishly.

The word in its various forms (as noun, verb, adjective, adverb) is
used seventy-eight times in the New Testament as a whole. Paul is responsible for over half the occurrences, forty-five of them. Paul can't
get enough of this word. He uses it every chance he gets.

Does Paul overdo it? I don't think so. In matters of God's grace,
hyperboles are understatements.

Gerard Manley Hopkins wrote poetry that was likewise wildly
extravagant in praise of God. Like St. Paul, this Irish Jesuit was not
timid in expressing the abundance of grace that he discovered all
around him. His poem "God's Grandeur" is no mean companion to
Paul's Ephesian exuberance.

> The world is charged with the grandeur of God.
> It will flame out, like shining from shook foil;
> It gathers to a greatness, like the ooze of oil
> Crushed. Why do men then now not reck his rod?
> Generations have trod, have trod, have trod;
> And all is seared with trade, bleared, smeared with toil;

And wears man's smudge and share's man's smell: the soil
Is bare now, nor can foot feel, being shod.

And for all this, nature is never spent;
There lives the dearest freshness deep down things;
And though the last lights off the black West went
Oh, morning, at the brown brink eastward, springs —
Because the Holy Ghost over the bent
World broods with warm breast and with ah! bright wings.[7]

*　　*　　*

Verb six: God *made known.* "With all wisdom and insight he has made known to us the mystery of his will" (Eph. 1:8-9).

We are not in the dark. We are in on what God does. We are not intended to be kept in a state of ignorance, asking no questions. We are not children "to be seen and not heard."

But — and this catches our attention — what God makes known to us is "the mystery of his will." But if a mystery is known, is it still a mystery? Not if it is a murder mystery in which the "mystery" is simply a literary device to keep us turning the pages in suspense until someone cleverer than we are solves the mystery, at which point it is no longer a mystery. But in Paul's use of the word, "mystery" is elaborated "as a plan for the fullness of time, to gather up all things in him, things in heaven and things on earth" (Eph. 1:10). It seems that "mystery" here does not refer to things kept in secret, classified information that is not accessible to people without proper clearance. "Mystery" here refers to something more like the inside story of the way God does things that bring us into the story. This is a kind of knowledge that cannot be gained by gathering information or picking up clues. It has nothing to do with satisfying curiosity. It is a far cry from the inquisitive, clamoring questioning that wants "answers."

7. Gerard Manley Hopkins, *The Poems,* ed. W. H. Gardner and N. H. Mackenzie (London: Oxford University Press, 1967), p. 66.

The way in which God makes known the mystery is "with all wisdom and insight." That is, the knowledge that God gives to us comes in the form of wisdom and insight. God does not dump information on us. He does not "home school" us in mathematics and biology. "Wisdom and insight" are knowledge lived out.

We have far too little experience of this in American schools. Education majors in dates and figures, explanations and definitions, how things work, how to use a library, doing experiments in a laboratory. None of this is without usefulness. But it has little to do with becoming a mature person, with growing up. We know a thing, a truth, a person only *in relationship*. There is a great deal of impersonal knowledge available. There is no impersonal wisdom.

We truly know something only by entering it, knowing it from the inside, lovingly embracing it. That is what wisdom is: truth assimilated and digested.

*     *     *

Verb seven: God *gathers up*. ". . . to gather up all things in him [Christ], things in heaven and things on earth" (Eph. 1:10).

"Gather up" is the summary verb in this sequence of "rocket verbs" that make us insiders to the comprehensive and action-filled conditions in the cosmos where we are growing up, becoming our created and saved selves, practicing resurrection.

When we review the verbs, the striking thing is that it is Jesus Christ who reveals and executes each of these actions. Eleven times, either as proper name or pronoun, Christ is named: "Lord Jesus Christ" (Eph. 1:3); "blessed us in Christ" (v. 3); "chose us in Christ" (v. 4); "destined us . . . through Jesus Christ" (v. 5); "bestowed on us in the Beloved [Christ]" (v. 6); "in him [Christ] we have redemption through his [Christ's] blood" (v. 7); "according to the riches of his [Christ's] grace" (v. 7); "that he [Christ] lavished on us" (v. 8); "that he set forth in Christ" (v. 9); "to gather up all things in him [Christ]" (v. 10).

There are also eleven matching pronouns ("our" twice, "us" six times, "we" once) that pull us personally into the action. Again, none of this is in general or by category.

The rest of this long sentence (Eph. 1:11-14) — there are another seventy words before we come to the full stop that lets us catch our breath — has eight more references to Christ and six more to us that elaborate and give texture to this huge blessing that orients us in this resurrection world. These are the on-the-ground results of the explosive, cosmic verbs. These results will be elaborated in the rest of the letter.

There is not a single item in the practice of resurrection, this life of growing to maturity, that takes place impersonally, or generally, or in abstraction.

It is an old habit among us, a habit subsidized by the devil, to depersonalize, to abstract, to generalize not only our language with or about God but also our language with and about one another. It is a bad habit. We avoid the personal in order to avoid responsibility. We find any way we think we can get by with to get control of God, our neighbors, or ourselves. We are relentless. We depersonalize God to an idea to be discussed. We reduce the people around us to resources to be used. We define ourselves as consumers to be satisfied. The more we do it, the more we incapacitate ourselves from growing up to a maturity capable of living adult lives of love and adoration, trust and sacrifice.

Paul won't let us get by with it by so much as a comma or semicolon. He keeps the seven verbs — God in person, in action — in our sights so that we keep our lives in resurrection focus.

Paul's summarizing verb "gather up" is both graphic and vivid, easily pictured and satisfyingly complete. The heart of the verb is a metaphor, "head" (kephale): put everything under the one head, that is, under the head of Christ, of which we are the body. Instead of a cosmos of clutter in which we are mired in rubbish, we have coherence. Instead of one thing after another, we have organic unity. Instead of fragmentation and dismemberment, we find ourselves part of a body with Christ as its head. "Head" keeps our orientation personal and relational — not hierarchical, not institutional.

This is a good picture to keep in mind. This Ephesian message is intended to gather us into the multifaceted, all-encompassing work of Christ in which we will become whole, healthy, complete men and women. None of us is the body in and of ourselves. We are an integral part of the body of which the head is Christ.

## God's Glory

One more thing. In this long, opening, cat's cradle of a sentence, with all its lines rapidly intersecting with one another, Paul introduces a phrase that succinctly states what is going on in this resurrection cosmos in which we grow up, and then, for emphasis, he repeats the phrase three times:

"He destined us ... to the praise of his glorious grace." (Eph. 1:5-6)

"so that we, who were the first to set our hope on Christ, might live for the praise of his glory." (1:12)

"marked with the seal of the promised Holy Spirit ... to the praise of his glory." (1:13-14)

Everything takes place "to the praise of his glory." "Praise" is grateful celebration. "Glory" is the bright presence of God. This is our destiny, this is what we are made for: a grand celebration in the full presence of God. Praise and glory.

*       *       *

Our subject, the subject of Ephesians, is "growing up." In dealing with something so critical and personal, so full of consequences for all of us, here is a surprise. This orienting introductory sentence places us in a cosmos in which God starts everything. Everything. There is not a single verb commanding us to do something, not so much as a hint or suggestion that we are to do anything at all. No requirements, no laws, no chores, no assignments, no lessons. We are born into a cosmos in which all the requirements and conditions for growing up are not only in place but in action.

Once we get this through our heads and assimilated into our imaginations, we are out of the driver's seat forever. The practice of resurrection is not a do-it-yourself self-help project. It is God's project, and he is engaged full-time in carrying it out.

This rescues us from small-mindedness, from thinking too small about our lives. This salvation-resurrection world is large. Anything we can come up with for ourselves in terms of goal or purpose is puny alongside of what is already in motion in the cosmos "to the praise of his glory."

Simultaneously, alongside this staggering revelation that God is actively involved within and overall — we rub our eyes, "can this be true?" — we are told in no uncertain terms that each of us is generously included in every aspect (all seven verbs!) of God's activity. Not a single verb leaves us outside the action. We are not spectators to a grand cosmic show. We are *in* the show. But we are not running it. All the conditions that make it possible for us to grow up to maturity, to the stature of Jesus Christ, are in place, even from "before the foundation of the world."

But this comprehensive involvement in this all-encompassing action of God in Christ by the Holy Spirit does require that we develop skills and aptitudes in a way of participation that none of us, excepting infants, is very good at. I mean receptivity.

All is gift. "Grace is everywhere." God in Christ is actively doing for and in us everything involved in the practice of resurrection. So what is there left for us to do? Receive. That is our primary response if we are to find ourselves no longer lost in the cosmos but at home in it. For the most part, receptivity is a learned response. Receive the gift. Paul's question to the Ephesian elders when he first met with them continues to be implicit in this letter he later wrote. It reverberates still: "Did you receive the Holy Spirit when you became believers?" (Acts 19:2).

## CHAPTER 4

# Paul and the Saints: Ephesians 1:15-23

*I have heard of your faith in the Lord Jesus and your love toward all the saints, and for this reason I do not cease to give thanks for you as I remember you in my prayers.*

EPHESIANS 1:15

*My Lord Jesus can hew heaven out of worse timber than I am.*

SAMUEL RUTHERFORD

Paul begins his letter with a blessing (Eph. 1:3-14): he blesses God for blessing us. He particularizes the blessing in seven God-activated verbs that provide a wide-screen panorama of the comprehensive ways that God works in this magnificent cosmos in which so many find themselves lost. God is on our side; he is not against us. God is actively at work among us for our good and our salvation; he is not passive. God is present and personal; he is not remote. God is totally involved in the cosmos; he is not indifferent.

We submit ourselves to the blessing. This does not come easy for us. It takes time; it takes a great deal of getting used to. As we submit, our imaginations are baptized. We are immersed in the icy, swift-flowing river of resurrection and come up with all our senses tingling, our imaginations cleansed. We see what we have never seen before. We thought we were looking for God. No, God is looking for us. We thought we were seeking God. No, God is seeking us.

This is the first thing: the blessing. We start with God. If we start with ourselves, we wander farther into the dark woods. Snow-blind, we circle our own tracks on polar ice. We trek across Sahara sands setting our hopes on one mirage after another. Pick your metaphor.

*     *     *

The primary language that we use as we grow up in Christ, which is to say as we practice resurrection, is prayer. But if we are to practice this resurrection prayer, a further renovation of imagination is required: we need to have an existential understanding of prayer as an all-involving way of life. It is not a special way of using language for holy things or sacred concerns. It is a way of using language personally in response to and in the presence of God, and in response to and in the company of the saints. Paul uses language in ways that bring everything — what we do and what we see, what we know and what we believe — into a syntax in which God is sometimes subject, sometimes predicate, sometimes preposition, sometimes conjunction, sometimes comma, and sometimes period. But always, always, somewhere in the sentence.

Baptism redefines our life as God's gift to be lived in the presence and within the operations of God. Our birth certificate is a record of our biological birth. Baptism is a record of God's eternal claim upon us. When we take that claim with full seriousness, we live out a far more comprehensive definition — son or daughter of God. The practice of resurrection consists in living out this definition day in and day out, "on the job." In order to do this, we need a language suited to the conditions given by the primacy of God's presence and action as Father, Son, and Holy Spirit in our lives in the particular circumstances of our place and responsibilities. That language is prayer.

There is a lot to understand and decide and express as we live out our baptismal identity in the practice of resurrection. Most of our social experience with language takes place with people who could not care less about our true God-given identity and who have little interest in resurrection. So it is going to take some time and require deliberate attention to acquire fluency in prayer, this language so consistent with who we really are, adequate for saying and listening as we practice resurrection.

Paul prays. From the moment we start reading Ephesians we are immersed in prayer language: "Blessed be the God and Father of our Lord Jesus Christ. . . ." It is an elaborate and richly textured blessing after the manner of the frequently repeated prayers of blessing that are so conspicuous in the lives of our Hebrew people-of-God ancestors. We bless the God who blesses us. The prayer language of blessing is part and parcel of God's revelation.

The blessings begin in Genesis as God blesses Adam and Eve, Noah, and Abraham. Before we know it, the people who God blesses are passing on the blessing: Isaac blesses Jacob, Jacob blesses his sons, Moses blesses the twelve tribes. The blessings accumulate, and in the pregnant phrase of G. M. Hopkins they "gather to a greatness"[1] in the Psalms, and punctuate the language of Jesus. The language of blessing comes to a flourishing finale in Revelation: seven blessings scattered through that text salt the magnificent apocalyptic poem and, in retrospect, flavor our entire Scriptures with blessing.

The language of blessing permeates the language of Scripture. We receive the blessing and absorb it into our obedience. It is not long before our language exudes what we are living.

### "I remember you in my prayers"

Paul started out praying (which is the blessing). He continues by redirecting his prayers from blessing God to praying for his friends, the

---

1. Gerard Manley Hopkins, "God's Grandeur," *The Poems of Gerard Manley Hopkins* (London: Oxford University Press, 1967), p. 66.

Christian congregation in Ephesus. He names them (and us) "the saints" (Eph. 1:15-23).

Not that any have been excluded from the blessing — all the ways that God blesses inevitably involve us — but there is a slight shift at verse 15 that brings the saints into particular focus. The saints are pulled into an act of thanksgiving: "I do not cease to give thanks for you as I remember you in my prayers" (Eph. 1:16). He gives thanks, and before you know it he is praying *for* them: "I pray that the God of our Lord Jesus Christ, the Father of glory, may give you . . ." (v. 17).

Give what? Paul enumerates five gifts that he is praying that the God of blessing will give them:

> wisdom and revelation,
> an enlightened heart,
> hope,
> the riches of his glorious inheritance,
> the immeasurable greatness of his power.

These gifts don't just float at random down out of the sky, scattered like confetti. They have energy behind them. They are the "working of [God's] great power" in Christ (vv. 19-20). The power that brings these gifts to us is ascribed to four successive and interrelated actions of God in Christ. After listing the gifts, Paul supplies four details that fill out exactly how God puts this power to work in Christ:

> He raised him from the dead.
> He seated him at his right hand.
> He put all things under his feet.
> He made him head over all things for the church.

The five anticipated gifts tell us what we can expect from God as we practice resurrection. God's way of putting "this power," this gift giving, at work in us is both personal ("in Christ") and cosmic (Jesus raised, ascended, ruling, and head of the church). The practice of resurrection is no hole-in-the-corner affair. This is not something to cultivate privately. We participate in everything that Christ does. The five prayed-for gifts and the four dimensions of the reach of Christ's power take their place in the context of the seven all-encompassing rocket verbs of blessing and the triply emphatic "praise of his glory" that tells us how all this is going to turn out.

This is a lot to take in. Extravagance compounded. Prayer extrapolated in every dimension. We can't help being impressed. This resurrection country, "the land of the living" that the psalmists so keenly anticipated, cannot be reduced to domesticated moralism or civilized good manners — or projected into a future that we will inhabit after death. This is the country that we live in. Here. Now.

*     *     *

Paul has used three verbs to name what he is doing: bless, give thanks, pray. And one noun: prayers. But prayer — and Paul at prayer is a conspicuous example — cannot be accounted for by grammar. It is fairly common among us to discuss the language of prayer by developing a vocabulary of nomenclature: adoration, petition, intercession, praise, thanksgiving, blessing, confession, even imprecation. This making of lists is not without its usefulness, but I have never been fond of the practice. Too much is excluded.

What we are after in the practice of resurrection is a way of language in which the word of God to us is continuously implicit in the way we use words, both in response to God and in relation to one another. It is a fluency and habit in the use of language that is comprehensive of all that God says and does and that is thoroughly dialogical, conversational.

Martin Thornton, one of our best teachers on the nature and practice of what is involved in prayer, often capitalized the word — Prayer — and treated it as the act and acts that bring everything together in attention and offering to God. When we pray we are not holy ghosts levitating, but bodies held firmly in place by gravity.

These are his words: "Written with an initial capital — Prayer — we have a generic term for any process or activity qualified by a living relation between human souls and God. It not only embraces all the usual divisions of prayer . . . but all such works, arts, and moral acts which truly spring from our communion with God. Prayer, quite simply, is the total experience of the Christian man and woman."[2]

We pray when we are meditatively quiet before God with Psalm 118 open before us; we pray while taking out the garbage; we pray when we are losing our grip and then ask God for help; we pray when we are weeding the garden; we pray when we are asking God to help a friend who is at the end of her rope; we pray when we are writing a letter; we pray when we are in conversation with our cynical and bullying boss; we pray with our friends in church; we pray walking down Main Street in the company of strangers.

I am not saying (nor is Thornton) that everything we do is prayer, but that everything we do and say and think *can* be prayer. It seems to have been that way with Paul. I am also saying that many of us pray far more than we are aware that we are praying. We pray when we are not in a conventional place of prayer. We pray when we are not using the conventional language of prayer. I am saying that "always to pray, and not to faint" (Luke 18:1 KJV) happens a lot, unnoticed and unremarked.

There are forms and models for prayer. It is important to know and be familiar with them. But looking for models, methods, and strategies that can be duplicated is not the way to mature in prayer anymore than learning stock phrases as a child ("You're welcome" . . . "Thank you" . . . "Please pass the potatoes" . . . ) is the way to become fluent in the English language. God works differently in each local context. We saturate our minds and memories in Christ and the Scriptures, and then go about our day's work without a prepared script, unself-consciously trusting the Holy Spirit language — its syntax and metaphors, its tone and rhythms — always working deep in our souls without awareness, sometimes articulate in our ears and on our tongues.

\*     \*     \*

2. Martin Thornton, *Pastoral Theology: A Reorientation* (London: SPCK, 1964), p. 4.

John Wright Follette was an itinerant teacher in the church world in which I grew up. At the time I am writing about, he was elderly, perhaps in his seventies. He never married. He was greatly revered as a "saint" all over the country. He was small of stature and slight of build, a kind of spidery figure with delicate fingers and ascetic mien. He spoke always in a soft voice and never smiled. My parents were fond of him and provided hospitality whenever he was in our area of Montana. He loved to spend days of retreat at our mountain lake cabin.

One summer day I accompanied my mother to the cabin for the day to prepare his meals and "sit at his feet" (her words). I was about sixteen and greatly in awe of his reputation as a holy man. After lunch he retired to a hammock on the shore of the lake to rest. I observed him from the deck of our cabin and wanted desperately to talk with him, the famous Dr. Follette. I wanted to talk to him about prayer. This was the chance of a lifetime. After an hour or so I got impatient — we were going to have to leave in a while, and I didn't want to miss my chance. I asked my mother how long she thought he would sleep. She said she didn't think he was sleeping: "He likes to be quiet and listen to the Spirit." She told me to go down and speak with him: "He won't mind." I was hesitant, shy — the "holy man"! She was insistent. Tentatively, cautiously, I approached the hammock.

"Dr. Follette, can I talk to you about prayer?"

He didn't open his eyes, but he spoke. He spoke in a kind of bark, louder than I had ever heard him, "I haven't prayed for forty years!"

I stood there. Stunned. That was it. I left.

I wandered off into the woods, puzzled and then scandalized. The venerable Dr. Follette — hadn't prayed for forty years! I never told my mother lest she also be scandalized at this fraud. I kept my secret.

Five or six years elapsed before what had taken place dawned on me. He *was*, in fact, wise and holy. He knew intuitively that the callow adolescent that was me that day would have swallowed whole anything he said and slavishly imitated it. No matter what he said, no matter how wise and holy, it would have sent me off for years of trying to be Dr. Follette at prayer — wasted years of imitating an icon — when I needed to be experimenting, practicing, internalizing the way of language that would bring me into the God-initiated conversation that is prayer. He was willing to risk my puzzled, but hopefully temporary, scandalized disillusion in order to save me from squandering my spirit in romantic spiritual "affairs." It was temporary. He did save me.

Meanwhile, having been disappointingly dismissed by the famous "man of prayer," through the next few years I gradually discovered David in the Psalms, Paul in Ephesians, and Jesus in his prayers. I was on my way.

## "All the saints"

Now: "all the saints." We come out of the river of our resurrection baptism, push our wet hair back from our eyes, and look around. There are a lot of people milling around in various states of dampness and undress. Who are these people? Most of them we have never seen before.

Understanding who these men and women are, this resurrection company that we now find ourselves among, requires a renovation of imagination as thoroughgoing as when we submitted to the blessing. Before the blessing, most if not all our conceptions of God were wrong. Or if not dead wrong, distorted by misinformation, ignorance, and sin. The blessing immersed us in a revelation that gave us a clear-sighted vision of God, gave us open ears to take in his "verbs."

Now it turns out that most of the conceptions that we have all along held of our neighbors have also been wrong. Or if not dead wrong, distorted by misinformation, ignorance, and sin. So Paul extends the "blessed be God" revelation that he started out with to what we might designate a "blessed be the people" revelation (Eph. 1:15-23), these people who are now our companions in this cosmos of salvation, these companions whom we are going to spend the rest of our lives with practicing resurrection, these friends (some of them most unlikely friends) with whom we are growing up to the stature of Jesus Christ. Did we think we were going to do this in the privacy of our own hearts? Did we think we were going to grow up in Christ by taking

moonlit walks on the beach? Did we think we would pick a few stimu-
lating friends for spiritual aerobics? Think again.

*   *   *

Paul began his letter by designating all of those who are in his congregation (and all of us in our congregations), without qualification, regardless of reputation or behavior, as "saints" (Eph. 1:1). Saint is, literally, a "holy one." Now, as Paul shifts from his opening blessing of God
to the people who are blessed, he picks up the designation again — "all
the saints" (1:15). He repeats it again halfway through this part of the
prayer as he describes what it is like to live "among the saints" (1:18). He
uses the term six more times (nine times in all) in the letter. "Saint," as
it turns out, is Paul's noun of choice for the people of God — men and
women who, no longer lost, follow Jesus in the cosmos. Throughout
every letter Paul wrote, "saint" is his word for us. In subsequent centuries "Christian" came to supplant "saint" as the common designation.
"Christian" occurs only three times in the New Testament, and never in
Paul's writings. As time went on, "saint" acquired an elitist patina, referring to an outstanding Christian. Eventually it was even further re-
stricted to persons officially installed after rigorous examination in a
kind of spiritual "hall of fame." The early usage, exemplified in Paul and
then fossilized in our creed — "I believe in . . . the communion of
saints" — is all but lost to common speech.

And so, accustomed as we are to hearing "saint" used as a term of
honor, when we hear the word used without qualification for the
mixed bag of people that is us, it creates dissonance. Are we hearing
Paul right? Did I really hear what I thought I heard him say? It is certainly not a word I would use when I look around at the Christians that
I am familiar with. Is Paul naïve? How well does he know these people?
How well does he know me? Know us? Or is this manipulative flattery?

Paul *does* mean what he says. And he does mean for the word to
take us by surprise, to create dissonance. He means for us to take a second look at these men and women that it would never have occurred
to us to name as saints. By identifying these blessed-by-God people —

77

we, of course, are included — Paul deliberately chooses a word that identifies us by what God does in and for us, not what we do for God. He re-identifies us as creatures of God, saved by Jesus, formed for holiness by the Spirit. He is retraining our imaginations to understand ourselves not in terms of how we feel about ourselves and not in terms of how others treat us, but as God feels about us and treats us. Not as our parents or our teachers or our physicians or our employers or our children define us, but God. Not in terms derived from our employment or our education or our physical appearance or our achievements or our failures, but God.

If someone is taken by surprise by something admirable that we do and that person says, "You're a saint," our automatic response is "I'm no saint." We protest, "If you knew me you would never say that." But Paul is not deterred. "Yes, you are. Pay attention to what I am saying. I want to give you a new word for yourself, a word that gets beneath all appearances, behind all roles and functions, a word that defines you primarily in terms of who God is for you and what God is doing in your life, a person who is growing up in Christ, a person who cannot be accurately identified apart from God's intents and persistent attention: saint." And so we do pay attention. Saint. Holy.

This involves a radical shift in perception both of ourselves and of others. We grow up in a society that evaluates us by appearance and role, by behavior and potential. We are endlessly tested, examined, classified, praised, damned, admired, despised, flattered, scorned, kissed, kicked . . . as thoroughly secularized *things*. Not by everybody, of course, but by most. The institutional way of looking at us in our schools and businesses and governments gives its imprimatur to this systematic and pervasive de-souling, de-personalizing, and, in the end, debunking of anything in or about us that has to do with God.

Still, if that opening "Blessed be the God and Father of our Lord Jesus Christ" is accurate in conveying the definitive action of the cosmos, those seven verbs, each one aimed precisely and personally at us, then any identifying term that fails to convey that basic reality fails. How can we hope to understand the world we live in and understand what living in this world involves for us if everyone addresses, promises, commands, and rewards us in terms that are indifferent, even oblivious, to the most significant thing about us, God's action and our orientation in that action? How can we have even a ghost of a chance to be known as we really are by leaders and teachers and parents, coaches and psychiatrists and poets, salespersons and judges and legislators, all of whom treat us on the working premise that we are all lost in the cosmos? With all these voices coming at us from every direction and at all hours, how do we acquire a God-oriented identity?

*     *     *

Looking in the mirror and naming what we see as "saint" is one way. We follow that up by redefining these people around us as saints. It is a start. It is where Paul starts. He names us saints — not because we are so wonderful but because he sees us truly as ever and always in the company of the Holy Trinity: holy men, holy women, holy children, holy, holy, holy.

In our identity-confused society, too many of us have settled for a pastiche identity composed of social security number, medical records, academic degrees, job history, and whatever fragments of genealogy we can salvage from the cemeteries. Christians can do better: we are *baptized*, baptized in the name of Father, Son, and Holy Spirit. By virtue of *that* name, not our family name, we are saints.

Paul does not name the readers (or hearers as the case may be) of his Ephesian letter saints because of their spiritual heroics or their moral athleticism. He has been around Christians for a few years and he knows us pretty well. And he knows himself. He has no pious illusions about these saints or himself. It has been several years since he was their pastor. He probably knows only a few of them by name. True, he knows a little: "I have heard of your faith in the Lord Jesus and your love toward all the saints, and for this reason I do not cease to give thanks for you as I remember you in my prayers" (1:15-16). But this is hearsay knowledge. How can he be serious in designating them as saints — holy?

Here's how: holy does not refer to them as they are in themselves;

it refers to who they are in God. Paul is not particularly interested in them psychologically. Their moral behavior doesn't top the list of what makes them who they are. It is God's intent for them and God's action for and in them that defines them. It is not what they think of themselves, or how well they are doing in life, or how good they are that defines them. God — those seven verbs! — is definitive for who they are. Paul knows that. He is not going to let them forget it.

One of the ways Paul reinforces this new way for Christ's followers to understand themselves is by calling them saints. "Holy" names not who they are on their own but who God is in and for them, not what they do but what God does in them. Paul understands them primarily and comprehensively in relation to the way God treats them, not the way they treat God. It is God's *calling* for us to be set apart from the ways of the world in order to be positioned to follow the assignments he gives us. The most important thing about any one of us is not what we do but what God does, not what we do for God but what God does for us. It is because we know what God does in and for us that we are no longer lost in the cosmos.

*    *    *

But there is also this. Anybody who has spent any time at all in the company of Christians knows that none of us whom Paul calls saints is a saint in any conventional sense. Most of us are not exceptionally good or good-looking. It is worse than that. Adultery and addictions, gossip and gluttony, arrogance and propaganda, sexual abuse and self-righteousness are as likely to occur — even flourish — in congregations of Christians as in any school or college, any bank or army, any government or business. Still, Paul doesn't hesitate to name these men and women in his congregation as saints.

And there is no use looking around for a congregation that is any better. It has always been this way. As far as we can anticipate, it always will be. Horrible crimes continue to be committed by these saints. Terrible injustices continue to be perpetrated by saints. But God, it seems, is not squeamish about keeping company with the worst and the vile.

80

He goes to work each day to redeem the worst. I can't imagine that he spends his time carefully screening through the best in order to recruit saints and then preempt heaven by launching utopian church communities on earth.

A few years ago I was in correspondence with a friend, also a pastor, on the difficulties and nearly continuous embarrassment of working week by week our entire vocational lives with, to our minds, such unsatisfactory saints. Tempted to outrage, he caught himself and reflected: "Jesus did not fool around with the drug of editorializing outrage. . . . Jesus went for the jugulars of real, specific persons God brought into his influence. He 'wasted his time' on small potatoes. He committed himself to the companionship of real people and the transformation of the motives and modes of these few souls. Holy paradox. Divine mystery. Trust in the present and personal God who loves. Jesus' temple cleansing and confrontations of authorities were not done to protest or fix. They were done to convict the worshiping people of God of blasphemy, to foster repentance before God, to honor the holy, to return his love. And they were done as part of Jesus' road to personally sacrificing his life. It's the way of the cross."

We talk about this, my friend and I, from time to time. We are trying to develop facility in using the "saint" word as easily and unguardedly as Paul did. Recently, my friend had to deal with a man fed up and angry with the church and its bad track record in matters of justice and righteousness. The man admired Jesus extravagantly but had quit on the church. He was declaring a formal self-excommunication from the unpromising collection of ne'er-do-wells that he found in churches.

The atmosphere didn't seem to encourage conversation, so my friend wrote him a letter. He sent a copy to me. I keep it in a drawer in my desk and pull it out occasionally to reread it. It helps to keep my head clear on saint language.

In his letter my friend confronted the man first by agreeing with him: "I agree. It's very hard to participate in church over time and retain your humanity. You correctly deplore what you criticize." Then he followed up with a blunt question, "Yet do you worship with a congregation, scrub its floors, change its babies, face its crises, humble yourself to its relational intricacies? The Jesus you admire did. He honored and observed worship and community. He formed a new communion while honoring the old. He lived as a participant. It was not from without but from within the 'people of God' that he confronted sin. And it was not from without but from within that he was censored and killed. It's the church that he came to build that killed him, not a network of autonomous idealists."

Then he zeroed in: "The church is woefully sinful, distorted, and inadequate. In its seasons and centuries it is often in bed with commerce, the military, and the political establishment, or just as bad, opportunistically leeching superficial life out of them by reactionism. But it's still in the bowels of the church, the worshipers, that God has chosen to work, live, and sometimes be crucified. It's the church, that Jesus says he will build, and that hell will not prevail against."[3]

Saints — the "bowels of the church." I like that. It is not much different from Paul's self-description that he wrote to the saints in Corinth: "we have become like the rubbish of the world, the dregs of all things" (1 Cor. 4:13).

Here is a marvel: from within these bowels comes a continuous witness, sounds of praise, the totally unexpected word "resurrection," talk of healing and forgiveness, preaching and praying. And all this in the bowels, from among men and women who are unashamed and unembarrassed to call the failed and sometimes unscrupulous, flawed and not infrequently scandalous men and women who are their "brothers and sisters" saints.

*     *     *

This improbable saint identity is affirmed and further clarified in the act of baptism. Holy baptism defines a person comprehensively as a creation, new creation and ongoing creation, of God the Father, God the Son, and God the Holy Spirit, a person totally immersed in all the operations of the Trinity. It is the one practice that the entire Christian

3. Letter from M.C., July 25, 2006.

church (Quakers excepted) worldwide and through all its centuries of existence has continuously carried out: "I baptize you in the name of the Father, the Son, and the Holy Spirit." Some baptize only adults. Some baptize infants. But for virtually everybody, baptism is the identity-defining act that marks us as saints, as Christians. Baptism is a public witness that this baptized person can be accurately understood only in relation to who God is, the way God reveals himself, and the ways that God works.

Baptism marks a radically new way to understand ourselves and one another: not by race, not by language, not by parents and family, not by politics, not by intelligence, not by gender, not by behavior. All of these various ways of accounting for ourselves are significant, but none is definitive. Holy baptism defines us as holy, as saints. Baptism is definitive.

*     *     *

Having acquired this identity, how do we maintain it? We maintain our baptismal identity in the practice of resurrection, *Jesus'* resurrection. We don't carry around our baptismal identity like a driver's license, a social security card, or a passport so that we can prove we are who we say we are. Our identity is not something exterior to us, a label, a nametag. We live out our identity in the practice of resurrection.

Jesus' resurrection is the convincing proclamation in the country of Palestine and in recorded first-century Roman history that everything revealed in our Scriptures can be lived by flesh-and-blood men and women like us. Not just assented to as true, not just admired as art, not just acted out as in a dramatic performance, but *lived* in the ordinary conditions of home and workplace in all kinds of weather — just as Jesus, baptized by John in the Jordan River, did. We are able to spend our lives doing this because we are saints, raised from the dead to a resurrection life.

We continue to maintain this identity by keeping company with people who have firsthand knowledge of who we are: men and women blessed, chosen, destined, bestowed, lavished, made known, gathered up — *by God!* These same people embarrass us with their haphazardness, exhilarate us with their joy, offend us by their inconsistent lives, comfort us with their compassion, bully and criticize us, encourage and bring the best out of us, bore us with their blandness, stimulate us with their enthusiasm. But we don't choose them. God chooses them. We keep company with the men and women God chooses. These saints.

### "It is here. We are on it. It is under us."

A few years ago I was with some writer friends. We were reading some of our recent writings to one another. What I am writing here (and you are reading) was in embryo within me at the time. Then one of the friends, Robert Siegel, read a poem he had recently written. I was trying to find a way to provide imagery and clarity to this saint language in the Ephesian letter that I was having difficulty keeping in focus. When Robert finished reading the poem I knew it was just the poem for me. I knew I wanted to use it at this juncture as I deal with the end of Ephesians chapter 1.

Before reading the poem, Robert described the incident that had prepared for its making. He and his wife Anne live in New England. For years they had driven through an intersection where there was a posted sign to Mt. Monadnock, a name familiar to Robert from a poem by Emerson. But they had never followed the sign to the mountain. This day, Robert saw the sign but out of habit kept going. But then on impulse he said to Anne, "Isn't it about time we saw this famous mountain for ourselves?" He returned to the intersection and turned on to the road. Afterwards he wrote this poem. It gave me the exact image I was waiting for: "Looking for Mt. Monadnock."

> We see the sign "Monadnock State Park"
> as it flashes by, after a mile or two
>
> decide to go back. "We can't pass by Monadnock
> without seeing it," I say, turning around.

We head down the side road — "Monadnock Realty,"
"Monadnock Pottery," "Monadnock Designs,"

but no Monadnock. Then the signs fall away —
nothing but trees and the darkening afternoon.

We don't speak, pass a clearing, and you say,
"I think I saw it, or part of it — a bald rock?"

Miles and miles more. Finally, I pull over
and we consult a map. "Monadnock's right there."

"Or just back a bit there." "But we should see it —
we're practically on top of it." And driving back

we look — trees, a flash of clearing, purple rock —
but we are, it seems, too close to see it:

It is here. We are on it. It is under us.[4]

*     *     *

This practice-resurrection life, this growing-up-in-Christ life, this
Christian life that some people talk about and many others hear about,
is a Mt. Monadnock kind of life. We read the words, we see the signs.
We hear the talk, read the poems, sing the hymns, pray the prayers. We
read the famous letter that the famous Paul wrote. We read Ephesians.

So we decide to take it seriously and see for ourselves, firsthand.
We see the words *Christian, resurrection, saints* all over the place. We
travel to holy places. We look through churches. But we never see what
we expected to see. We never see the mountain. We read all the extravagant words, the rocket verbs, the gift nouns, the all-encompassing

---

4. Robert Siegel, *The Waters Under the Earth* (Moscow, ID: Canon Press, 2003),
p. 70.

strategies, the grand purposes that are associated with this mountain. But we never see the mountain.

This is nothing new. It's been going on a long time. Most of the people who saw Jesus during those thirty years he lived in Palestine didn't see anything in him to write home about. Jesus: the eldest in a family of brothers and sisters growing up in small-town Nazareth, a working carpenter most of his life, came to a bad end, a common criminal dying on a cross. A few of the important people of the time noticed him only to dismiss him: King Herod Antipas, anticipating a show-and-tell miracle, was disappointed; Governor Pilate was puzzled but unimpressed; High Priest Caiaphas was contemptuous. In resurrection Jesus was still unimpressive: Mary Magdalene mistook him for a gardener; Cleopas and his friend walked seven miles with him without recognizing him, in conversation all the way. An interesting conversation, to be sure, but *God?* "We had no idea" — no idea that they were in conversation with the Savior of the world. For seven miles, walking with Jesus, discussing Holy Scriptures, they didn't know they were in conversation with the Word made flesh. Why didn't they get it? Maybe because they were preoccupied with more important things, spiritual things, Bible study. Then he picked up a loaf of bread, blessed it, broke it open, and passed it around. Now with the texture of bread on their fingers, and the taste of bread on their tongues — grounded in the ordinary — they recognized him. Paul had to walk around blind for three days before he saw him.

Why do so many of us who see Jesus every day of the week never see him? Are we looking for Jesus walking on water, a cosmic light show, a charismatic circus, a transfiguration on Denali that we can take a picture of or use as a metaphor in a poem? "What went ye out for to see?" (Matt. 11:8 KJV).

Why doesn't Jesus advertise himself? If he wants to be known as God present with us, to heal and save and bless, why doesn't he get our attention and let us know pointblank what is going on? If all those verbs and nouns that Paul has spread out for us to consider and receive are the real thing, why doesn't Jesus at least raise his voice?

The short answer: God reveals himself in personal relationship and only in personal relationship. God is not a phenomenon to be considered. God is not a force to be used. God is not a proposition to be argued. There is nothing in or of God that is impersonal, nothing abstract, nothing imposed. And God treats us with an equivalent personal dignity. He isn't out to impress us. He's here to eat bread with us and receive us into his love just as we are, just where we are.

Resurrection is an immense and glorious mountain, all right — there is no exaggeration in Paul's verbs and nouns. But the practice of resurrection in which Paul engages us is not climbing the mountain. All the immensity and glory are under our feet. It's a Monadnock kind of mountain: "It is here. We are on it. It is under our feet."

**CHAPTER 5**

# Grace and Good Works: Ephesians 2:1-10

*For by grace you have been saved through faith, and this is not your own doing; it is the gift of God — not of works, so that no one may boast. For we are what he has made us, created in Christ Jesus for good works, which God prepared beforehand to be our way of life.*

EPHESIANS 2:8-10

*This was the first time he had been passive like this. Before it had been his idea, his aggression, his carnal desires. Now this passivity seemed to open something up.*

ROBERT PIRSIG, *Lila, An Inquiry into Morals*

We turn a page: a new chapter. We find ourselves moving into new territory. We enter into the country that we have been looking at from a distance, the country of resurrection. We have been taking in the contours of the landscape, the grand horizons, Paul's dispatches back from the front — the action of God "for us and for our salvation." Paul anchored this landscape in Jesus' resurrection: "God put this power to work in Christ when he raised him from the dead" (Eph. 1:20). Now we find ourselves in it, our feet on the actual ground. We smell the wild fragrance of resins and blossoms, touch the textured tree bark, feel the rain on our heads and the wind in our faces. We are in the country of salvation, the land of resurrection, in the company of resurrection men and women.

It is one thing to look at the grandly profiled horizons and thrill to the weather gathering behind mountain ranges, launching huge light shows with sudden bursts of sunlight through fissures in the clouds, fireworks of lightning scored by organ thunder. It is quite another to leave the car or bus or train and walk into the forest and climb those mountains.

The transition is abrupt: "You were dead" (2:1) but now you are "alive together with Christ" (2:5). God raised Jesus from the dead (1:20); he also raised *us* from the dead: "raised us up with him" (2:6). Resurrection defines Jesus' life; resurrection defines our lives. We were sin-dead; we are resurrection-alive.

Paul's language is black and white: death and life. We left the roadside vista where we busied ourselves in taking pictures and sending postcards to the people back home. We walked into the forest. Resurrection country is no longer an extravagant landscape before which we stand in reverential awe. It is the land we live in, entering into the detailed intricacies of resurrection living. It is the same country that we heard about and looked at. But now we are in it, actively participating with all our bodily senses.

Resurrection life, as defined by Jesus' resurrection, is totally different from what we are used to, as different as death is from life. When we were oohing and aahing on the roadside of resurrection, we were basically spectators, able to pick and choose from the visual extravaganza spread out before us, and then to talk about it. We could leave whenever we wanted to. If we were bored we could retreat with a guidebook and anticipate the view around the next bend. Paul calls it "following the ruler of the power of the air" (Eph. 2:2). But here everything and everyone is born anew, or has the potential of becoming born anew: "the whole creation . . . groaning in labor pains" (Rom. 8:22).

Nothing and no one is a mere object, a thing that we can ignore or dispose of as we like. This is *resurrection* country. Resurrection is not something we add on to everything we are already accustomed to; it *makes alive* what has been "dead through . . . trespasses and sins" (Eph. 2:1). It is understandable that we will carry old cemetery habits and assumptions into this resurrection country. We have, after all, been living with them a long time (if you can call it living). And so we require a patient, long-suffering reorientation in the resurrection conditions that prevail in this country, living into the "full stature of Christ" (4:13), our resurrection pioneer and companion. Paul begins our reorientation with the word "grace." It is a word that he uses a lot.

## Acquired Passivity

A good part of growing up in the land of resurrection, growing up in Christ, involves practicing a kind of acquired passivity. The word "passivity" carries a bad odor in the American language: insipid, spineless, no-good, lazy, lacking gumption, couch potato, good-for-nothing, shiftless, hangdog. We are brought up to admire and imitate get-up-and-go, hustle, drive, take-no-prisoners strategies.

Energy and ambition, single-minded purpose, an undistracted and unswerving race for the finish, and eye-on-the-ball concentration go a long way in making money, acquiring academic degrees, winning wars, climbing Mt. Everest, and hitting home runs. This is indisputable. But such goals, all of them much lauded by our culture, have very little to do in themselves with living a mature life, living "to the praise of his glory."

Competitive ambition and the accompanying disciplines that bring about its achievement can be pursued, and more often than not are pursued, without conscience, without love, without compassion, without humility, without generosity, without righteousness, without holiness. Which is to say, quite apart from maturity. Immature entertainment celebrities are on display on every street corner. Immature millionaires routinely walk out on their families. Immature scholars and scientists who collect Nobel Prizes make do with estranged and godless lives. Immature star athletes regularly embarrass their coaches and fans by infantile and adolescent, sometimes criminal, behavior.

These are the men and women who set the standards for a life fueled by ambition, getting to the top, making a name for themselves, beating out the competition. These are the men and women who provide the images and examples for North Americans of what it means to be standout human beings. Do any of us want to live, I mean really *live*, that way? Is that living? Has that ever, in the entire history of humankind, been living — fully alive?

I don't think so. And I don't think many other people think so when they stop to think, if they ever do. The misery, the emptiness, the superficiality, the boredom, the desolation that accompanies this kind of living is devastating, not only to the individuals involved but to their families and communities. And the seepage of such lives into our culture — for no man is an island unto himself — impoverishes us all.

When we observe these people, as we can't help observing — they are in our faces every day in our daily newspapers, our history textbooks, our media reporting — we realize how radically different they are from the life of Jesus and the resurrection life of Jesus that Paul uses as his text for living a mature human life. They are not so much different in appearance as different at the very root, the *radix*.

This is nothing new. Contemporary life is no different from life in the ancient world in this regard. What is different is that North Americans, by and large, exempt themselves from any sense of cultural and societal kinship, especially in terms of immaturity, with the ancients. We assume that we are different, better, more advanced. We have a higher standard of living, immensely improved health care, a high rate of literacy, psychological testing that gives us amazing and profound insights into who we are and how we function (IQ tests, Myers-Briggs profiles, family systems, Enneagrams), and a technology that provides instant access to anything we want to know and that can put men and women on the moon and who knows where else in the years to come. It is obvious, is it not, that we are far more advanced than our ancestors, much farther along in becoming fully developed human beings? Not only that, but many of us, whether we think much about it or not, also have this rich Judeo-Christian heritage, forming our identity as "Christian." A Christian nation. A Christian culture. A Christian person.

It is commonplace among us to combine our cultures, American and Christian, taking what we think is the best of each to produce a hybrid: American Christian, Christian America. The best of the modern world, American, and the best of the biblical world, Christian: hybrid Christians.

But why would we suppose that the best of the modern world is any different from the best of the ancient world? Assyria, Babylon, and Egypt possessed sophisticated technology and mathematics with which they engineered astonishing architectural feats, including pyramids and intricate irrigation systems. Persia, Greece, and Rome had artists and philosophers who carved statues and wrote books that continue in the top ranking of what human beings are capable of making and thinking.

Our Hebrew people-of-God ancestors lived as neighbors with these high-achieving ancients. But however they may have accepted and benefited from their libraries and technologies, they were fiercely jealous of the integrity of their souls and vigilantly guarded their image-of-God identity. They did not admire the leaders of those kingdoms and cultures. They did not adopt the successful ways of life that produced the power and wealth of those civilizations.

The stories of Abraham and Moses, Elijah and Jeremiah, Daniel and Esther are all energetically countercultural. Our pioneering Christian ancestors lived as neighbors alongside the descendants of the highly civilized and accomplished Greeks and Romans, and they participated in the economies that were provided for them and the learning that was accessible to them. At the same time, they were uncompromising in their rejection of the divine pretensions and sexual profligacies of their leaders in government and the arts, and the superficial idolatries in all the so-called best families.

Matthew, Mark, Luke, and John wrote the definitive texts of their God as crucified — *crucified!* — texts that shaped their participation in living a well and whole *mature* life. The cross was a "stumbling block to

Jews and foolishness to Gentiles" (1 Cor. 1:23) in the time of Jesus. It continues to be an unassimilable stumbling block and folly in our North American culture that worships power and self-indulgence, a culture that divinizes human achievement.

Christians, then and now, are the only persons on the face of the earth who worship a *crucified* Savior — to all appearances in every and all cultures a rejected, humiliated, and failed Savior.

But, unlike our Hebrew people-of-God identities and unlike our pioneering Christian ancestors who worshiped a crucified Savior as the revelation of God, the popular religious practice in our culture is to cross-fertilize American with Christian and come up with a hybrid. In botany and animal husbandry hybridization is practiced by grafting or cross-breeding to bring out the best in both species: hybrid corn and hybrid sheep, for example. But if you don't know what you are doing, no matter how well intentioned you may be, you can end up with something that is worse than either on its own: a mongrel. The Latin *hybrida,* literally translated, is just that, a mongrel, the offspring of a tame sow and a wild boar. When the wild bull of American ambition is bred with a tame Christianity with no cross, the result is mongrel spirituality — a "Christian" with both the image of God and the crucified Savior lost in the cross-breeding. The distinctive element in the human is lost. The distinctive element in Jesus is lost. An antichrist?

\*     \*     \*

These are background observations for understanding why what I am calling "acquired passivity" is so difficult for us to take seriously and then embrace — and why it is absolutely necessary to embrace it if we are to accustom ourselves to living in a world characterized by the grace of God, for "by grace you have been saved." There are no other options. It's grace or nothing. There is no "Plan B."

The air we breathe and the atmosphere we inhabit as believers and followers of Jesus is grace. If we don't know what grace is, the last place to go looking for help is the dictionary. Grace is everywhere to be experienced but nowhere to be explained. We need to look to Moses and Isaiah, Jesus and Paul, as they tell us the story of our lives as immersed, conditioned, and experienced in the grace of God.

Grace is an insubstantial, invisible reality that permeates all that we are, think, speak, and do. But we are not used to this. We are not used to living by invisibles. We have work to do, things to learn, people to help, traffic to negotiate, meals to prepare. When we need a break, there are birds to watch, books to read, walks to take, a cup of tea to drink, maybe even a chapel to sit in and meditate for ten minutes or so. But these so-called "breaks" are not what we call the real world, the world in which we make a living, the world in which we make something of ourselves. They are brief escapes from it so that we can go back to the "real world" refreshed.

I received a most helpful and enduring reflection on what grace consists of from William Stafford, an American poet. I was reading a book he wrote on creative writing, specifically the writing of poems. In the middle of a page I came across what I immediately recognized as something very much like what followers of Jesus name grace. He was using swimming as an analogy for writing. As I read, I began substituting the language of grace (the bracketed words in what follows) to transfer Stafford's analogy of swimmers and water to the Christian experience of grace.

Stafford observed that

> any reasonable person who looks at water [grace], and passes a hand through it, can see that it would not hold a person up. . . . But swimmers [followers of Jesus] know that if they relax on the water [grace] it will prove to be miraculously buoyant; and writers [followers of Jesus] know that a succession of little strokes on the material nearest them — without any prejudgments about the specific gravity of the topic or the reasonableness of their expectations — will result in creative progress [growing up in Christ: maturity]. Writers are persons who write; swimmers [believers] are . . . persons who relax in the water, let their heads go down, and reach out with ease and confidence. . . . Just as the swimmer [be-

liever] does not have a succession of handholds hidden in the water, but instead simply sweeps that yielding medium and finds it hurrying him along, so the swimmer and writer [follower of Jesus] passes his attention through what is at hand, and is propelled by a medium [grace] too thin and all-pervasive for the perceptions of nonbelievers who try to stay on the bank and fathom his accomplishment.[1]

Grace originates in an act of God that is absolutely without precedent, the generous, sacrificial self-giving of Jesus that makes it possible for us to participate in resurrection maturity. It is not what we do; it is what we participate in. But we cannot participate apart from a willed passivity, entering into and giving ourselves up to what is previous to us, the presence and action of God in Christ that is other than us. Such passivity does not come easy to us. It must be acquired.

\*     \*     \*

And works? Why is there such unending and often acrimonious argument and contention about faith and works? Doesn't the way Paul places our working lives in the deep and wide ocean of grace, an ocean that we enter only by diving in, put an end to all that tedious gossip? Faith in Christ is an act of abandoning the shores of self, where we think we know where we stand and where if we just try hard enough we can be in control. Faith in Christ is a plunge into grace. Grace: "not your own doing; it is a gift of God."

\*     \*     \*

But that terra firma, feet-on-the-ground self is hard to give up. We have grown up on this ground, learned the way the world works on this ground, become pretty good at finding our way around on this

1. William Stafford, *Writing the Australian Crawl* (Ann Arbor: The University of Michigan Press, 1978), pp. 23-25.

ground. We have maps and guidebooks, know all the best restaurants, know where to shop for bargains. All our habits have been formed on this ground.

In fifty years of being a pastor, my most difficult assignment continues to be the task of developing a sense among the people I serve of the soul-transforming implications of grace — a comprehensive, foundational reorientation from living anxiously by my wits and muscle to living effortlessly in the world of God's active presence. The prevailing North American culture (not much different from the Assyrian, Babylonian, Egyptian, Persian, Greek, and Roman cultures in which our biblical ancestors lived) is, to all intents and purposes, a context of persistent denial of grace.

\*    \*    \*

A couple made an appointment to come talk with me. We had lived in the same neighborhood for several years but we had never met. A friend of theirs, a man from my congregation, suggested me to them. I introduced myself, "I'm Pastor Peterson."

The man said, "My name is Eben. My wife, Sylvia."

"Good to meet you, Evan and Sylvia."

"No, not Evan. Eben."

I said, "Oh, like in Eben-ezer."

"How did you know that?"

"I read it in the Bible. And sometimes I sing it in a hymn. Eben, stone; Ebenezer, stone of strength. And Sylvia, forest. I like that, an appropriate pairing of names — Eben and Sylvia, stone and forest — for the country of marriage."

"It's marriage we came to talk to you about. We're having some difficulties."

We talked. They were about fifty years of age, thirty of those fifty years married to one another. Eben was a non-practicing Jew, Sylvia a non-practicing Southern Baptist. Since they were non-practicing, the contrasting religious backgrounds had never seemed to be a problem. They had both been schooled in their respective faiths, but had long ago quit paying much attention to what they had been taught. Eben was something of an entrepreneur — imaginative, hardworking. He had left a secure government desk job several years before to risk a new start by forming a rental business. It had flourished. He rented all kinds of things from backhoes for digging ditches to coffee urns for wedding receptions. I knew the store: I had once rented a rototiller there to help cultivate our vegetable garden. Sylvia worked with him in the business, doing the bookkeeping and welcoming and helping out with customers. I remembered her easy congeniality from the time I had been in their store.

We talked. They liked their work and worked well together. They made more than enough money and lived comfortably. They had raised three children. One lived several states away; the other two were away in college. They liked their lives. But now, for the first time, they weren't getting along with one another. They didn't know what had changed, what was different. Everything seemed the same, but nothing seemed the same.

We talked. Every week or so we would spend an hour together. I liked them. Eben always paced the room as he talked — language involved using his legs as much as using his mouth. Sylvia kept her hands busy smoking cigarettes. In our conversations the realization emerged among the three of us that as long as they were working together they did just fine, but when they locked the doors of the business and went home things fell apart. And Sundays were hell. Their lives and their relationship with one another were largely defined by their work. When there was no work to do they didn't know what to do. Now that the demanding work of raising children and getting a new business running had been accomplished, they had time on their hands that they had never had before. There was no adrenaline in leisure.

Eben had been raised in a Jewish work world of reaching and striving, making a mark. His energy and extensive know-how in tools and machines kept the customers coming. Sylvia had been raised in a Baptist moral world of getting it right, of making a good impression. Her warm Alabama hospitality, enhanced by a practiced smile and a well-kept body, brought in high approval ratings during store hours.

But out of the workplace there was no market for Eben's know-how and no one to confirm Sylvia's performance.

We talked. So what do you do when you aren't getting paid for what you do? What do you say when what you say and the way you say it doesn't affect the cash flow? Our conversation developed into exploring how things change in a relationship when you don't have to earn your keep. Insights began to surface from unseen depths, the invisibilities that buoy performance.

We talked. In the middle of the conversation one day, Eben stopped in mid-stride and said, "Grace! Is what we are talking about *grace?* I've always wondered what that word meant. Is *this* what it means?" Sylvia lit another cigarette.

I didn't know it at the time, but that Eureka! — exclamatory, surprised — *grace,* marked the winding down of our conversations. I hadn't ever used the word in their presence; it was Eben who introduced it. But something underground in Eben's Jewish heritage, latent for forty years or so, ignited. He was on to something. I brought Abraham into the conversation. Eben introduced the name of Jesus. Sylvia was increasingly bored. The gap between them widened.

So close. A near miss. I don't think they ever divorced. I saw them occasionally in their store when I went to rent a tool. We made friendly small talk and did our business. But the conversations were over. Eben and Sylvia had, in effect, abandoned their marriage and gone back to their workplace.

## Good Works

But work and workplace are not antithetical to grace. In fact, grace is absolutely and insistently at home in work and workplace. Paul makes sure we get this right by placing the term "good works" in the same sentence in which he discusses grace: not only saved by grace but "created in Christ Jesus for good works, which God prepared beforehand to be our way of life" (Eph. 2:10).

Fundamentally, work is not what we do; we are the work that

God does: "We are what he has made us," also translated "We are [God's] workmanship" (RSV, KJV).

Grace does not displace work. Work, whether pre- or post-resurrection, remains as pervasive as ever. Resurrection Christians are not awarded the bonus of a reduced workweek. Work is not downgraded to something sub-spiritual. The mature life in Christ does not exempt us from punching the clock, laboring long hours with too little help in harvesting a field of grain, putting in time in a boring occupation until we reach retirement, holding on to a thread of sanity in the chaos of raising three preschool children. Work is often exhilarating. It is just as often debilitating, demoralizing, and exhausting. The only thing worse than bad work is no work, unemployment.

So what changes when Paul sets "work" as a companion word alongside "grace" if the next day, having been "raised up with him," we return to the same jobs, the same responsibilities, the same workplace conditions?

This: we are no longer working for General Electric, the government, the school board, the hospital, Safeway. We are God's work and doing God's work: "we are what he has made us, created in Christ Jesus for good works, which God prepared beforehand to be our way of life" (Eph. 2:10).

*       *       *

Work is first of all what God does, not what we do. Genesis 1–2 is our entrance story of God in his revelation to us. Most significantly, it is a story of God at work, working in the very same environment in which we do our work. The first thing we learn about God is that God works. God goes to work making the world and all that is in it (Genesis 1) and then invites us into his work, giving us work to do that is commensurate with his work (Genesis 2).

The Christian community has a long tradition of reading, meditating, and praying Genesis 1–2 in order to form our understanding and experience of work in the company of God at work. All our work is preceded by his work. All our work takes place in God's workplace. All our work is intended to be a participation in God's work. As we prayerfully imagine God's first "workweek," we get a feel for what is involved.

God makes light. What a gift. God's work. God's gift. We can see what is going on, we can see where we are going. "Light dawns for the righteous" (Ps. 97:11). Every lamp, every candle, every torch, every chandelier is a witness to what is continuously revealed around us.

God makes sky. Sheer gift. God's work. God's gift. This huge Above. Space and spaciousness, this immense Beyond. Far, far more than we can take in. Far, far more than we can control. Everything visible stretching into invisibility.

God makes earth and sea, plants and trees. Sheer gift. God's work. God's gift. Oak forests and wheat fields, apple trees and rose gardens. A place to stand. A place to be at home. A home furnished with what we need. A home beautiful.

God makes sun and moon and stars, marking seasons and days and years. Sheer gift. God's work. God's gift. Time to look around and see the sights, sunrise and sunset. Time to listen to the wind in the willows and the rain on the roof. Time to sleep and dream and "awake the dawn" (Ps. 108:2). Time to remember and count blessings. Time to hope and pray.

God makes fish and birds. Sea and sky resplendent with life. Sheer gift. God's work. God's gift. Rainbow trout and belted kingfishers. The dazzle and elegance of every kind of life.

God makes animals domestic and wild. Sheer gift. God's work. God's gift. Cattle and caribou, ants and lizards, grizzly bears and honeybees. Life on the move. Life profuse in form and color. Life dancing.

God makes man and woman. Sheer gift. God's work. God's gift. Wherever you look, wherever you go, man and woman. Man and woman on every street and road, each one unique. But on this sixth day of work, there is something different. Each man and woman is not only an instance of God's workmanship but is capable of participating in God's work, working in God's workplace and continuing God's work, continuing the gift-making.

And then it is done, complete, "finished." The seventh day, a day for God to look back across the workweek, take stock of "all the work that he had done." "The work that he had done" is repeated three times (Gen. 2:2-3). A day of rest. A day for quiet reflection on all the good work. A day of hallowing and blessing the good work.

Seven times in this week of work, God paused, looked over his work, and pronounced it good. The final "good" was intensified to "very good." Good work, indeed.

*    *    *

A week of work. A week of gifts. All work at its heart and origin gives form to a gift. Or, to put it another way, it is the nature of work to provide a container for a gift. The reason that work is called good is that it is the means for delivering a gift.

To call something or someone a gift does not tell us what it is but how it comes to us. "Gift," as such, has no shape or color or texture. "Gift" merely says that it comes to us freely. It arrives neither out of necessity nor on demand. It is free. It arrives in an ambience of generosity, with no strings attached.

A prayed attentiveness to the workweek of creation develops within us a realization that we live in a world of sheer gift, that we ourselves are sheer gift, and that whatever we do replicates and continues to express and give form to this basic giftedness — *God*-giftedness. And we receive this gift in the form of works.

The most common term in our biblical languages for this underlying and comprehensive God-giftedness is "grace." And Genesis, with the emphasis provided by the repetitions across the seven creation days of God at work — "Let there be" (12x), "made" (3x), "created" (5x), "work" (3x) — dramatically underscores that it is the nature of work to provide a material form for the invisibilities of grace.

## Works as a Form for Glory

The mature Christian life involves a congruence of grace and work. Nothing in the Christian life matures apart from work and works. The invisible Word that was in the Genesis beginning (John 1:1) "became flesh" in Jesus. In Jesus, a human form "full of grace" (1:14), we see God at work ("the works that the Father has given me to complete," 5:36). Jesus insists that the God no one has ever seen (1:18) is visible in the works that Jesus himself does right in front of their eyes. "The works that I do," Jesus said, "testify to me" (10:25).

It is one of the great ironies of Jesus' life that what people saw Jesus do — Jesus at work feeding the hungry on a hillside, Jesus in their neighborhood, Jesus reaching out to the marginal, Jesus healing a "mother-in-law" and a twelve-year-old child (both unnamed) in the houses they lived in, Jesus reading familiar Scriptures in the synagogues where they worshiped each Sabbath — were the very things that provoked criticism and mistrust and outright rejection of him as the incarnation of God. His contemporaries found it far easier to believe in an invisible God than in a visible God.

Jesus' work is the form in which the invisible God can be seen. The fourth Gospel, John, puts it succinctly: we have seen God's glory in Jesus. Glory is God's invisibility become visible in Jesus at work. And — this is Paul's point in Ephesians — we also are "created in Christ Jesus for good works, which God prepared beforehand to be our way of life" (Eph. 2:10). Our work is a form for the glory.

*     *     *

It is essential that we assimilate God's Genesis week of work if we are to live what "God prepared beforehand to be our way of life." The Genesis week is the story of God pouring all the Trinitarian invisibilities into forms that are accessible to our five senses. God's grace, the basic giftedness of everything that God is and does, becomes present to us exclusively in the form of work. The works of God — light and sky, earth and sea, trees and vegetation, time and seasons, fish and birds, cattle and kangaroos, man and woman — are the forms by which we see, hear, touch, taste, and smell grace. The works of creation, including we ourselves as part of those works, provide the forms by which we enter into and participate in the world of grace.

The visible creation is the form, the context, in which we experience grace. Invisible grace permeates the forms of creation, filling them with content. The Genesis gift-work of creation becomes visible and audible in the forms of creation. Creation is all gift. We receive the gift and participate in the gift in the forms of work. Salvation is all gift. It takes form in a world of work.

A meditative understanding of Genesis forms us in continuity with the Genesis works that God pronounced good and very good. Formed in submission and obedience by Genesis rhythms and images, we mature into a life of "good works, which God prepared beforehand to be our way of life." These Genesis rhythms and images free us from secularized and pietist distortions that result from pitting grace and work against one another. Good work and good works are to grace what a pail is to water: a container to get it from the well to the supper table. God's grace is the content. Our work (after the manner of Jesus) is the container.

We are not angels. This world that we inhabit is God's work. Everything we experience we experience under God's sky and on God's earth and sea, in God's time marked by sun, moon, and stars, in the company of God's menagerie of dolphins and eagles, lions and lambs, and in the company of image-of-God men and women who come to us as parents and grandparents, children and grandchildren, brothers and sisters, neighbors and relatives, playmates and workmates, students and helpers — and Jesus. Nothing in the practice of resurrection is experienced or participated in apart from a body, a form, fingers and feet, eyes and ears and tongue. And nothing in the practice of resurrection takes place apart from stuff to work with — dirt and clay for shaping pots and mugs, stone and timbers for constructing homes and churches, nouns and verbs for conveying wisdom and knowledge, cotton and wool for weaving clothes and blankets, semen and eggs for making babies: good works. Work is the generic form for embodying grace. All Christian spirituality is thoroughly incarnational — in Jesus, to be sure, but also in us.

*       *       *

Distortions of "good works" abound. I just named the distortions as "secularized" and "pietist." The distortions occur when we don't take the Genesis context of work with attentive and meditated seriousness on one hand (the secularist hand), or when we don't observe and listen carefully to the Jesus context of work on the other hand (the pietist hand).

The secularist romanticizes work. The pietist spiritualizes work. Either is a distortion of God's Genesis work and of God's Jesus work. Both disregard what Paul is teaching us about growing "to the measure of the full stature of Christ," namely, that in the practice of resurrection we live not in terms of what we make of ourselves but in terms of what God makes us.

Work is romanticized when it is understood as a way to be significant, to become well known, to make a lot of money, to "make a contribution." Romanticized work tends to be glamorized work. Romanticized work relies heavily on payoffs, whether in salary and stock options, in recognition and prominence, or in "job satisfaction" and "fulfilled potential."

But in the Genesis workweek, there is nothing glamorous in the narration. Each day's work is matter-of-fact, set down without embellishment. The only comment that is made is a single syllable: "good." This is the way it is. The worker, God, is nearly invisible in the work: "No one has seen God at any time" (John 1:18). The work itself is what is seen, a container for receiving the unseen.

Work is romanticized when it is conceived and practiced quite apart from God's Genesis style and context. It is romanticized when it becomes a way to extend our significance and influence and importance — when we become the worker with no relation or thought that we are God's work, before we ever go to work. Work becomes a way to become godlike without dealing with God.

The most conspicuous distortion among romanticizers comes through the omission of Sabbath. Sabbath is rarely practiced — no seventh day, no rest. There is always more to be done because the work itself is never finished. Romanticized work has a high adrenaline component. The satisfactions of doing a great job, accomplishing a difficult task, and being recognized and appreciated are considerable . . . and easily addictive. Romanticized work is self-idolatrous.

Pietistic work develops when we fail to observe the way Jesus went about his work. The pietist "spiritualizes" work. Work is desecularized into religious acts: prayer, worship, witness. Or it is professionalized into occupations of pastor, preacher, missionary, evangelist. This spirit-ualization of work de-spiritualizes most of the world of work, the work that Kathleen Norris has named "the quotidian mysteries."[2] This is the daily work of what is often dismissively referred to as "women's work" — laundry, meal preparation, child-rearing, typing, and carpooling. It also, across the board, removes unskilled work from the Christian workweek: work for hire, assembly-line work, grunt work. The only work left for honoring and practicing "good works" is church work, of-ten identified as "the Lord's work" or "Christian work."

But this pietistic distortion of work can be accomplished only by ignoring Jesus at work. Almost all of the metaphors Jesus used to an-chor our work in the world that he himself inhabited come out of the ordinary, the everyday: seeds and flowers, bread and salt, farmers and builders, sparrows and scorpions, widows and children. The people he spent most of his time with were either outcasts or the underclass: tax collectors, fishermen, prostitutes, lepers. None of the apostles he called into discipleship training had any credentials from the religious workplace. He openly avoided the standard religious practices of fast-ing, praying in public, and conventional Sabbath keeping — and was heavily criticized for it. With very few exceptions, all the works of Je-sus took place in a secular setting.

*       *       *

Genesis and Jesus develop a congruence of grace and good works in us, and Paul assures us that we can, in fact, live this way. Keeping company with them is the best way I know for getting free of romanticized and

---

2. Kathleen Norris, *The Quotidian Mysteries: Laundry, Liturgy, and "Women's Work"* (New York: Paulist Press, 1998).

spiritualized distortions of work. In the company of Genesis and Jesus, the conditions for the integration of grace and good works are favorable. However difficult this is, it is not alien to us. We are created for this. The Genesis origin and the Jesus practice will gradually but surely find their way with us. As we grow to the "measure of the full stature of Christ" we will find that whatever job we get and whatever task we are assigned can serve as a container for grace, can provide a form for God's grace, as we practice resurrection.

# III

# THE CREATION OF CHURCH

*Why do people in churches seem like cheerful brainless tourists on a packaged tour of the Absolute? . . . On the whole I do not find Christians, outside the catacombs, sufficiently sensible of conditions. Does anyone have the foggiest idea what sort of power we so blithely invoke? Or, as I suspect, does no one believe a word of it? The churches are children playing on the floor with their chemistry sets, mixing up a batch of TNT to kill a Sunday morning. It is madness to wear ladies' straw hats and velvet hats to church; we should all be wearing crash helmets. Ushers should issue life preservers and signal flares; they should lash us to our pews. For the sleeping god may wake someday and take offense, or the waking god may draw us out to where we can never return.*

ANNIE DILLARD, *Teaching a Stone to Talk*

## CHAPTER 6

# Peace and the Broken Wall: Ephesians 2:11-22

*But now in Christ Jesus you who once were far off have been brought near by the blood of Christ. For he is our peace; in his flesh he has made both groups into one and has broken down the dividing wall, that is, the hostility between us.*

EPHESIANS 2:13-14

*I know God only through Jesus. The unique grandeur of Christianity is its belief in a poor God, like a wound in the absolute. God, the child in a manger. No man could invent that; it requires revelation.*

JEAN SULIVAN, *Morning Light*

Paul's message on growing up in Christ breaks in on us in a dazzling exposition of what is going on in this world we live in (Eph. 1:3-14). Hard on its heels comes a surprising redefinition of how we who live in this world understand ourselves (1:15-23).

What is going on is this: God is continuously in action in ways that are comprehensively glorious.

And what we understand is this: every part of our lives is affected by these actions of God.

\*     \*     \*

Most of us have a pretty thorough schooling in understanding this world in terms of astronomy and geography and history. We learn that the earth revolves around the sun, which takes some getting used to because it certainly doesn't look that way. We learn that we live on a globe, not a flat surface — that's something we never would have guessed without a teacher. We learn that a lot more has been going on than what we have observed in our homes and neighborhoods: Columbus (or was it Leif the Lucky?) discovering America; Helen of Troy's face launching a thousand ships; Napoleon, a man who Ezra Pound remarked couldn't build a chicken coop, becoming famous by starting a big war and killing a lot of people; Rachel Carson waking up the country to the damage we were doing to one another and the trees and air, the water and birds around us, and getting us to do something about it.

But there is not much about God in all this. By the time we leave elementary school most of us know more about the phases of the moon, the life cycle of frogs, and the adventures of Lewis and Clark than we know of God. There is a huge irony here, for God accounts for most of what is going on in the world. If we are going to grow up, we need to know what's going on in the neighborhood. We need to know about *God* in the neighborhood. We need to know that God is continuously active in this world. We need to know that in and with, before and after everything that is and takes place, God is present and active. Paul tells us. Paul tells us that everything that is going on in this world, including us, is intended "to the praise of his glory" (Eph. 1:14).

\*     \*     \*

Most of us know a good bit about ourselves. We learn the language of the country. We learn the rudiments of what we need to stay alive and healthy. With a good bit of parental reminding, we learn that our teeth need brushing and our hands need washing. We learn how to tie our shoes. We know what we need to do to keep from getting in trouble with our parents and friends. We learn other survival things along the way: how to get through school, how to get a job, how to get married and raise a family. We find out what we like and are good at. We learn about aptitudes and emotions. We fall in love. We fall out of love. We learn how to fit in and get along — or not.

But how God figures in all this on a day-by-day basis is vague. We know in considerable detail what is involved in being a child and having (or not having) parents. We know what our teachers think of us and what their place is in our lives. We know what it feels like to have a good friend. We know what it feels like to be left out. We know the adrenaline thrill of running fast, riding a bike, riding on a rollercoaster. But it is not readily apparent that God is present to us in these immediate ways that contribute to our self-understanding.

If we don't know what God thinks of us and what we have to do with God, we have missed a huge part of what it means to grow up. We need to know that God is not just "deity in general," not off doing something big in the universe, remote from who we are or what we think of ourselves. God is not remote; God is present and active in us. The way God thinks of us and treats us is not just another item in a continuum of all these other ways in which we learn to understand ourselves. It is, in fact, quite different. It is a surprise — and a good surprise. It is a radical redefinition of who we are in a way that is different from anyone else. We need to understand that God has to do with every part of our lives, not just the religious part. Paul tells us. Paul tells us we are saints.

What Paul tells us involves a comprehensive reorientation of the way we have learned to know the world and to understand ourselves. It doesn't exclude what we have learned from our parents and teachers and friends. But it places all of it in a much larger reality — a way of seeing the world and a way of understanding ourselves that changes everything.

Here's the concluding sentence in this comprehensive reorientation: "And he has put all things under [Jesus'] feet and has made him the head over all things for the church, which is his body, the fullness of him who fills all in all" (Eph. 1:22-23).

Church: the final entry in the litany of God's actions that establishes the conditions in which we grow up in Christ. One of our most discerning writers on Ephesians says that with this sentence "we begin one of the most difficult sections of the letter."[1]

## The Brambles of Individualism

Paul must sense that it is going to be difficult to move from what our parents and teachers and friends tell us about the world and ourselves to what God reveals, and so he takes his time with us. He doesn't just jump into it. Before taking up "church," this climax topic that comprehends everything that has gone before, Paul clears the way by helping us through some rough terrain. What he does is guide us through the thorny brambles of individualism.

Individualism is the growth-stunting, maturity-inhibiting habit of understanding growth as an isolated self-project. Individualism is self-ism with a swagger. The individualist is the person who is convinced that he or she can serve God without dealing with God. This is the person who is sure that he or she can love neighbors without knowing their names. This is the person who assumes that "getting ahead" involves leaving other people behind. This is the person who, having gained competence in knowing God or people or world, uses that knowledge to take charge of God or people or world.

We, of course, are inherently individuals responsible for our intentions and the use of our free will. God does not eviscerate us of individuality when we enter church. Church, rather, is where we cultivate a submission to the care and authority of God.

America, compounded with a degraded form of evangelicalism, is the individualism capital of the world. So it is understandable that American Christians experience such a high rate of injuries, and even casualties, in getting through the thistles and boulders and potholes of individualism that so severely impede growing up in Christ.

1. Ernest Best, *A Critical and Exegetical Commentary on Ephesians* (Edinburgh: T. & T. Clark, 1998), p. 181.

For as long as individualism has free rein in our lives, we will not be capable of embracing church. Individualism severely handicaps us in growing up to the measure of the full stature of Christ. If unchecked it can be fatal, fating us to lifelong immaturity.

Paul understands this. He wants *us* to understand it. And so before he takes up God's gift of church, he helps us through the subtle treacheries of individualism by showing us how grace and good works (the subject of the previous chapter) are integrated. If grace and good works are separated, either one by itself becomes a breeding ground for individualism: living a "spiritual" life (or intellectual or caring or devout) without it taking bodily form; living a "practical" life (working for God, helping humanity, leading good causes) without personal relationship. Briefly, specializing in God (grace) without being bothered with people; specializing in people (good works) without bothering with God.

Why is it so difficult to overcome the soul-debilitating effects of individualism? After all, in Jesus, who shows us the way in all things, there is no perceptible dissonance between grace and good works. None. He was totally God and totally human. His being (grace) and his doing (good works) were fused. And it is in Jesus that we are growing up. If we focus on Jesus instead of ourselves, I don't think it is so difficult to understand. What is difficult is getting used to it. We are too full of ourselves. It is Christ — not me, not you, not us — who "fills all in all." Get used to it.

## "A serious house on serious earth"

With the ground cleared of the brambles of individualism, Paul is ready to explore his final entry in the catalogue of conditions in which we become mature men and women of God: the church — "the church, which is his body, the fullness of him who fills all in all" (Eph. 1:22-23). Church is not simply the final entry. Church summarizes all that God does, all that Christ is, all that we are in Christ. Church comprises all that is involved in living the mature life in Christ.

This is important. We cannot understand or experience church as a discrete thing. And we do not become mature by taking a course in maturity or reading a book on maturity. Maturity is everything we are becoming attentive and responsive to, everything that Christ is. It cannot be entered into apart from everything that first leads up to and then proceeds from it. The first thing that leads up to it is that there is far more to the church than meets the eye.

What meets the eye for most of us is a building we see on the street in our neighborhood. It usually, but not always, looks like a church. But there is no mistaking it, for there is usually a sign that identifies it as "church."

For some of us it is a church that we were brought to by our parents when we were young. Others make their way inside the doors later in life, sometimes out of curiosity, sometimes at the invitation of friends. We go to this church most Sundays. We get to know the names of the people there; some of them become friends. We are called to worship God by the pastor or priest. We sing hymns and listen to sermons. We receive the sacrament of the Lord's Supper. Sometimes there is a baptism.

For others of us it is a building that we enter only on the occasion of a wedding or a funeral. Our only reason for being there is affection for the persons being married or respect for the person who has died.

But what takes place in the church building, for both the insiders and the outsiders, is pretty ordinary stuff with ordinary people — at least that is what it looks like. There is no training required, no skills to be mastered, just people praying and singing and listening, exchanging vows, being blessed, receiving Jesus in the bread and wine, celebrating marriage, honoring the dead. Millions of men, women, and children do it every Lord's Day all over the world, and some of their friends join them for special occasions. We've been doing it for two thousand years now.

Anyone entering one of these buildings expecting entertainment or relief from a dull and boring life is not likely to come back a second time. Anyone entering a church hoping to see a miracle or have a vision will almost certainly leave disappointed. There is nothing out of the ordinary to see in churches. What you see is what you get. And what you see is painfully ordinary.

*     *     *

Midway through the twentieth century, church attendance in Europe, with North America not far behind, began a slow and then precipitous decline. The obituary of God — God is dead! — was reported endlessly in the newspapers and elaborated in books. "Spirituality,"[2] a promising but hopelessly vague trend, seemed on the rise. Meanwhile church, the traditional gathering place for worshiping God, was losing ground.

While all this was going on, Philip Larkin, a British poet, wrote a poem entitled "Church Going."[3] It was a poem about going to a church in which no one was going to church. At least not going to church to worship God, which is why churches are built in the first place.

I read the poem during a time when I had been given an assignment to organize and develop a church. It was the early 1960s. I was going house to house in an area of population growth northeast of Baltimore, introducing myself and what I was doing. It was not what I set out to do, but it turned out that I was gathering firsthand evidence that fewer and fewer people were going to church. Many of them commented by way of explanation that they were "into spirituality." I felt as if I was selling and repairing bicycles in a country where bicycles had once been the primary mechanized means of transportation but were now suddenly replaced by automobiles. Bicycles were obsolete. Cars were the thing — far faster, far easier. No pedals!

Pedaling a bicycle was church going. Driving a car was spirituality.

2. The word has a good pedigree, originating in that which has to do with the Holy Spirit. But in common American usage now, it is usually reduced to the human spirit with only marginal, if any, reference to God's Spirit. I place the word in quotation marks to indicate this reduced, individualistic usage of the word. I provide an extended comment on the term in *Christ Plays in Ten Thousand Places: A Conversation in Spiritual Theology* (Grand Rapids: Eerdmans, 2005), pp. 25-30.

3. Philip Larkin, *The Less Deceived* (Hessle, Yorkshire: The Marvell Press, 1955), p. 28.

Was there any future in organizing and building yet another church when more and more people were abandoning church-going and taking up with spirituality? Had a paradigm shift from church to spirituality taken place when I wasn't looking and church would soon be on a scrap heap along with one-room schools, phrenology, and smoke-signal communication?

This was the setting in which I first read Larkin's poem. It caught my interest, but it wasn't long before my attention was riveted. After numerous readings I was ready to take up church again.

*　　*　　*

The poem is narrated by a man riding a bicycle, who stops at a country church in the middle of the week and steps inside. He removes his hat and cycle-clips "in awkward reverence." A church is not home ground for him, certainly not a place to worship God. But something draws him in. He observes his surroundings, among them "sprawlings of flowers cut for Sunday." He moves forward to the chancel, runs his hand around the baptismal font, stands behind the lectern, reads a few lines of Scripture in mock seriousness, and leaves. He signs the book at the door and donates an "Irish sixpence" on his way out.

He wonders why he did it: "the place was not worth stopping for." Yet he did stop. He often stops at empty churches on his bicycling excursions and walks in. What are they good for? he muses. What will happen to them when no one shows up to worship in them, which is sure to happen sooner or later? Maybe a few of the big ones will be kept on display as architectural museum pieces while rain and a few grazing sheep complete the slow demolition of the rest. Following the inevitable disintegration of belief, superstition will also die out (ghosts and ghost stories, cures for cancer, and wind-whispered oracles through the ruins). With both belief and superstition gone, what will be left? Nothing but a site for gravestone rubbings and maybe whiffs of recently evaporated sanctity. Or a rest stop for a casual bicyclist like himself, "bored and uninformed," wondering what a church is good for when God or the worship of God is no longer in fashion.

Then, unbidden, his reflections, in spite of his cynical skepticism, deepen. He recognizes that this is "a serious house on serious earth," where "someone will forever be surprising a hunger in himself to be more serious." And that hunger "can never be obsolete."

Is a church a church when everyone quits going to church? If Larkin is right, and I am now convinced he is, the answer is yes. Church "can never be obsolete." I was ready to go back to carrying out my church assignment.

*   *   *

As it turns out, there is far more going on in the matter of church than meets the eye. Paul tells us what it is. Even as Larkin's bicyclist moves from the externals of what he sees in the empty church, "the sprawlings of flowers," Paul makes us insiders to the much documented fact that it is a place where "someone will forever be surprising a hunger in himself to be more serious." As we let Paul form our understanding of what goes on in church, what strikes us is that the church is primarily the activity of God in Christ through the Spirit. God and Jesus are the subject of nine active verbs that tell us what is going on in church: Jesus is our peace (Eph. 2:14), he made us one (v. 14), he broke down the dividing wall of hostility (v. 14), he abolished the law (v. 15), he created one new humanity (v. 15), he made peace (v. 15), he reconciled (v. 16), he put to death (v. 16), he proclaimed peace (v. 17).

And insofar as we are included in the action, the action is not something that we do but something done to us. Paul uses five passive verbs to tell us how we get included in the action: we are brought near (v. 13), the Spirit gives us access (v. 18), we are built upon the foundation (v. 20), we are joined together (v. 21), we are built together (v. 22). Simple copulas name the identities that we acquire by God's action. We are identified as citizens and members of church. When we are pulled into the action, it is God who pulls us in. We acquire our identity not by what we do but by what is done to us.

This is what transforms the church we see into the church we don't see, "a serious house on serious earth," a place where someone is surprised by "a hunger in himself to be more serious."

## The Ontological Church

But this understanding of church is hard to come by — maybe especially in America. Americans talk and write endlessly about what the church needs to become, what the church must do to be effective. The perceived failures of the church are analyzed and reforming strategies prescribed. The church is understood almost exclusively in terms of function — what we can see. If we can't see it, it doesn't exist. Everything is viewed through the lens of pragmatism. Church is an instrument that we have been given to bring about whatever Christ commanded us to do. Church is a staging ground for getting people motivated to continue Christ's work.

This way of thinking — church as a human activity to be measured by human expectations — is pursued unthinkingly. The huge reality of God already at work in all the operations of the Trinity is benched on the sideline while we call timeout, huddle together with our heads bowed, and figure out a strategy by which we can compensate for God's regrettable retreat into invisibility. This is dead wrong, and it is responsible for no end of shallowness and experimentation in trying to achieve success and relevance and effectiveness that people can see. Statistics provide the basic vocabulary for keeping score. Programs provide the game plan. This way of going about things has done and continues to do immeasurable damage to the American church.

This way of understanding church is very, very American and very, very wrong. We can no more understand church functionally than we can understand Jesus functionally. We have to submit ourselves to the revelation and receive church as the gift of Christ as he embodies himself in this world. Paul tells us that Christ is the head of a body, and the body is church. Head and body are one thing.

"Ontology" is a word that can get us past this clutter of functionalism. Ontology has to do with being. An ontological understanding of church has to do with what it is, not what it does. And what it is is far wider, deeper, higher than anything it does, or anything we can take charge of or manipulate. The Singapore theologian Simon Chan puts his finger on our persistent misunderstanding of the church as instrumental, as pragmatic, when he writes, "When it comes to understanding the church, sociology takes over."[4] The *being-ness* of church is what we are dealing with. Church is not something that we cobble together to do something for God. It is the "fullness of him who fills all in all" (Eph. 1:23) working comprehensively with and for us.

\*       \*       \*

Having introduced the term "church" into his "growing up in Christ" letter (Eph. 1:22-23), and having guided us through the treacherous terrain of individualism, Paul is ready to cut to the chase. He sets out to stimulate a praying imagination in us that is adequate for taking in all that is involved in church.

He begins his renovation of the Ephesians' understanding of church by reminding them of what church is not. "Remember," Paul says, what your pre-church life was like (2:11). He repeats the imperative "remember" (2:12). This is important; if you are going to understand what it is to be a church, you must keep in mind what church is not, remember your pre-church life. Do you remember how you were defined entirely by what you were not? Paul assists their remembering by hammering home seven negatives: Gentiles (all the Ephesians were Gentiles, that is, not-Jews), uncircumcised, without Christ, aliens to the commonwealth, strangers to the covenants, having no hope, godless.

Improvising on Paul's *remember,* I hear him saying, "Remember what that transition was like when you crossed the threshold into church, the transition from exclusion to inclusion? Remember the surprise of being an insider to God and his revelation after being an out-

---

4. Simon Chan, *Liturgical Theology* (Downers Grove, IL: InterVarsity Press, 2006), p. 36.

sider? Remember this well, for church cannot be comprehended by negatives, by what it is not. And neither can you."

There is considerable irony in the probability that this negative definition was given to the first Gentile Christians by Jewish Christians representing church. But it is understandable. Jews had a long history as the people of God with ancestors like Abraham, Moses, Samuel, David, Elijah and Elisha, Isaiah and Jeremiah in their family tree. They had a well-developed sense of being a chosen people, which they were. That was a good thing. But along with that, they had also developed an entrenched prejudice against non-Jews as a rejected people, which they were not. The originating covenant with Abraham was that "in thee shall all families of the earth be blessed" (Gen. 12:3 KJV, quoted by Paul in Gal. 3:8); over a thousand years later the inclusiveness of the covenant blessing was reaffirmed in the Isaianic preaching of all nations streaming to "the mountain of the LORD" (Isa. 2:2-3) and God's "house of prayer for all peoples" (56:7) — Larkin's "serious house on serious earth."

This prejudice, formed contrary to the magisterial authority of Abraham and Isaiah, was not a good thing. And so when Jesus, with a solid Jewish pedigree, was recognized as the Messiah and his crucifixion and resurrection became definitive for salvation, it was hard for the Jews, who were the first Christians, to accept Gentiles into the family of faith. They eventually did accept them, but it was not easy going for the first Gentile Christians.

Paul, with impeccable credentials as a Jew, self-identified as "apostle to the Gentiles" — those perceived as outsiders, aliens, strangers — was tireless in insisting that church brooks no divisions, no condescension, no rejection of anyone for any reason. He allows no exceptions: "There is no longer Jew or Greek, there is no longer slave or free, there is no longer male and female; for all of you are one in Christ Jesus. And if you belong to Christ, then you are Abraham's offspring, heirs according to the promise" (Gal. 3:28-29) — that promise of blessing cited from Genesis 12:3.

*　　*　　*

The preconditions of church are not unlike the preconditions of creation: "without form and void, and darkness was upon the face of the deep; and the Spirit of God was moving over the face of the waters" (Gen. 1:2 RSV). God speaks over that formless void, that dark and watery chaos, and brings forth the forms of creation.

The "Father's only Son," who was "in the beginning with God," through whom "all things came into being," Jesus Christ (John 1:1-14), also speaks over a wreckage following the fall — disintegration, disconnection, depersonalization, the chaos of splintered humanity, empty souls, divided families — and brings forth "out of the womb of the morning" (Ps. 110:3 ASV) . . . church.

The church that Jesus Christ speaks into being is formed against the backdrop of the creation that the Word, who was in the beginning with God, spoke into being.

This is the ontological church. This is the church in its Isness. This Isness is previous to whatever we do or don't do. We do not create the church. It *is*. We enter and participate in what is given to us. What we do is, of course, significant. Our obedience and disobedience, our faithfulness and unfaithfulness — what we *ought* and *ought not* to do — are part of it. But what I am wanting to say is that there is more — far more — to the church than us. There is Father, Son, and Holy Spirit. Most of what the church *is*, not all, is invisible. We miss the complexity and glory of church if we insist on measuring and defining it by the parts that we play in it, if we insist on evaluating and judging it by what we think it *ought* to be.

\*     \*     \*

Fifty years ago I fell in love with a woman who would soon become my wife. I was in graduate school at Johns Hopkins University in Baltimore; she was about to graduate from Towson State University. Our studies were demanding, and we didn't have much time to spend with one another, not even to go to Druid Hill Park to stroll through the zoo or to the Inner Harbor to enjoy the jugglers and magicians and musicians who provided sidewalk entertainment. Nor did either of us have much money to spend going to the theater or concerts. The university gave graduate students a free pass to all athletic events, and so we went to every game that was played, whether we cared about it or not — it was free space to be together. Because everyone else was watching the game, it also turned out to be essentially private space in which we could continue to get to know one another without interruption, which was the primary reason we were there anyway.

When spring arrived, the game was lacrosse, a game neither of us had ever seen. At our first game, out of curiosity, we gave it our attention, hoping to get some idea of what was going on. We couldn't make out anything. To our unpracticed eyes it seemed like organized mayhem, the players on the field caught up in a vortex of legitimated violence. We soon went back to what we were there for in the first place. Every Saturday afternoon we were in the bleachers at the lacrosse field, mostly oblivious to the game that we had failed to figure out. We were learning to understand one another, and we were getting better and better at that, but pretty much gave up on lacrosse.

During this time I had to go to the hospital to repair an old athletic injury to my knee. A few days after being dismissed from the hospital I was diagnosed with a staphylococcus infection contracted in the surgery. I was placed in the university infirmary on the campus. The infirmary was a single room about thirty feet square with beds arranged around the periphery. There were three other students there, all of them lacrosse players who had been injured playing the game — one with a broken ankle, one with a broken collarbone, the other with a broken rib. They had their lacrosse sticks and a ball with them and spent their convalescence using their lacrosse sticks to throw the ball to one another, caroming it off the walls, bouncing it off the floor.

Their stickwork was impressive. The ball went around that room with incredible speed but also with precise accuracy. Sometimes I feared for my life as the ball passed inches from my head, but I needn't have — they knew what they were doing and they were good at it. I was there a week. During that week I had an intensive seminar in lacrosse. They patiently instructed me in the ways of lacrosse. Out of my original perception of chaos and mayhem an amazingly intricate and exquisite game, graceful and beautiful in execution, emerged.

I have spent the fifty years since that week in the infirmary as a pastor in a church with people, a lot of whom seem to have no idea what is going on. What they see is chaos: hostility, injury, brokenness, church fights, church sleaze, church grandstanding, religious wars. Many of them find a place in the bleachers with a few other likeminded people and make do with what they find there. They survive by ignoring what they find confusing and disorienting. They remove their attention from what is taking place on the field (in the congregation, in the denomination). They do pray together, study together, socialize together. Life in the bleachers isn't all that bad.

There are other people who are so disturbed by what they perceive as chaos on the playing field that they decide to "do something about it." They want a game that looks like a game, a church that looks like a church, where no one gets hurt and everything is orderly and stays in place. They understand church as something they need to take charge of. And of course there are a great many people who just walk out and look for a game that they are already familiar with or go home and turn on the television where they can satisfy, if you can call it that, their religious needs by picking a brand without dealing personally with either God or people.

*     *     *

None of these three responses to the perceived messiness and bewildering chaos of church is without value, whether it is finding a comfortable niche, finding something to fix, or looking for something that is congenial to one's individual temperament and circumstances. But all of them, by reducing church to matters of function and personal preference, miss church in its richness, its intricacy, the complex aliveness that is inherent in everything that is going on.

Paul wants us to first understand and then participate in church as it is, as the living Christ. He wants us to understand church first of all and primarily in terms of ontology, its being, not its function. There are, of course, functions — things happen, things are done, there are jobs to do, there are tasks to be obeyed. But if we don't grasp church as Christ's body, we will always be dissatisfied, impatient, angry, dismayed, or disgusted with what we see. We will never see the elegance and intricacy of church; we will entirely miss the "praise of his glory"; we will fail to discern what is going on right before our eyes in our congregation. A great deal of what is observable in church is simply incomprehensible as church if we have no ontology of church.

## "[Jesus] is our peace"

Peace is Paul's word of choice to help us into an ontological understanding of church. He begins by identifying Jesus as "our peace" (Eph. 2:14). He goes on to describe Jesus as "making peace" (v. 15) and "proclaim[ing] peace" (v. 17). He elaborates on this triple evocation of peace by telling us that we are "brought near" by Jesus (v. 13), that Jesus "has made both groups [Jews and non-Jews] into one" (v. 14), that Jesus "has broken down the dividing wall, that is, the hostility between us" (v. 14), that Jesus has "abolished the law . . . that he might create one new humanity in place of the two" (v. 15), all this so that Jesus "might reconcile both groups to God in one body" (v. 16) — five distinct actions of Jesus that add up to peace. Each of these five actions contributes detail and texture to our understanding of peace: Jesus brings us home, Jesus brings us together, Jesus breaks down hostility, Jesus re-creates us as a unified humanity, Jesus reconciles all of us to God. Peace is complex and many-layered. A lot of action goes into making peace — and Jesus *is* the action.

So far so good. But here's a puzzle: If Paul is right — and I would not be writing this if I wasn't convinced he is — then why isn't church with Christ as its head the most conspicuous place on earth as a place of peace and peacemaking?

Three things account for this dissonance between Jesus "our peace" and the church that more often seems like a war zone. All three things have to do with the way that Jesus is our peace.

First, Jesus is a person. That means that peace is personal. It is nothing if not personal. There are no other ways. Peace cannot be achieved in impersonal ways. It is not a strategy, not a program, not a political action, not an educational process. Jesus is always relational, never a disembodied idea, never a bureaucratized arrangement. Peace doesn't come into being by fiat. It requires participation in the ways of peace, participation in Jesus who is our peace.

Second, Jesus respects us as persons. He does not force himself upon us. He does not impose peace. He does not coerce. Jesus treats us with dignity. His peace is not a decree that everyone must get along without hurting or killing or despising one another. Peace is never external to us. It is not the absence of war or famine or anxiety that makes it possible to live in peace. It is not accomplished by getting rid of mosquitoes, rebellious teenagers, and contentious neighbors, or burning heretics at the stake.

All of us are participants in peace. Jesus is at work bringing us, all that is us — our eternal *souls* — into a life of connectedness, of intimacy, of love. There is a lot going on, a lot involved. We are all involved, whether we want to be or not. It takes a long time, because Jesus doesn't push us around and make us shape up, doesn't shut us up so that we don't disturb the peace. Peace is always in process, never a finished product.

Third, the way that Jesus becomes our peace — and this is the crux, literally! — is by an act of sacrifice. The sacrifice of Jesus is what makes Jesus Jesus; it is what makes peace peace; it is what makes church church. Paul says it two different ways: "by the blood of Christ" (Eph. 2:13), and "through the cross" (2:16).

Church is the one place in the world that holds all these three components of peace together, refusing to simplify by eliminating any of the aspects. Church is the place where God cannot be depersonalized into an idea or force. The evidence? Jesus, the "word made flesh."

Church is the place where men and women cannot be depersonalized into abstractions such as insider and outsider, in-group and out-group, friends and enemies. The evidence? Our worship: Holy Baptism, in which we are personally named in the Name of the Trinity, and the Holy Eucharist where peace is inextricably identified with sacrifice — the broken body and shed blood of Jesus, given to us to focus, clarify, and bring us into participation with the life, death, and resurrection of Jesus, who *is* our peace.

\*     \*     \*

I don't think we have to make any apologies that church is not conspicuously prominent as a place of peace. Peace is continuous, complex, and strenuous. If we are serious about it, and many of us are, we soon learn that there are no shortcuts. We accept the conditions given to us as church: Jesus, who does not force peace upon us; our neighbors, backyard and worldwide, upon whom we don't impose peace; and sacrifice, the only way — the Jesus way — of bringing about peace without violence.

The church in its deepest being, as it is in itself, the ontological church comprises a vast company of men and women in all stages of maturity: crawling infants and squalling babies, awkward and impulsive adolescents, harassed and fatigued parents, and occasional holy men and holy women who have it all together. All of us who understand and practice peace in the company of Jesus, who is our peace, have a lot of maturing to do. About the time we are becoming mature (if we ever do), we find that we have brought another generation into the world that has to go through the whole process once again. Humankind does not mature all at once. And so peace is constantly in the making, and also constantly at risk. Church is where Jesus is proclaimed as "our peace."

Church is where peace is understood comprehensively as Christ present and working among us. But none of us who meet and worship together as church were admitted into the company on the strength of our peace skills. We all have a lot of growing up ahead of us: learning to worship God as personal; learning to accept and embrace one another as personal, as family members, and not as competitors or strangers; learning to accept and follow Jesus sacrificially on the way of the cross. Given the twin set of circumstances — that we use the vocabulary of peace a lot, and that like children learning to walk none of us are very good at it — when anyone looks at church as a performance, whether from inside or outside, mostly what they see is skinned knees and sprained ankles, awkward, bungled attempts at keeping the peace. But we also know that at the source and center of church, Jesus is our peace. And so we don't quit.

But neither are we intimidated by our critics, critics who know nothing of the ontological church, when they are scandalized by our failures.

## The Hospitable Church

The centerpiece of the fivefold action by which Jesus made and proclaimed peace is found in the proclamation designated near the end of the letter (Eph. 6:15): "the gospel of peace" is Jesus himself, breaking down the wall — "the dividing wall, that is, the hostility between us" (2:14).

Jesus demolishes the wall that separates insiders and outsiders, lost and homeless men and women, aliens and strangers. In its place he builds a place of peace. As soon as the rubble is cleared away, a structure is built to welcome these once-upon-a-time alienated, hostile men and women into a place of hospitality.

Three metaphors fill in the details of what is involved in this God-originated and God-inhabited reality: "household of God" (2:19), "holy temple in the Lord" (2:21), "dwelling place for God" (2:22) — all metaphors for church.

The usefulness of a metaphor is that it is something that we can see or handle but at the same time draws us into participation with something we cannot see or handle. We can see a house, a barn, a store — or in this case a household, a temple, a dwelling place. We cannot see God — Father, Son, and Holy Spirit. But the building we see and the God we cannot see are the same, occupy the same space, fused by the prepositions "of," "in," and "for."

Church on one level is something we can see. It is a building. It is a place on earth. It is local. We can walk into it through its doors, gather with others within its walls, talk and study and pray under its roof. It is not uncommon to hear people dismiss a church building as "nothing but bricks and mortar." In a world that gets its meaning from "The Word became flesh and dwelt among us," that is a very unspiritual thing to say. That is like saying "She's nothing but a pretty face," or "He's nothing but a doormat," or "Jesus is nothing but blood and bone." Nothing is "nothing but."

Church is also something we can't see. We can't see the ascension of Jesus. We can't see the "descent of the dove." We can't see sins washed away. We can't see the birth of a soul. We can't see the river of life. It is not uncommon for people to walk into a church out of curiosity, look around, leave, and later report to their friends, "I couldn't see that there is anything to it." That is also a very unspiritual thing to say, for a great deal of what we live by is unseen, the air we breathe and the promises we make, for a start.

*    *    *

Paul's three church metaphors pick up various aspects of church as *place*, not just an idea but a feet-on-the-ground place of hospitality where we are welcomed as participants with Jesus, who is our peace: "household of God," a place where God gathers his family together; "a holy temple in the Lord," a place where we are set apart to worship God; and "a dwelling place for God," a place where God makes himself known to us in our language and circumstances, in word and sacrament.

The local, immediate, participatory aspects of church are extended by describing us as the building materials used to construct church. Men, women, and children are just as material as boards and bricks. Apostles and prophets are foundation stones. Jesus is the cornerstone (or keystone). And we are whatever else makes up the structure: rafters and joists, flooring and roofing, door and window frames.

When we consider church, we must not be more spiritual than God. Church is a place and a building, church is people and relationships, church is Father, Son, and Holy Spirit. And all of this at the same time: one, holy, catholic, apostolic.

## CHAPTER 7

# Church and God's Manifold Wisdom: Ephesians 3:1-13

*[T]he Gentiles are fellow heirs, members of the same body, and partakers of the promise in Christ Jesus through the gospel . . . that through the church the manifold wisdom of God might now be made known to the principalities and powers in the heavenly places.*

EPHESIANS 3:6, 10 RSV

*Take care you don't know anything in this world
too quickly or easily. Everything
is also a mystery and has its own secret aura in the moonlight,
its private song.*

MARY OLIVER, "MOONLIGHT"

Paul is on his way and gathering momentum as he makes us insiders to understanding and participating in church. The single most significant thing to know is that Christ is involved in everything that is going on whether in redemption or judgment, in rebuke or blessing. Paul uses the word "church" for the first time in Ephesians 1:22-23. He gives us to understand that Christ and church are organically joined as head and body: Jesus Christ is the head of the church; the church is the body of

Christ. You can't have a head without a body; you can't have a body without a head. It is essential that this head-and-body metaphor be taken seriously, for one of the more frequent misunderstandings of both Christ and church comes when head and body, Jesus and church, are severed and then studied or discussed in isolation.

From its opening lines, Ephesians has saturated us in the primacy and presence of God in everything. The Christian life is too often treated in our culture as an extra, something we get involved in after we have the basic survival needs established and then realize that things aren't yet quite complete. So we become a Christian. That is all well and good, but there is no B.C. in our lives, no "Before Christ." Neither is there any B.C. in anyone else who is not a confessed Christian. Christ is *always* present, for *all* of us. Just because we have no awareness of the presence and action of God previous to our knowledge of it does not mean that God was absent. We must not naively assume that the Christian life begins with us. As long as we think in those terms, we are apt to judge everything and everyone else by our experience and circumstances. That kind of thinking is understandable in adolescents. But we are called to grow up.

Paul vigorously counters B.C. assumptions: he fills us in on what has been going on "before the foundation of the world" (Eph. 1:4). The world is immense, and God is at work in it comprehensively. Not only that, but everything that God does, is doing, and will do involves our total lives (1:3–2:10). Growing up in Christ means growing up to a stature adequate to respond heart and soul to the largeness of God.

Ephesians continues to expand and deepen what this Christian life involves by taking up the way we think about church (2:11ff.). The church that is the body of Christ has a long pre-history. The formation of the people of God that began with Abraham came into its own as the church took form at Pentecost. The church is formed in continuity with Israel as an expansion of Israel, the "Israel of God" (Gal. 6:16). Just as Israel, in the language of many a prophet (Hos. 1–3; Jer. 3:1-5; Isa. 54:4-7), was the wife of God, so the church is the bride of Christ (Eph. 5:22-33; Rev. 21:2, 9-11). On becoming Christians we are "grafted" into the olive tree that is the people of God (Rom. 11:17-24). We become conscious participants in holy history, a people whose lives are given their identity in Jesus and his resurrection, the incarnation of the Son who was "before the foundation of the world" (Eph. 1:4).

In parallel with the way we wrongly think of "Christian" as an extra tacked on to life, an improvement or a completion of what turned out to be not enough, so "church" in our culture is wrongly considered to be something more or less tacked on to "Christian." Church is not an "add-on," a program or cheerleader, to help us be faithful and better Christians. We think wrongly if we consider church in terms of what it does for us, or (and this is perhaps even worse) in terms of what we can do for it. As long as we think of church in those terms, we will evaluate it in terms of how it meets our self-identified needs, or in terms of how it needs us and how we can help out. In the process we cut ourselves off from our intricate and rich pre-history in Israel.

Paul will have none of that: in his opening foray into church (Eph. 2:11-14), Paul uses the name of Christ four times and pronouns for Christ eight times — twelve times in all — as he lays the groundwork that will show us just how church comes into being and how we fit in. Interestingly, one of the verbs he uses is the great Genesis word "create" ("in the beginning God created the heavens and the earth"). Paul here uses it of Christ creating church ("create in himself one new humanity"). It is useful, I think, to let our imaginations gather around that first great creation story so that it can provide perspective to this second great creation story, the creation of church with its long pre-history in people-of-God Israel. Just as creation provides the context for living in God's covenant, church provides the context for the practice of Jesus' resurrection.

But as Paul continues his reordering of the way we think of and experience church, we notice a change of pace (Eph. 3:1-13). There is a shift from the intensity that has marked his writing so far. We detect a slight relaxation in the tension. It is not exactly a digression, for the subject is the same, but Paul lets himself enter into the conversation. The tone is more narratival than doctrinal. The metaphors that are so conspicuous in chapters 1–2 recede to give room for personal witness.

## "I am the very least of all the saints"

Paul is characteristically reticent when it comes to talking about himself. He has a much larger subject to deal with than himself. He is working through the vast territory of Christian living, the deep and wide realities of God's action in creation and salvation, the resurrection of Jesus that brings us from death to life, the church in which we are all built "into a dwelling place for God" (Eph. 2:22). He doesn't want to distract us from the gospel message, from the Jesus presence, by intruding himself.

But every once in a while the door opens just a crack — a word, a phrase. We get a glimpse of Paul the man at work, writing, praying. There is a living person involved behind these sentences: a prisoner (3:1), a servant (3:7), an allusion to his story, "how the mystery was made known to me by revelation" (3:3). His self-deprecating reference as "the very least of all the saints" (3:8) catches our attention by creating a novel form of the adjective "least" that doubles its comparative emphasis. Translated literally it comes out "I am the *leaster* or *smallester* of all the saints." In 1 Timothy 1:15 he identified himself as "foremost" of sinners. Last in the roll call of saints; first in the roll call of sinners.

First-person personal pronouns, "I" and "me" pronouns, start appearing, eleven of them in this paragraph. Fragments of his story come into view. Paul lets himself into the story, but as inconspicuously as possible.

It's enough, just enough to be reminded that the language of mature spirituality cannot be depersonalized into abstract propositional "truths." This man is living everything he is saying. This resurrection life is never disembodied, never abstract, never an objective truth that can be analyzed and argued and defended.

The mature, resurrection life is irreducibly personal; it is about us. But it is also a life that is mostly *not* about us. It is about God. Paul keeps it personal, but he does it with considerable reticence. Christian spirituality is not well served by confessional monologues. Egotistic verbosity diminishes the authenticity of the language of witness. Paul is unmistakably present. But he is also unassumingly present. He doesn't take over.

\*   \*   \*

Here's another observation: this unexpectedly relaxed tone interrupts a very intense, packed, single-minded focus on the action of God that has carried us along thus far. This undeviating intensity is very effective. Our imaginations are being retrained to think first "God" and "Christ" and "Spirit" and then, as we have a chance to catch our breath, to think "me" and "I." But the intensity is also exhausting. We cannot sustain it for long. We need time to step back, pause, get our bearings.

The Christian life has a goal, famously put by Paul in an earlier letter: "I press on toward the goal for the prize of the heavenly call of God in Christ Jesus. Let those of us then who are mature be of the same mind" (Phil. 3:14-15). The mature life in Christ does not dillydally. It doesn't chase after fads. But any focus on a goal that dismisses, ignores, and avoids spouse, children, and neighbors who are perceived as impediments to pressing on to the "heavenly call" simply doesn't understand the way the *goal* functions in a mature life.

The Christian life is not a straight run on a track laid out by a vision statement formulated by a committee. Life meanders much of the time. Unspiritual interruptions, unanticipated people, uncongenial events cannot be pushed aside in our determination to reach the goal unimpeded, undistracted. "Goal-setting," in the context and on the terms intended by a leadership-obsessed and management-programmed business mentality that infiltrates the church far too frequently, is bad spirituality. Too much gets left out. Too many people get brushed aside.

Maturity cannot be hurried, programmed, or tinkered with. There are no steroids available for growing up in Christ more quickly. Impatient shortcuts land us in the dead ends of immaturity.

## Meshech and the Tents of Kedar

Coming on the heels of Paul's all-encompassing presentation of Christ "our peace" (Eph. 2:14) as a way of understanding church, there is one other item that requires attention before we return to Paul's further elaboration of church, namely, the conspicuous absence of peace in the world and in his life as he writes. This Ephesians exposition of the mature life in Christ in which peace has the prominent place is written out (or dictated) in a prison cell. All the time that Paul is using a broken wall as a metaphor for church that welcomes all, church that is open to all, church that is hospitable to all, he is locked behind the walls of a Roman prison: "I Paul am a prisoner for Christ Jesus for the sake of you Gentiles" (3:1). At the same time we know that there was considerable contention in most if not all of the first-century churches that are reported on and addressed in the New Testament. And in the two thousand years since, conflict and even killing have been waged in the name of Jesus. Whatever happened to that broken wall?

I have a photograph that I have kept propped on my desk for several years, the same desk on which I prepared my sermons. The photo is an aerial view of a suburban subdivision of cookie-cutter homes, each neatly fenced, and each with an identical swimming pool in its backyard.

I labeled the photograph, "Meshech and the Tents of Kedar."

I came upon the photo at a time when I was organizing a church in a suburb northeast of Baltimore. I was new to suburbia. I had grown up in a small town where there were occasional fences to keep in a dog, but mostly the dogs roamed free and my friends and I were free to take shortcuts across our neighbors' backyards. And we had a municipal swimming pool to which everyone in town had free access.

One swimming pool. No fences.

When I started my work in this suburban neighborhood, I soon realized that everyone was a stranger to his or her neighbors. Naively, I assumed that everyone would welcome me and the proposed church as a safe place to make friends, to find surrogate brothers and sisters, cousins and aunts and uncles, to replace the families and neighbors they had left behind to get a better job.

I wanted to keep things as simple and straightforward as I could. I would concentrate on two things: I would gather and lead a congregation in the worship of God, and I would invite them into a life of community with one another. I anticipated that calling these men and women into worship would be the hard part and developing a sense of community would be easy.

My sense was that these people were pretty thoroughly secularized, with little sense of reverence, no practice in entering into the mystery of God. They were used to taking life as a succession of problems to solve or overcome. They interpreted the world around them in terms of the commodities they could get for themselves. They had little sense of need for God. To cultivate that sense would be uphill work. On the other hand, they were all uprooted from their previous homes and strangers to one another. They were displaced and lonely. They missed friends. I would introduce them to one another, provide a safe place for getting acquainted and being a part of something larger than their own family rooms and responsibilities. They might not be interested in God, but surely they would be interested in the neighborhood. That's what I thought. As it turned out, I was wrong.

It wasn't long before I had people worshiping God on Sunday mornings. They weren't totally at ease. They had a lot to reimagine about the God they hadn't paid much attention to. Their vocabulary needed some stretching in order to acquire a language adequate for talking about what they couldn't go to the shopping mall and buy. But they were there, worshiping God.

But getting them interested in each other was another thing entirely. They didn't want neighbors. They wanted to be self-sufficient, independent. After we had been living in the neighborhood for six weeks, a community association that had been recently formed met to discuss what kind of community we wanted and what we could do to bring it about. I went, not knowing what to expect. (I grew up, remember, in a small western town. We didn't have community associations there. We *were* a community.)

But what happened at this meeting was a total surprise. It was the most contentious gathering of people I had ever attended. After half an hour I realized, "These people don't *like* one another." They didn't know one another, but what they didn't know, they didn't like. When someone spoke, there was an immediate challenge or refutation. There was a lot of talk, most of it rude. There was virtually no listening. I sat there, taking it all in, and realized that I had my work cut out for me.

That was when the phrase arrived out of my memory: "Woe is me, that I sojourn in Meshech, that I dwell in the tents of Kedar!" (KJV). It's a phrase out of Psalm 120. Meschech and Kedar were barbarian tribes with a reputation for wildness. They were neighbors to the biblical Hebrews. The person who prayed Psalm 120 was praying in the company of people who were on their way to worship God in Jerusalem, but feeling immersed in enmity, "lying lips" and "a deceitful tongue." He is committed to a way of peace, God's peace, but he feels hostility all around him. "I am for peace," he says, "but when I speak, they are for war."

That's the way I felt that night in the community association meeting. I had come to the neighborhood to gather a people into a church where we would worship God. I had barely started when I found myself surrounded by the offspring of Meshech and Kedar, men and women whose vocabulary consisted primarily of rude hostilities, war talk, who had somehow made their way to this American suburb where I was hoping to start a church whose head was Christ, "our peace."

*   *   *

It was a sobering moment. From that moment I was faced with the complex difficulties of gathering a congregation of warring factions into a place where the wall of hostility had been broken down and a church was being built on its site. Many of those in the community meeting later became members of my congregation. Some of them took a long time before submitting to being the building materials that Jesus fitted and joined together (literally, "harmonized," 2:21) into a dwelling place for God. One man, Reuben, the most vituperative in that early community meeting, never did submit. Twenty-seven years later I conducted his funeral in the church he had sat in every Sunday, as angry and sullen as the night I first met him.

I knew that there were wars and rumors of wars all over the world for thousands of years, and that it wasn't getting any better. But somehow I didn't expect it in "peaceful suburbia" and in a congregation that gathered regularly to be formed into a "household of God," a "holy temple" and a "dwelling place for God" to worship Jesus, "our peace."

But gradually I learned. I learned that growing up in Christ entails a lot of growing pains. I learned that the "ontological church" is the reality in which we worship and become community, and that maturity consists in a long, unhurried, prayerful life of becoming reconciled to God and to one another, and in the process realizing that each of us is part of a "whole structure" (2:21) and is not permitted to impatiently "go it alone," leaving the slower or unpromising ones behind. Not even Reuben.

Church, glorious as it is, built as a household of God, and growing into a holy temple in the Lord, comes into being in hostile country, among people who are strangers to one another — some who think they are better than others and are quite willing to help God do what he has to do, some who think they are inadequate and ill-equipped for anything that has to do with God. Long before my encounter with Kedar, Isaiah saw Kedar with its stubborn history of warring against God gathered into his household: "all the flocks of Kedar shall be gathered to you" (Isa. 60:7).

That's why I kept that photograph, Meshech and the Tents of Kedar, on my desk for so many years.

## Inscape

Church cannot be objectively described or defined from the outside. Church can only be entered. It is a creation of Christ for growing up in Christ. It is not a museum through which we can stroll and see exhibits of what has happened throughout history, precisely labeled with names, dates, and locations. Church takes place in history, just as Jesus takes place in history. But there is more than history here. There is the life of Christ, the work of the Spirit, the plan of God.

Many things about the church can be defined and described: creeds and leaders, conflicts and persecutions, architecture and politics. But the pieces don't add up to church.

This complex interior heart of church is captured in the phrase "that through the church the manifold wisdom of God might now be made known" (Eph. 3:10 RSV). "Manifold" has a picture in it: an intricately embroidered pattern in a tapestry.[1] And wisdom carries the sense of lived knowledge, or the revelation of God as lived. Wisdom is knowledge in action, embodied in the life of the church. Wisdom is the practice of resurrection.

Church is where this wisdom, this embodiment of the knowledge and revelation of God, takes place, where the resurrection is practiced. Church is the workshop for turning knowledge into wisdom, becoming what we know.

\*　　\*　　\*

Gerard Manley Hopkins, a Jesuit priest and poet in nineteenth-century Wales and Ireland, coined a term that is useful in grasping what is involved in the "manifold wisdom" made known in the church. The term is "inscape." Inscape is formed on analogy with but in contrast to landscape. Landscape is what we see spread out before us against the horizon. It is relatively stable and can be described and painted and cultivated: groves of trees, fields of mown grass, a meandering river, a range of glacier-carved mountains. Inscape is the intuitive sense that what we see is a living, organic form that strikes through the senses and into the mind with a feeling of novelty and discovery. Inscape is what something uniquely is, that which holds together whatever you are looking at or listening to, gives it distinction — proportions, shades of light, tints of color, shapes, relationships, sounds.

An editor of Hopkins's poems, W. H. Gardner, notes that "this feeling for the intrinsic quality of the unified pattern of essential char-

---

1. J. A. Robinson, *St. Paul's Epistle to the Ephesians*, 2nd ed. (London: Clark, 1922), p. 80.

acteristics [inscape] is the special mark of the artist."[2] Painters use oils and canvas to bring into visibility what left to ourselves we might never notice in a human face or a bowl of fruit. Sculptors carve and shape granite and clay and bronze to draw our attention to the way shape and form and texture affect our awareness. Poets arrange metaphors and similes, vowels and consonants, and alert us to meaning and significance in words that we miss in our preoccupation with mere information or getting out the vote. Musicians mix and give rhythm to various sounds — a singing voice, breath pushed through a reed or horn, a taut bow stroked over a gut or metal string — and create participation in and responsiveness to what we do not have words for. Artists make us insiders to the complexity and beauty of what we deal with every day but so often miss. They bring to our attention what is right before our eyes, within reach of our touch, help us hear sounds and combinations of sounds that our noise-deafened ears have never heard.

Often an element of surprise accompanies this experience of inscape: "I never saw that before" . . . "I've never heard anything like that" . . . "I've never been so moved." . . . But in fact nothing that the artist brings to our attention was unheard, unseen, untouched previously. It was all there before us in the tree we walked past every morning on our way to work, in the face that we thought we knew through and through, in the whispers of wind in the willows and the lapping of waves on the beach.

The artist helps us see what we have always seen but never seen, hear what we hear daily but don't hear, feel what we have touched a hundred times but never been touched by, recognize that we are living a story and not just drifting through fragments of journal jottings or disconnected bits of gossip.

Why are artists so necessary? And how do they do this? A great deal of attention has been given to understanding what is involved. The stock answer is that the artist makes us aware of beauty in con-

2. *Poems and Prose of Gerard Manley Hopkins,* selected by W. H. Gardner (Baltimore: Penguin Books, 1953), p. xx.

trast to the dull or the ugly or the commonplace. But that is obviously an unsatisfactory answer. For much of what the artist brings to our attention, with our grateful appreciation, is not so much beauty as reality — the way things actually are, whether it is the excruciating pain portrayed in a Rouault painting of the crucifixion of Jesus or the unrelenting ordinariness of a red wheelbarrow in a poem by William Carlos Williams, neither of which is "pretty."

Gerard Manley Hopkins never defined the term he coined. But he used it frequently enough in his journals and notes to give us a feel for what he is reaching for. One day he walked into a barn and was surprised by the way the timbers mingled light and shadow. Later he "thought how sadly beauty of inscape was unknown and buried away from simple people and yet how near at hand it was if they had eyes to see it and could be called out everywhere again." Another time he looked out of his window and caught the inscape in the random clods and broken heaps of snow made by the cast of a broom. He later remarked, "All the world is full of inscape and chance left free to act falls into an order as well as purpose."[3]

Reading and reciting the poems of Hopkins is an immersion in inscape, a thorough and glorious apprenticeship in sensing the invisibles and inaudibles that give cohesion and wholeness to everything that we see and hear and taste, not just its superficial appearance but the inner core of individuality.

\*     \*     \*

Norman H. MacKenzie, a most perceptive reader of Hopkins, sums it up like this: "Inscape is the distinctive character (almost a personality) given by the Creator to a particular species of rock or tree or animal. Each separate species through its inscape reflects some fractional part of God's all-inclusive perfection."[4] I want to add church to MacKenzie's

3. Norman H. MacKenzie, *A Reader's Guide to Gerard Manley Hopkins* (Ithaca: Cornell University Press, 1981), p. 130.

4. MacKenzie, *A Reader's Guide*, p. 233.

list of "particular species." I want to consider the inscape of church, the "manifold wisdom of God" that gives structure to the reality of church.

Many people (most?) look at the church and see only the exterior with no sense of what holds it together, no sense of pattern or proportion, no perception of the inner energy that pulses through it, no feel of being in harmony with the reality of what is there, no imagination adequate for responding to the "manifold wisdom." It is a building, more often than not undistinguished. It is a gathering of people, more often than not undistinguished. It has a history, much of it an embarrassment.

Inscape means that there is a lot more to church than we can see, hear, or read. It also means that everything we do, see, hear, and read in church is *church*. There is no invisible church that exists apart from what our five physical senses bring to us. Those who want to save themselves the embarrassment and trouble of dealing with the church as God's "manifold wisdom" by creating out of thin air a "mystical church" are headed up a dead-end street. Markus Barth impatiently names such practice as "sacrilegious nonsense."[5]

It is true that a superficial survey of church brings up a lot of disconnected and random things, ideas, and people. But dismissing all that offends our spiritual sensibilities by brushing it aside, and creating our own sanitized and idealized church rejects the church God gave us. The task is to see everything in relation and in proportion, see all light and shadow at once, see all the colors and tones working together, recognize all the men, women, and children as thews and sinews in the body that is the church, with Christ as its head.

Another poet, Czeslaw Milosz, one of the great Christian poets of the twentieth century, expressed in other words what Hopkins conveyed by inscape. In writing about growing up in Poland and maintaining his Christian identity in the midst of the warring forces and ideologies of Soviet communism, Nazi fascism, and French secularism, he wrote of his developing realization that "one had to master a skill, like

---

5. Markus Barth, *The Broken Wall: A Study of the Epistle to the Ephesians* (Chicago: Judson Press, 1959), p. 121.

swimming or running, rather than a body of knowledge capable of being set forth in theories. Reality [Paul's "manifold wisdom"] . . . was a changing, living tissue; it was woven out of countless interdependencies in such a way that even the tiniest detail germinates infinitely; and at the joints that keep its structure mobile, man is able to insert the lever of a conscious act."[6]

\*　　\*　　\*

This is what I was getting at earlier using the term "ontology": *the ontological church.* When we have our eyes and ears, our feelings and our memories activated to see all of this working together, there it is, *inscape.* Without a developed sense of inscape we are held captive by ephemeral irritants and enthusiasms: the gossip who always manages to be in the way of our vision during worship; the sixteen-year-old with gushing naiveté who reports on how three weeks of mission work in Mexico building homes for hurricane victims "changed my life"; a free-floating memory of the inquisition and crusades that intrudes on the sermon; the plodding pedestrianism of Christians we meet in the shopping mall slapping their small children into submission; the hallelujahs at Easter; the latest sex or financial scandal of a church celebrity. All of that too, but within and throughout the "manifold wisdom."

Gregory of Nyssa expands on the "manifold wisdom" in a sermon on the Song of Songs. He lists the difficult juxtapositions that make up church: life created by death, the attainment of glory by dishonor, of blessing by curse, of power by weakness, and more.[7] This is church as God gives it to us. This is *real* church. Are we going to receive what God gives us? Or make up our own? "He who has ears to hear, let him hear."

---

6. Czeslaw Milosz, *Native Realm: A Search for Self-Definition* (Berkeley: University of California Press, 1968), p. 267.

7. See Markus Barth, *Ephesians 1–3*, The Anchor Bible, vol. 34 (Garden City, NY: Doubleday, 1974), p. 356.

## Shadow Work

Judith is an artist. Her primary medium is textiles. Most of the time she begins her work with raw cotton or wool. She cards, spins, dyes, and then weaves her fabrics. Her weavings are usually on a small scale — a nest of birds' eggs, a portrait of David's Abigail, three crows — which she frames and gives as gifts to her friends. She makes her living by repairing tapestries in museums.

Judith had an alcoholic husband and a drug-addicted son. She had kept her life and her family together for years by attending twelve-step meetings. One Sunday, she was about forty years old at the time, she entered the church where I was the pastor. She came at the invitation of some friends she knew from her meetings — "You need to come to church. I'll meet you there." She had never been to church before. She knew nothing about church. She was raised in a morally upright home but had no acquaintance with institutional or formal religion. In her family God was not part of their working vocabulary. She was well read in poetry and politics and psychology, and knew a great deal of art and artists. But she had never read the Bible. If she had heard the stories in the Bible she had paid no attention. As far as she could recall she had never been inside a church.

Something, though, caught her attention when she entered this church, and she continued to come. In a few months she became a Christian and I became her pastor. I loved observing and listening to her. Everything was new: Scriptures, worship, prayer, baptism, eucharist — *church!* It was a tonic to me to hear and see through her excited perceptions everything that I had lived with all my life. All her questions were exclamations: "Where have I been all my life! These are incredible stories — why didn't anyone tell me these! How come this has been going on all around me and I never knew it!" We had delightful conversations. We became good friends.

Meanwhile, her primary community was made up of artists — painters and poets and sculptors, mostly, with a few of her twelve-step friends sprinkled in among them.

After four years or so of this, I moved across the continent to take up a new assignment. Letters replaced voiced conversations. The following is a portion of a letter that is a witness to what the church's inscape and the manifold wisdom of church feels like to a newcomer.

"Dear Pastor: Among my artist friends I feel so defensive about my life — I mean about going to church. They have no idea of what I am doing and act bewildered. So I try to be unobtrusive about it. But as my church life takes on more and more importance — it is essential now to my survival — it is hard to shield it from my friends. I feel protective of it, not wanting it to be dismissed or minimized or trivialized. It is like I am trying to protect it from profanation or sacrilege. But it is strong, it is increasingly difficult to keep it quiet. It is not as if I am ashamed or embarrassed — I just don't want it belittled.

"A long-time secular friend, and a superb artist, just the other day was appalled: 'What is this I hear about you going to church?' Another found out that I was going on a three-week mission trip to Haiti and was incredulous: 'You, Judith, *you* going to Haiti with a church group! What has gotten into you?' I don't feel strong enough to defend my actions. My friends would accept me far more readily if they found that I was in some bizarre cult involving exotic and strange activities like black magic or experiments with levitation. But going to church is branded with a terrible ordinariness.

"But that is what endears it to me, both the church and the twelve-step programs, this façade of ordinariness. When you pull back the veil of ordinariness, you find the most extraordinary life behind it. But I feel isolated and inadequate to explain to my husband and close friends — even myself! — what it is. It's as if I would have to undress myself before them. Maybe if I was willing to do that they would not dare disdain me. More likely they would just pity me. As it is they just adjust their neckties a little tighter.

"I am feeling raw and cold and vulnerable and something of a fool. I guess I don't feel too badly about being a fool within the context of the secular world. From the way they look at me, I don't have much to show for my new life. I can't point to a life mended. Many of the sorrows and difficulties seem mended for a time, only to bust open again.

But to tell you the truth, I haven't been on medication since June and for that I feel grateful.

"When I try to explain myself to these friends I feel as if I am suspended in a hang glider between the material and immaterial, casting a shadow down far below, and they say, 'See — it's nothing but shadow work.' Perhaps it takes a fool to savor the joy of shadow work, the shadow cast as I am attending to the unknown, the unpaid for, the freely given."

\*     \*     \*

Judith gets it right. She has no romantic illusions about church. She knows she can't defend or explain it to the satisfaction of her friends. Nobody has any idea of what she is doing. She feels apologetic about that. But she embraces what she was given — that seemingly fragile hang glider church suspending her in the mystery, the unpaid for, the freely given. She is here. She can't *not* be here. She didn't expect to find nice people, people of accomplishment, artists. She is an artist of church: "Don't look at me — see the shadow down there. Look at the shadow work. You might see what God is doing."

Newcomer as she is, unschooled as she is in the intricacies and controversies of church, Judith knows what church is, visible but not glamorous, suspending her in its mystery, in her words, "the unknown, the unpaid for, the freely given." She knows so little about church, yet she knows what it is. She is an artist who knows something about inscape and the manifold wisdom. With an artist's intuition she perceives the energy (the Holy Spirit) that keeps aloft the ligaments and sinews and fabric of the hang glider that she is strapped into, this seemingly fragile church that casts on the earth what she calls shadow work.

\*     \*     \*

Church as the body of Christ is not obvious. But neither is Jesus as the savior of the world obvious. We learn to penetrate the obvious ordinariness when we think in terms of inscape and manifold wisdom and shadow work. But for as long as we employ secular values and insist on having church as we think it ought to be, formulating this "ought" from what we see work in our culture quite apart from God, we will never recognize the church that is right before us. For as long as we think that the church is in competition with the world, a way of outdoing the world, we will never get it.

The contrast between world and church in this regard is stark: American culture is doing its dead level best with its celebrities, consumerism, and violence to keep us in a perpetually arrested state of adolescence. Yet all the while the church is quietly and without false advertising immersing us in the conditions of becoming mature to the measure of the full stature of Christ.

# CHAPTER 8

# Prayer and All the Fullness: Ephesians 3:14-21

*I pray that you may have the power to comprehend, with all the
saints, what is the breadth and length and height and depth, and to
know the love of Christ that surpasses knowledge, so that you may be
filled with all the fullness of God.*

EPHESIANS 3:18-20

*We must re-learn the essential truth that Christian prayer is rather
like cleaning a car. When we are lucky enough to have a new one we
wash and polish away with enthusiastic fervour, it is a devotional job.
When the novelty wears off it becomes rather a nuisance and rather a
bore, but we can still clean it efficiently, and here is the one vital point:
there is no difference whatever in the result.*

MARTIN THORNTON, *Christian Proficiency*

Prayer is the cradle language of the church. This is our mother tongue.
So it is both natural and fitting that Paul's "churchiest" letter be articulated in the language of prayer. Paul has opened with an extensive, explosive (!) volley of prayer: "Blessed be the God and Father of our Lord
Jesus Christ . . ." (Eph. 1:3-14). He goes on to address his readers, but af

ter only a single sentence he is again praying: "I pray that the God of our Lord Jesus Christ . . . give you a spirit of wisdom and revelation . . ." (1:17-23).

Now, at the transitional center of the letter, Paul is at it once more, on his knees, praying before the Father (3:14-21). In a couple of pages we will find him concluding his letter by urging his readers (us!) to enter into what he has been praying and writing by praying it all themselves: "Pray in the Spirit at all times. . . . Pray also for me. . . . Pray that I may declare [the mystery of the gospel] boldly . . ." (6:18-20).

Paul prays. Even when the prayers are not explicit, the language is prayerful. Paul lives his prayers. He is praying even when he doesn't know he is praying. He begins by laying a foundation in a prayer of blessing and then goes on to pray for those to whom he is writing. Now here, at the center of the letter, we come upon this strategically placed prayer that keeps the letter centered in prayer. At the end of the letter, Paul's admonition to pray will keep the church praying — not discussing church, not talking about prayer, but praying.

Church begins in prayer, stays centered by prayer, and ends up praying.

## "Glory in the church and in Christ Jesus"

This centering prayer is a single sentence that is controlled by its final phrase, "glory in the church and in Christ Jesus" (Eph. 3:21). This is a succinct compression of the entire letter: the motif of glory (1:6, 12, 14) as it comes to expression in Christ and church.

Christ and church, church and Christ. When we are dealing with church we are dealing with Christ. When we are dealing with Christ we are dealing with church. We cannot have one without the other — no Christ without church, no church without Christ.

The unique thing about Jesus Christ is that he is both human and divine. Not just human. Not just divine. Both at the same time. To keep these two seeming opposites together, simultaneously, is the hardest thing followers of Jesus have to do.

The unique thing about church is that it is both human and divine. Not just human. Not just divine. Both at the same time. The parallels between Christ and church are not exactly the same, for what is divine in church is derivative from the divinity of Christ. Still, to keep these two seeming opposites together, simultaneously, is one of the hardest things that members of the church have to do.

\*     \*     \*

It is fairly easy to understand Jesus Christ as human. We have a personal investment in being human — that is what *we* are. And we know that we are not very good at it. There is a lot of trial and error involved. If there is help available, we will give it a try. Jesus seems worth a try. He has a widespread reputation as the greatest and finest instance of humanity in the long history of humankind. His wisdom, compassion, love for enemies, voluntary suffering, teaching us who God is and the way he works, teaching us who we are and how to live a good life, care for the poor and acceptance of the outcast, pithy aphorisms and imagination-enlarging stories — all this and more is both easy to discern and easy to admire in Jesus. There are not many who would dissent.

There are many, of course, who know all this but do not follow Jesus. It is not because they think he is (or was) a bad person. They just don't think following Jesus will get them where they want to go in this world, get them success or wealth, satisfy their ambitions or lusts, guarantee them obedient children and a comfortable retirement.

It is also fairly easy to believe that Jesus Christ is divine. Throughout the history of the human race, in every time and place that we know anything about, men and women have believed in and worshiped a god or gods. There is more to life than being born and getting a job, getting married and having children, playing golf and going fishing, climbing the ladder and "making a mark." There is truth to be known, love to be experienced, heaven and hell to consider, souls to be nurtured, beauty to be embraced, eternal mysteries yet to be revealed. Robert Browning's question — "A man's reach should exceed his grasp or what's a heaven for?" — keeps us open and responsive to what is beyond us, what we cannot control, to the divine mystery that infuses our lives with meaning. There are widely circulated reports of Jesus Christ on record as being the Son of God, miraculously born on this earth to show and tell us these things, and then miraculously returning to the "right hand of the Father" enthroned in heaven. We humans seem to have a built-in propensity to believe in the supernatural. Christ is for many the leading candidate as the revelation of God, "God with us."

There are many, of course, who do not believe in Jesus as divine, as the revelation of God, but not because they don't know about the reports as such. They just don't think belief is an adult option. Belief that Christ is God is superstition. Taking the supernatural seriously is for children. It is naïve, there is nothing to it. If there is anything to God or gods it is simply a way of talking about ourselves, the "god within." If there is any divinity around to be believed in, it is me. To seriously believe that Christ is God means that I am *not* God, that I don't possess godlike attributes. Becoming an adult means that I make the big decisions on my own terms. Gods don't like competition. If you insist on the divinity of Christ, I'm not interested.

Christians have worked long and hard and thought and prayed and conversed with one another in order to understand and follow and believe Jesus Christ as both fully human and fully divine: very God, very Man. It hasn't been easy, and there continue to be assaults on the unity from both sides. Still, in the church at least, the consensus holds.

*     *     *

Christians are interested in understanding and participating in the life of church on the same terms that we use to understand and participate in the life of Christ — human and divine simultaneously, without diluting or compromising either element. Ephesians, more than any other text in Scripture, pairs Christ and church. Eleven times in this brief letter, Christ and church are set alongside one another as intertwined, inseparable.[1]

---

1. Ephesians 1:22-23; 2:15, 26; 3:6, 7-10, 21; 4:15-16; 5:23, 25, 29, 32.

When the divinity of church is diminished or slighted, "human" fills the vacuum: we get a religion that we cobble together on our own as we indulge ourselves as aesthetes of the sublime, with God honored at the periphery. It is often magnificent religion: splendid music, dazzling tapestries and altar work, dramatic liturgies, elegant language, emotionally charged rhetoric, breathtaking architecture, carefully written and intellectually competent (but prayerless) theologies. All to the glory of God, of course, but mostly *pro forma*. Jesus doing the works of the Father — healing, saving, blessing, forgiving — is reverently ignored.

When the humanity of church is diminished or slighted, a subtly disincarnate faux "divinity" replaces it and we get a spirituality that is mostly about us as individuals with eternal souls to save and spiritual tasks to perform. The name Christ is in conspicuous use, but it is also very apparent who is calling the shots: *we* are, with Christ as backup if a miracle should be required. Sometimes Christ is enlisted to help us develop our interior lives of devotion through Bible studies and the practice of prayer. Sometimes Christ is called upon to help us carry out programs or crusades or missions. Church that depreciates humanity often develops an impressive spirituality: intense Bible studies, prayer and fasting, programs and causes, dreams and visions, crusades and inspirational appeals to move mountains. But it is also a spirituality curiously deficient in human relationships, welcoming, and hospitable intimacies. Men and women, including our own souls, are depersonalized and abstracted into causes to be pursued or problems to be fixed. Church becomes an impersonal project. All in the name of Jesus, of course, but there doesn't appear to be much of Jesus' humanity in the details.

When church fails to embrace the divinity of Jesus as its own imputed divinity — God's forgiveness and salvation, God's love and sanctification — it betrays its core identity as Christ's body.

And when church fails to embrace the humanity of Jesus as its own humanity — personal, local, earthy, humble — it betrays its core identity as a dwelling place for God.

\*     \*     \*

Church, Christ's body, when deficient in either the divinity or humanity of its head, ceases to be Christ's body and is no longer church. I want to take seriously Paul's bold and forceful yoking of the identity of church as derived from the identity of Jesus. We are not looking for perfection but for marks of maturity however imperfectly realized. There has never been a perfect, sinless church, and there never will be.

I find it useful to bring the experience of John of Patmos and his seven churches to set alongside Paul and his Ephesian church to post a warning notice: "Danger! Be mindful that church is not a safe conclave, insulated from sin." Constant vigilance is required to keep the humanity and divinity of Jesus Christ organically one. An identical vigilance is required to keep the humanity and divinity of church organically one.

Paul wrote his letter to the Ephesians thirty years or so before John took up his responsibilities as pastor of a circuit of seven churches that included Ephesus. This letter shaped the Ephesian self-understanding of church in continuity with what they understood of Christ. A generation later, that Christ-formed identity is under assault in John's congregations by false teachers and Satan and by the evil presence of idolatry and violence, lying and persecution that permeated the Greek and Roman world. Paul in his foundational, identity-forming letter had told them that this kind of thing was part of being church, warned them that church did not have diplomatic immunity from the forces of evil.

Now it's John's turn. The Spirit-discerned indictments that Pastor John of Patmos delivered to the seven churches he served (Rev. 2–3) is a sobering caution against making the church in "our image" at any time or in any form. He uses his vision of the resurrection body of Jesus Christ as his text for understanding church (Rev. 1:12-20). He then goes on to use strong language to face his seven congregations with their careless, indifferent, or willful betrayals of Christ's body.

The Ephesian church is the first to be indicted on the grounds that it "abandoned the love you had at first" (Rev. 2:4). The insipidity ("you are lukewarm") of the last-named church, the Laodicean, leads Jesus to say, "I am about to spit you out of my mouth" (3:16). He uses the name Satan ("synagogue of Satan," 2:9; "Satan's throne," "where Satan lives," 2:13) to shock some of the other congregations into recognizing that what is going on right before their eyes is diametrically opposed to the Christ who has revealed himself as very God and very Man among them. Are they so naïve and innocent of sin and evil that they don't see through the "angel of light" sleight-of-hand of Satan? Christ nails them for the false teaching and practice that is apparently getting a hearing among them: "the works of the Nicolaitans" (2:15), the "teaching of Balaam" (2:14), "that woman Jezebel" (2:20), "the deep things of Satan" (2:24). Can't they hear the radical difference between the teachings that have come like a flaming two-edged sword from the mouth of Jesus Christ and what these pretended prophets and prophetesses are saying? We aren't told the specific nature of these teachings, but three of the names associated with them — Balaam, Jezebel, Satan — clearly identify them as lies, perversions, and distortions of what these churches know from Moses and Elijah, Jesus and Paul, and more recently John himself.

It is unlikely that the terms "Satan" (four times), "Nicolaitans" (twice), "Balaam," and "Jezebel" refer to any conspicuously outrageous sin or teaching that was taking place in John's churches. Church, the head and body of Christ, is rarely defied and challenged outright from within. Sin and lies within the church work at a more subtle level. They almost always show up as a promised improvement or an extension of what has been already definitively revealed in Jesus Christ.

What John named for his churches as Satan and the Nicolaitans, Balaam and Jezebel, and the deep things of Satan, Paul had earlier named "the wiles of the devil . . . cosmic powers of this present darkness . . . spiritual forces of evil in the heavenly places" (Eph. 6:11-12). Church has always been prey to enemy assault and infiltration. It always will be. The Ephesian church had been well-warned from the outset by Paul. Now John picks up the pastoral task of discerning the ways in which evil people and "this present darkness" were dissembling and deconstructing the fundamental Jesus identity of the churches under his pastoral care.

John countered the threat posed to his congregations with a grand vision of Jesus alive, in action, and present in the midst of the church. By means of the vision, each church saw itself as part of church on a grand scale, worshiping God and watching as Jesus takes on the entire world of Satan and Balaam and Jezebel, the wiles of the devil, the present darkness, the forces of evil, "conquering and to conquer" (Rev. 6:2).

The vision was a tour de force. Ever since, it has played a major part in church through the centuries and all over the world in reimagining and reinforcing the central, exclusive, and irreplaceable place of Jesus Christ as the head of the church, which Paul had identified as Christ's body.

## "I bow my knees before the Father"

The physical act of bowing "my knees before the Father" (Eph. 3:14) is an act of reverence. It is also an act of voluntary defenselessness. While on my knees I cannot run away. I cannot assert myself. I place myself in a position of willed submission, vulnerable to the will of the person before whom I am bowing. It is an act of retreating from the action so that I can perceive what the action is without me in it, without me taking up space, without me speaking my piece. On my knees I am no longer in a position to flex my muscles, strut or cower, hide in the shadows or show off on stage. I become less so that I can be aware of more — I assume a posture that lets me see what reality looks like without the distorting lens of either my timid avoidance or my aggressive domination. I set my agenda aside for a time and become still, present to God.

This posture is not in vogue in a world in which the media, our parents, our employers, our teachers, and, perhaps most demanding of all, our egos are telling us to make the most of ourselves. On his knees before the Father, Paul prays.

*   *   *

Prayer is the lingua franca of humankind. Everybody prays. At least everybody starts out praying. So why is the practice of prayer in so-called

Christian America so sporadic and confused? Why is prayer for so many either a personal embarrassment or a political cause? I ask that question a lot.

As a pastor, much of my work involves encouraging and teaching people to pray. But I have never found this work to be easy. Why is the teaching so difficult? If prayer is evident virtually everywhere and, at least vestigially, in everyone, why is there so little fluency? The men and women I have worked with all my life don't mind being prayed for — in fact, they often ask me to pray for them. Why are people so ready to appoint a representative to do their praying for them? Why is there so much more talk about prayer than actual praying? Why are so many more doubts expressed and questions raised about this form of language than any other?

An adequate answer, at least the beginning of an answer, begins to take shape when we observe the way we use language when we are not on our knees. When we listen carefully to the language used around us every day as we go shopping, go to school, go to the bank, go to work, and boot up our computers, we can't help noticing that the primary use of language is impersonal.

Language can be used in a variety of ways: to name things, describe actions, provide information, command specific behaviors, tell the truth, tell lies, curse, bless. Language is incredibly and endlessly versatile. But in our heavily technologized and consumerized world, most of the words said and heard in most ordinary days have little or no relational or personal depth to them. They deal with a world of things and activities, machines and ideas.

But language at its core and at its best reveals. Using words, I can speak myself into relationship with another. I can tell another who I am, what I feel, the way I think. And by listening to words another speaks to me, I can become relationally involved with him or her. Language at its best initiates and develops personal relationships. It does all the other things I mentioned also, but it is as revelation that it comes into its own.

From infancy, all of us learn language in this personal, relational, revelational way. Before we can articulate words, the sounds we make develop intimate affections, basic trust, promises, and comfort. But too soon we learn to name and demand things. Language objectifies both the world before us and the people around us. As we become increasingly proficient in the language of naming and defining and describing, the personal, relational aspects of language recede as we learn to talk our way competently through a world made up mostly of things to arrange and work to do. In the process, sadly, we "thingify" persons. More often than not, the words we use and listen to are in the context of the roles that we are given to play: students, customers, employers, workers, competitors, all of whom could just as well be, and often are, nameless. Gradually, our early language instinct with intimacy erodes, and along with it the very capacity for intimacy. Before long, most of our language is used, as Wordsworth lamented, in "getting and spending." As language becomes impersonal, the world becomes depersonalized. By the time we decide to get married we hardly know how to say "I love you," and so we go out and buy a Hallmark card with doggerel verse to do it for us.

But here's the thing: prayer is personal language or it is nothing. God is personal, emphatically personal: three-personed personal. When we use impersonal language in this most personal of all relations, the language doesn't work. And when we listen in Scripture and in silence to what the personal God has to say to us in our unique personhood, anticipating information or answers and not hearing anything remotely like that, we don't know what to make of it. We walk away saying or thinking, "God doesn't speak to me. . . . He never even listens to me." The language we are really fluent in, the language we are most used to, deals with impersonal data and functionalized roles. The practice of prayer, if it is going to amount to anything more than wish lists and complaints, requires a recovery of personal, relational, revelational language in both our listening and our speaking.

The classic textbook for recovering the personal language of prayer is the Psalms. A thorough immersion in the Psalms is the primary way that Christians acquire fluency in the personal, intimate, honest, earthy language of prayer and take our place in the great company of our praying ancestors. For while prayer is always personal, it is never individual. At prayer we are part of a great congregation whether we see them or not. Praying the Psalms gets us used to being in a praying congregation of men and women. We are never less alone than when we pray, even when there is no one else in the room. We are praying for others who don't know we are praying for them. Others are praying for us although we don't know it. This is important, for while prayer is language at its most personal, it is also inherently interrelational — it is *church* language. The more intimately we are in relation to Christ, the more aware and relational we are with the body of Christ. When we pray, we are not self-enclosed. Praying the Psalms keeps us in a school of prayer that maintains wakefulness and an open ear, alertness and an articulate tongue, both to the word of God and to the voices of praise and pain of God's people.

## "All the fullness"

Paul's prayer for his congregation is nothing if not exuberant. There is nothing cautious or restrained in his prayer. As he prays for the Ephesians, the intercessions exude generosity: "riches of his glory . . . power through his Spirit . . . rooted and grounded in love . . . power to comprehend . . . breadth and length and height and depth . . . the love of Christ that surpasses knowledge . . . filled with all the fullness . . . abundantly far more than all we can ask or imagine. . . ." We pray in a household of extravagance.

This is nothing less than astonishing, this prayer of intercession for the Ephesian Christians. Intercession usually takes its start in praying for someone who needs help: interceding for families who are grieving a death, interceding for the healing and health of the sick, interceding for wisdom on behalf of our political leaders, interceding for clarity and direction for the confused, interceding for peace in the Middle East, interceding for the hungry of the world, interceding for the homeless, interceding for an end to racial discrimination and strife, interceding for the jobless.

This is understandable. In any congregation, on any given

Sunday, it doesn't take long to look around and locate and name a dozen people whose identity is synonymous with need: a single mother of three with a newly diagnosed inoperable cancer; a father who has just placed his teenage drug-addicted son in rehab; a grandmother recently abandoned by her husband of thirty-five years; a scruffy stranger who doesn't "fit" here in *this* congregation, an obvious misfit. There is not a pew in any sanctuary that does not reserve space for needs that require and receive prayers of intercession.

Paul's prayers of intercession add another dimension, the huge reservoir of plenitude out of which the intercessions flow. His prayers of intercession flow out of the plenitude of God. The plenitude of God, not the penury of the human condition, undergirds the intercessions. Paul is certainly not unaware of the neediness of the congregation to whom he is writing — he is, after all, a pastor. But his prayers do not arise out of pity or desperation over the human condition. These intercessions are shaped and energized by God: Father, Son, and Holy Spirit. The eight God-detonated "rocket verbs" in his opening prayer (Eph. 1:3-14), the resurrection-created "saint" identity that he gives thanks for as he remembers his congregation in prayer (1:15-25), the "immeasurable riches" of salvation that replace anxious effort with amazing grace (2:1-10), the wall that Christ broke down in order to give access to everyone everywhere to "our peace" (2:11-22), the "manifold wisdom" — the "inscape" and shadow work of church — all give us eyes to see and ears to hear what is going on in the world, *really* going on.

Herman Melville once wrote to a friend, "I love all men who *dive.*" Paul dives. He goes deep and explores the conditions that keep us afloat. He is not unaware of or indifferent to what takes place on the surface, but in his intercessions he dives, listens for and names what God is and is always doing beneath us — and as he comes up from the depths, he prays that "he may grant . . . power through his Spirit" (3:16), "that Christ may dwell in your hearts" (3:17), "that you may have the power to comprehend" (3:18), and "that you may be filled with all the fullness" (3:19). Here are four intercessions, praying us into the presence of and participation in God, the God who is previous to who we are and what we are doing, the God who is previous to what has gone wrong in our lives. Our problems don't define us; God defines us. Our problems are neither the first nor the last word of who we are; God is.

*   *   *

Two friends, Fred and Cheryl, went to Haiti twenty-five years ago to pick up a child they had adopted. Addie was five years old. Her parents had been killed in a traffic accident that left her without a family. As she walked across the tarmac to board the plane, the tiny orphan reached up and slipped her hands into the hands of her new parents whom she had just met. Later they told us of this "birth" moment, how the innocent, fearless trust expressed in that physical act of grasping their hands seemed almost as miraculous as the times their two sons slipped out of the birth canal 15 and 13 years earlier.

That evening, back home in Arizona, they sat down to their first supper together with their new daughter. There was a platter of pork chops and a bowl of mashed potatoes on the table. After the first serving, the two teenage boys kept refilling their plates. Soon the pork chops had disappeared and the potatoes were gone. Addie had never seen so much food on one table in her whole life. And she had never seen so much food disappear so fast. Her eyes were big as she watched her new brothers, Thatcher and Graham, satisfy their ravenous teenage appetites.

Fred and Cheryl noticed that Addie had become very quiet and realized that something was wrong — agitation . . . bewilderment . . . insecurity? Cheryl guessed that it was the disappearing food. She suspected that because Addie had grown up hungry, when food was gone from the table she might be thinking that it would be a day or more before there was more to eat. Cheryl had guessed right. She took Addie's hand and led her to the bread drawer and pulled it out, showing her a back-up of three loaves. She took her to the refrigerator, opened the door, and showed her the bottles of milk and orange juice, the fresh vegetables, jars of jelly and jam and peanut butter, a carton of eggs, and a package of bacon. She took her to the pantry with its bins of potatoes, onions, and squash, and the shelves of canned goods — tomatoes and peaches and pickles. She opened the freezer and showed Addie three or four chickens, a few packages of fish, and two cartons of ice cream. All the time she was reassuring Addie that there was lots of food in the house, that no matter how much Thatcher and Graham ate and how fast they ate it, there was a lot more where that came from. She would never go hungry again.

Cheryl didn't just tell her that she would never go hungry again. She showed her what was in those drawers and behind those doors, named the meats and vegetables, placed them in her hands. It was enough. Food was there, whether she could see it or not. Her brothers were no longer rivals at the table. She was home. She would never go hungry again.

My wife and I were told that story twenty-five years ago. Ever since, whenever I read and pray this prayer of Paul's, I think of Cheryl, gently leading Addie by the hand through a food tour of the kitchen and pantry, reassuring her of the "boundless riches" (Eph. 3:8) and "all the fullness" (3:19) inherent in the household in which she now lives.

## "The inner man"

Prayer is attentiveness to God, which Paul has certainly been diligent in doing. But prayer is also the practiced cultivation of what we sometimes designate our inner life. That is to say, there is far more to God than just knowing about him and "the riches of his glory" (Eph. 3:16). Prayer weds what we know of God to a personal responsiveness to God. And so Paul prays — that the Father "may grant that you may be strengthened in your inner being with power through his Spirit, and that Christ may dwell in your hearts" (3:16-17).

The phrase "inner being" is literally, in Paul's Greek, "inner man," and it is translated as such in the King James Version and Revised Standard Version. Most students of this text take the meaning to be our inner life, our heart, the life of the soul. But Markus Barth sets out a comprehensive (and to me convincing) case for keeping to the literal rendering, "inner man," and then goes a step further by capitalizing it

"Inner Man" as a title for Jesus. He translates, ". . . grant that through his Spirit you be fortified with the power to grow toward the Inner Man that through faith the Messiah may dwell in your hearts." Inner Man is synonymous with Messiah, who dwells in our hearts.[2]

Earlier Paul used similar language in writing to the Galatians: "I have been crucified with Christ; and it is no longer I who live, but it is Christ who lives in me. And the life I now live in the flesh I live by faith in the Son of God" (Gal. 2:19-20).

\*   \*   \*

The attractiveness for me of Barth's exegesis of the Inner Man as Jesus is the protection it provides against the danger of divinizing our inner lives quite apart from Jesus. Hyper-subjectivity in prayer threatens the very nature of prayer, the *relational* core of prayer. While I am on my knees before the Father, Christ is praying for me (John 17) and in me, strengthening me with power through his Spirit. In contrast, the translation "inner being" is sometimes seen as a colorless spiritual abstraction that I am free to color in with any or all of the colors of the rainbow. But if "Inner Man" is specifically Jesus — God revealed in words that I can ponder, actions that I can participate in — my prayers are rooted in real history, in actual incarnation, and are not controlled by my moods or fantasies, guilty fears or wishful thinking.

Prayer is subjective; it *does* have to do with my inner being, my heart. But there is so much more than that, so much more to what is within me than "me." There is God, revealed in Jesus. There is the "interior castle" celebrated and elaborated by Teresa of Avila that necessarily includes me, all of me — body and soul, emotions and thoughts, memories and dreams, parents and family, and all the people who have played a part in my life story. But the "castle," the person at prayer, includes so much more: there is also all of God, in all the operations of the Trinity — Father, Son, and Holy Spirit. At prayer I am not myself by

---

2. Markus Barth, *Ephesians 1-3*, The Anchor Bible, vol. 34 (Garden City, NY: Doubleday, 1974), p. 391.

myself before God: the Inner Man is there, a partner in my praying, speaking the word of God. Prayer transcends "me, myself, and I" by bringing me into attentive participating relationship with the Inner Man, with Jesus, who reveals the Godhead.

Prayer is not "getting in touch with your true self," as is so often said. It is the practice of shifting preoccupation away from yourself toward attentiveness and responsiveness to God. It is a deliberate walking away from a me-centered way of life to a Christ-centered way of life. It is certainly true that in weakness and thirst and desperation we reach out to God, but the larger and more encompassing reality is that God is already reaching out to us. Prayer has its origin in the movement of God toward us.

This is consistent with the entire tenor of Ephesians. Everything begins and is completed in God. Growing up in Christ is not a matter of being "born again" and then, with this wonderful gift of life, handed the responsibility of nurturing it into maturity.

*     *     *

By installing the Inner Man on the premises where we pray, Paul protects us from becoming preoccupied with the state of our "inner being." It is not uncommon in the Christian way for people to get sidetracked in prayer by becoming more interested in themselves than in God, sometimes to the point of obsession. This shows up when we talk a lot about prayer, run here and there to places of prayer, read a lot of books about prayer, make a specialty of prayer. Self-consciousness in matters of prayer is not a good sign, not a sign of health, not a mark of holiness. With Jesus, the Inner Man, in our prayers we are protected from prayers that spiral into neurotic self-absorption.

Another perversion of prayer that Paul protects us from is treating prayer as a depersonalized curiosity: phenomena of the supernatural, signs and wonders, laboratory experiments to validate ESP (extrasensory perception), the effects of prayer on plant growth, collecting testimonies from remote places on bilocation and levitation. This curiosity easily degenerates into groping for methods for getting in contact with transcendental spheres through meditation techniques or astrological charts or inducing psychological states through dance or fasting or drugs, which have nothing to do with Jesus or anybody else, and certainly nothing to do with living "to the praise of his glory." But if we know that Jesus, the Inner Man, is here "dwelling" with us in the place and act of prayer, his Spirit strengthening us to grow to the "full stature of Christ" (Eph. 4:13), we are not going to be distracted into episodes of spiritual voyeurism. If the context of prayer is an aspect of myself, my inner being, it is easy enough to develop unseemly curiosities about what might be going on. But with the Inner Man in the room, any such curiosity would be exposed as sacrilegious.

Paul prays, we pray, in the company of the Trinity.

\*     \*     \*

To understand church we must immerse ourselves in the God-revealing vocabulary and the prayer-saturated syntax in which it is given to us, a vocabulary and syntax that are so conspicuous in Ephesians. Apart from such an immersion, church cannot be comprehended. Outsiders cannot understand church. Lacking a God-revealing vocabulary and a prayer-saturated syntax, they can only misunderstand it.

The misunderstandings are numerous, but two that consistently dog the church stand out. One is that church is what we do. It is commonplace to think that church is what we build, what we organize, what can be measured and counted. It is people and bricks, causes and programs, liturgies and altar calls. Church is our assignment in the business of mission and salvation. The form that church takes can range from a Byzantine religious bureaucracy to a Ma and Pa storefront to a sentimentalized church in the wildwood — state churches, established denominations, independent "free" and "Bible" churches. What takes place in church is up to us.

The second misunderstanding is that the church, the "real church," is invisible. Church is a mystical company of souls who have little to do with one another apart from occasional gatherings of like-minded souls, people who share the "right vibes." It has little, maybe nothing, to do with bodies and buildings. Bodies and buildings are all right in their place, but they are not the church. The church is entirely spiritual.

There are variations in the way these misunderstandings are expressed, but both of them are an essential denial of what our Scriptures reveal as church. The first misunderstanding, that church is what we do, is a denial of the central action of Father, Son, and Holy Spirit in the making and continuation of church. Not that these people don't believe in or pray to or serve God. Some of them do it with great devotion. Others do it out of religious habit, or moral obligation, or a fondness for sacred aesthetics. What they have in common is that they themselves, whether they are conscious of it or not, are the measure of church. The decisions they make and the feelings they have trump anything that they *don't* have a voice or decision in. These forms of church can be formal or spontaneous, traditional or innovative, but pragmatism is the bottom line — what we do for God and in the name of God. Sometimes the pragmatism presents itself clothed in robes of religion; other times it is blatantly blue-jeans-in-your-face.

The second misconception, that the church consists of a mystical elite who cannot be identified with named places and people, is essentially a denial of the distinctive belief and experience of the Christian faith, the Incarnation: God became flesh and dwelt among us, we who are also flesh. God does not work apart from flesh and bones, timber and brick. The Christian church is historical. It exists in time and space. The Christian faith came to birth in a human body born in Bethlehem. The Christian church came to birth thirty or so years later in a company of human bodies in Jerusalem.

There are plenty of people around — they have always been around — ignorant of or indifferent to both Trinity and Incarnation, determined to remake the church along the lines they have learned from marketers and sociologists. They can be safely ignored. They don't know what they are talking about. We do better to return to the text of Ephesians with its God-revealing vocabulary and prayer-saturated syntax and work with the cornucopia of images for understanding church: the fullness of him who fills all in all (1:23), new humanity (2:15), household of God (2:19), holy temple (2:21), dwelling place for God (2:22), body of Christ (4:12), marriage (5:31-32), community (6:23).

God does know what he is talking about when it comes to church, even if we do not know what we are talking about.

## CHAPTER 9

# One and All: Ephesians 4:1-16

*... making every effort to maintain the unity of the Spirit in the bond of peace. There is one body and one Spirit, just as you were called to the one hope of your calling . . . until all of us come to the unity of the faith and of the knowledge of the Son of God, to maturity, to the measure of the full stature of Christ.*

EPHESIANS 4:3-4, 13

*[T]he baptized are brought into relation with God and with each other in the same act, by virtue of sharing in communion with the one Father, mediated by the Son and realized by the Spirit. Those who are in Christ are in the church: brought into relation to God and into community simultaneously.*

COLIN GUNTON, *The One, the Three, and the Many*

We are at a transition point in Ephesians, moving from an exuberant exploration of who God is and the way he works to a detailed account of who we are and the way we work. "Therefore" is the hinge word. But the transition is not abrupt. It is not as if we can separate the being of God from being human and treat them separately. But we do separate them. The practice of resurrection puts together what we "put asunder." Jesus' resurrection restores the original intimacy that our first parents enjoyed in those uninhibited evening conversations with God in Eden. "Life" cannot be divided into compartments. Even less can the Christian life be divided into compartments: first, who God is and what he does for us, and then, after we have mastered that, who we are and what we do for God.

We are anticipating coherence, integrated wholeness, maturity "to the measure of the full stature of Christ" (Eph. 4:13). Paul is not in a hurry; he has patiently and skillfully drawn us into an understanding of church as created by God. He displays an equivalent patience and skill in discerning our part in it. Church is the appointed time and place of conversation between the two "beings" — the being of God and the human being. Both "beings" get equal time.

God created church as a place on earth accessible and congenial for being present to us, listening to us, and speaking to us on our home ground. Simultaneously it is his gift to us, a place in our neighborhood within walking or driving distance for being present to God, listening to God, and speaking to him. Everything that God is and everything that we are intersects locally in the company of family and friends and the immediate circumstances of our lives.

We don't have to leave our neighborhood to find a congenial time and place to be present to God. We don't have to "ascend into heaven" (Rom. 10:6) to get an audience with God. We don't have to "descend into the abyss" (10:7) to find out what God is doing deep in souls, deep in history, and behind the scenes. Church welcomes us, just as we are, into the conversation. God is not abstract, remote, inaccessible. Church — ordinary, local, immediate, personal — welcomes us into the company of Jesus, who is God with us, who embraces the human condition and speaks our language. Don't be intimidated: nothing here is too deep for ordinary people to get.

Church at its simplest and most obvious is a protected place, an available time for God to have conversation with us and for us to have conversation with God in company with God's people. At the same time it is far more than this. God speaks and acts whenever and wherever he wills, but it is at least this: a congenial place and time to cultivate the presence of God.

When we embrace church, we find ourselves part of a conversation in progress between what we know and experience of God and the way we live with one another, with our families, in the workplace — morally, ethically, and personally. There are many who absent themselves from the conversation so that they can go off by themselves and develop a Rube Goldberg religious contraption out of God-fragments or God-rumors picked up in back alleys, flea markets, and talk shows — a kind of makeshift, do-it-yourself belief (or unbelief) system that suits their particular lifestyle. Others, impatient with the complexities and ambiguities in the conversation, set themselves up as freelance connoisseurs of transcendence, searching out experiences of ecstasy, taking photographs of sunsets, collecting books and music that inspire.

For many people these practices seem to work pretty well in relieving the tedium of the humdrum. What they amount to, though, is a kind of spiritual pastiche of disconnected moments of diversion or escape from the confines of the self. Neither of these abstentions from the conversation that takes place in church is without its attractions. There is nothing that appears destructive in what they are doing. It is not as if the absentees were out trashing the neighborhood or secretly pursuing a life of crime. At the same time, neither way contributes to maturity — growing up, and more specifically to the point, growing up in Christ.

There is far more to God, who he is and what he is doing, than we can cobble together out of our own resources. And there is far more to us, our earthly life and our eternal souls, than can be comprehended by making a mosaic out of shards of beauty. There is God in all the operations of the Trinity: "how majestic . . . in all the earth!" (Ps. 8:1). And there is us, only "a little lower than God, and crowned . . . with glory and honor" (8:5). Becoming mature means refusing to live a reduced life, refusing a minimalist spirituality. Church is the gift we have been given for maintaining conversational relationship with everything that God is and everything that we are, so that we can gradually come to live "to the praise of his glory," so that we can finally — it is going to take a long time! — grow to "the full stature of Christ."

*   *   *

Showing up in church on this earth and in our history doesn't guarantee that we will live attentively to the full revelation of God in our lives and understand everything we are and do conversationally with God. Gifts by the very nature of being gift can be freely received or rejected. There is no coercion in a gift.

Paul through the first three chapters of Ephesians has been training our imaginations to recognize and embrace the nature of God's gift of church. He is about ready to elaborate in detail (from 4:17 to the end) the ways in which we get in on the action, live the gift. But he doesn't push us through the door. He lingers, pondering the intricacies involved in becoming mature in Christ in company with all the others who are growing up with us, and along with the considerable number who are not, or at least not yet, interested in growing up. Ephesians 4:1-16 is transitional, easing us along so that we don't abruptly shift our attention from God to us and thereby lose our distinctive *church* orientation: head *and* body, Christ *and* us, in continuous and reverent conversation.

## "The calling to which you have been called"

Paul gathers everything that he has written so far into a single word that gets us ready for what comes next. The word is "calling." God's word to us is inherently a call, an invitation, a welcome into his presence and action. When we respond to the call, we live a calling.[1] The calling gives us a destination, determines what we do, shapes our behavior, forms a coherent life. We live into the world and the relationships into which we

---

1. This is the fulcrum at the center of Ephesians that I elaborated on in chapter 2, "The Message to the Ephesians."

**169**

have been called. Our English word, derived from the Latin for "call" (*vocare*), is "vocation." Vocation, calling, is a way of life. A job is different. A job is an assigned piece of work. When the work is done, the job is over and we go back to being just ourselves, free to do anything we choose to do. A vocation, by contrast, is comprehensive.

Jesus calls us. When we hear the call and respond, we live the calling. From then on the call shapes our lives, gives content to our lives, characterizes the way we live our lives. "I therefore, the prisoner in the Lord, beg you to lead a life worthy of the calling to which you have been called" (Eph. 4:1).

The verb "call" is the root of the Greek word for church, *ekklesia*. Paul uses the word nine times in Ephesians.[2] For the Greeks it was not a religious or cultic word. It simply meant assembly, a gathering of people, men and women who have been called together in a designated place. In the Greek translation of the Hebrew Bible the word it translates is "congregation" (*qahal*), but always with the implicit meaning "God's congregation," the "assembly of God's people." Some have strapped the word to a chair and tried to etymologically torture a spiritual or theological meaning out of it. Our best scholars have advised us of the futility of such forced exegesis.[3] No. It is an ordinary word taken out of ordinary life — public meetings, celebrations, family reunions, whatever — to refer to an assembly of people. That in itself seems to me to be significant, for it offers sturdy resistance to romanticizing or glamorizing or spiritualizing the word "church" apart from the conditions in which it is given to us.

The useful thing the word does at its root is keep us mindful that this assembly, this congregation, this household of God, this temple of God, this body of Christ, is the community of the called — who now have a calling. God's call and our calling fuse into church. Verbs are the circulatory system of church. The call and the calling are the systolic and diastolic heartbeat of the body of Christ.

---

2. Ephesians 1:22; 2:10, 21; 5:23, 24, 25, 27, 29, 32.

3. See *Theological Dictionary of the New Testament*, ed. Gerhard Kittel, trans. Geoffrey W. Bromiley (Grand Rapids: Eerdmans, 1965), vol. 3, pp. 530-36.

## The Language of Paraclesis

The characteristic tone of Paul's language up to this point has been kerygmatic. *Kerygma* is the transliteration of the Greek word for preach, proclaim, post a decree, herald urgent news. "Preach" is the usual translation. But since American ears often pick up overtones of condescension and pious nagging in the word ("don't preach to me") I want to use "kerygmatic" to catch the bold, urgent, excited, extravagant exuberance that permeates Paul's language as he writes of God and glory, Christ and grace, church and abundance, Spirit and prayer.

And I want to contrast it with another, quite different use of language that Paul now brings into play: "I therefore, the prisoner in the Lord, beg you to lead a life worthy of the calling . . ." (Eph. 4:1). This verb, "I beg you," in contrast to the bold kerygmatic vigor of Paul's language that we have been immersed in, introduces a quieter, more conversational tone, something on the order of "I'm here at your side, let's talk this over, let's together consider how we can get in on everything that God is doing." At the conclusion of Ephesians, Paul will use the same verb again, translated this time "to encourage your hearts" (6:22). The language style that develops out of this verb is sometimes referred to as *paracletic*. Like church *(ekklesia)*, which has the verb "call" *(kaleo)* at its root, "I beg you" or "encourage you" *(parakaleo)* also has "call" *(kaleo)* embedded in it. "Paracletic" names the style of language used in church as we discern and embody the calling to which Christians have been called.

Three kinds of language are in common use in church: kerygmatic, didactic, and paracletic. Preaching, proclamation (kerygmatic language), is most obvious. The gospel must be preached. Paul, writing to the Romans, put it memorably: "how are they to hear without someone to proclaim [*kerussontos*] and how are they to proclaim [*keruxosin*] unless they are sent? As it is written [he is quoting Isaiah], 'How beautiful are the feet of those who bring good news!'" (Rom. 10:14-15). Preaching takes pride of place as the church's distinctive language. "Yes, the world's a ship on its passage out, and not a voyage complete;

and the pulpit is its prow."[4] Jesus Christ is God's revelation of salvation: "Repent and believe the gospel!" Churches have sanctuaries and pulpits to keep the language of preaching front and center. Preaching is directed to the will, calling us to decide on and follow the way of Jesus.

Teaching (didactic language) follows. There are the Scriptures to understand. There is a world of unbelief to diagnose. There are questions to ask and answer. The Christian life involves re-understanding our entire lives and the whole world in the light of God's revelation. There is much to learn and understand. Creation and covenant map our existence, and we need to learn how to read the maps and use a compass to find our way through the territory. Churches have classrooms and lecterns to keep our minds sharp and active in understanding who God is and who we are, who this complex and various company of people (church) is that we are grafted into. Teaching is directed to the mind, to knowing the mind and ways of God revealed in Scripture and experienced in church.

Discernment (paracletic language) doesn't have the high-profile visibility of its siblings, but it is no less important. Yet because it is spoken in a quieter voice, it is often not noticed, or if it is noticed, not taken as seriously as its sister languages. Preaching has pulpit and sanctuary to dignify its authority. Teaching has lectern and classroom to spatially define its task. But discernment takes place informally, anytime and anywhere, with no one officially in charge. The settings for this kind of speech range from a pair of rocking chairs on a nursing home porch, to two men bent over coffee in a diner, to a telephone conversation between mother and daughter across three state lines. It could take place in a letter or succession of letters dealing with matters of heart and soul, or among three or four friends at a weekly meeting before going to work, reading and pondering together the ways in which Jesus' discourse in John 6 intersects the hours that they have before them that day.

Discernment is conversation directed to the insights and deci-

---

4. Herman Melville, *Moby Dick* (1851; New York: W. W. Norton & Company, Inc., 1976), p. 40.

sions, the behaviors and practices, that emerge from hearing the preached good news and learning the truth of the Scriptures as they then get prayed and embodied in my life where I am just now. These insights are not always obvious given my emotions, history, parents, baggage from old sins, and misunderstandings accumulated from a secular culture. The gospel message that seemed so simple and straightforward in the sanctuary on Sunday develops severe complications when I enter my workplace on Monday. Our families muddy the waters that seemed so clear, outlined, and in order on a chalkboard while we were sitting in a classroom.

Gerhard von Rad, for me the most percipient Hebrew scholar from the twentieth century, observed that the first appearance in our Scriptures of the language of paraclesis is in Deuteronomy, where it takes its place alongside the indicative "gospel" and the imperative "law." It is not to be confused with law, and it assumes that there is ongoing participation in the gospel of salvation. It is quite distinct from either gospel *(kerygma)* or law *(didache)*. Paraclesis is language used with men and women who already have received the word of preached salvation and have been instructed in the teaching of the law, but who are in need of comfort or encouragement or discernment in the muddled details of dailiness.[5] This is a way of language commonly identified in the church's life as "cure of souls" and "spiritual direction."

And this is the style of language that is absolutely required in the church in the process of becoming mature, of growing up in Christ. All three ways of language — kerygmatic, didactic, and paracletic — work together in this, but the one most often slighted, at least in the American church with its fondness for the indicative (telling it like it is) and imperative (ordering people to do something about it) is the paracletic. This is the kind of language that pays attention to the way the preceding languages of preaching and teaching enter into the personal particulars of each person while in the company of brothers and sisters, strangers and neighbors. Individuality is given dignity, but always in

5. See Gerhard von Rad, *Old Testament Theology*, trans. D. M. G. Stalker (New York: Harper & Row, 1965), vol. 2, p. 393.

the context of congregation. Listening, which requires silence, is a substantial element in the language of paraclesis.

Paraclesis is a language that permeates Isaiah, one of our leading guides into a mature life of faith: "Comfort, O comfort my people . . . speak tenderly to Jerusalem" (Isa. 40:1-2). It is the language of Psalm 23 that has guided many a confused soul through a wilderness: "your rod and your staff — they comfort me" (Ps. 23:4). This is the language that Jesus used in the second beatitude, blessing those who mourn: "for they will be comforted" (Matt. 5:4). In each of these representative passages the lead-off verb is *parakaleo*: "comfort" . . . "be encouraged" . . . "you are not alone in this" . . . "I am with you always."

And this is the language that Jesus uses in his final conversation with his disciples (John 13–18). Throughout their years with him, they have heard great preaching: "The kingdom of God is at hand!" They have heard incredible teaching: "The kingdom of God is like. . . ." But this night, his last night with them, he engages them in a long, unhurried, intimate conversation. He uses the language of paraclesis. They know what has happened in Jesus: kingdom, salvation. They know what the calling means. Parables and discourses and prayers have made everything vivid. All this now needs to get assimilated and digested. It needs to get metabolized into the muscle and bone, the nerve endings and brain cells of the body of Christ. They have a new basic identity: friends, disciples, followers of Jesus. But they have just begun. They need to grow up, become what they know, mature — grow up in Christ.

In order to clarify exactly what will be taking place and how, Jesus introduces them to a new word, "Paraclete," translated in our English Bibles as "Advocate" (NRSV), "Counselor" (RSV), "Comforter" (KJV), "Friend" (*The Message*). He uses it four times (John 14:16, 26; 15:26; 16:7). He doesn't leave them guessing at who or what the Paraclete is; he identifies the Paraclete as the "Spirit of truth," the "Holy Spirit." Jesus promises his disciples that the Paraclete, the Holy Spirit, will continue speaking Jesus' words in their lives. Jesus is not leaving them to figure out how to do this on their own — "I will not leave you orphaned" (John 14:18).

Paracletic language is the language of the Holy Spirit, a language of relationship and intimacy, a way of speaking and listening that gets the words of Jesus inside us so that they *become* us. It is not new information. It is not explanation. It is God's word on our side, within us, working out the details in the circumstances of our lives.

*     *     *

As Paul shifts into this paracletic mode of language, he describes the paracletic life that authenticates the language. Paracletic language is only credible if it is spoken from a paracletic life, a life he describes as lived "with all humility and gentleness, with patience, bearing with one another in love, making every effort to maintain the unity of the Spirit in the bond of peace" (Eph. 4:2-3).

Not one of these five marks of the "calling to which you have been called" that contribute to fluency in paracletic speech has anything, as such, to do with knowing the right words or understanding the correct meanings. They refer to the way the words are spoken and the relational element in which they are conveyed. The only adequate, "worthy" way to articulate this calling in and by the church, this company of the called (the *ekklesia*), is with humility, gentleness, and patience. Which means without arrogance, without harshness, without hurry. Becoming mature takes a long time, with many rest stops along the way; it cannot be hurried. Becoming mature is a complex process that defies simplification; there are no shortcuts.

The only atmosphere congenial to paracletic speech is a community in which love and peace are actively pursued. Which means that treating others in a depersonalizing way (*not* bearing with one another in love) violates the very nature of those who share the calling. And it means that treating others in a competitive way (*not* treating others as companions bound together in a covenant of peace) violates the "broken wall" conditions created by Christ that make the church *church*.

What I want to say, following Paul, is that no matter how brilliantly and forcefully we preach the good news of salvation (the *kerygma*), and no matter how accurately and thoroughly we teach the truth of the kingdom (the *didache*), if we don't master the idiom of paraclesis, the chances of growing to the "measure of the full stature of Christ" are dim.

## Deometry

This is a lot to take seriously in our calling: the torrent of church metaphors, the cascade of God-activated verbs, the lavish dimensions involved in every direction — "breadth and length and height and depth" (Eph. 3:18). It leaves our heads swimming, dizzy with the profligacies of grace. And now Paul is edging us into actually living here, taking up permanent residence in this country, getting jobs, learning the language, raising families, making ourselves at home in this, our new homeland, growing up and growing old here.

This is all well and good. But we are in danger of being overwhelmed, paralyzed into inaction by all that is before us. Where do we start?

Good Jew that he is, thoroughly schooled in the Hebrew Scriptures, Paul begins with a single word, "one," lifted out of Israel's creed: "Hear, O Israel: the LORD our God, the LORD is one" (Deut. 6:4 NIV). One. He repeats the word seven times: one, one, one, one, one, one, one. ONE. One is emphatic.

Yes, there is a lot going on. And yes, there is a lot to do. But it is not a lot of isolated things, and it is not a lot of different tasks, random, disconnected people, a junkyard of parts out of which we try to piece together something livable. Living a calling develops into a "unity of the Spirit . . . until all of us come to the unity of the faith and of the knowledge of the Son of God, to maturity" (Eph. 4:3, 13). The underlying and all-encompassing oneness that is church flows from the underlying and all-encompassing oneness that is God. The oneness reverberates in the underlying and all-encompassing oneness that is the Christian calling, the Christian life.

The repetitions in this context are not, I think, a nagging insistence on monotheism as a dogma to be believed; this is gentle pastoral reassurance that we are involved in a life of basic simplicity. But it is not oversimplified simplicity. The simplicity of our participation in the unity of the Trinity is profound and hard earned. Not a life of competing priorities, but a life in which "all things work together for good for those who love God, who are called . . ." (Rom. 8:28). Not a life teeming with anxieties on how best to please God, but simply "to will one thing" (Kierkegaard). Not a Martha life of worry and distraction over many things, but a Mary life in which "there is need of only one thing" (Luke 10:41-42).

This basic and inherent oneness is at hand wherever we look and in whatever we touch. Paul gives us a running start of recognition by identifying seven dimensions of the unity: "one body . . . one Spirit . . . one hope . . . one Lord, one faith, one baptism, one God and Father of all, who is above all and through all and in all" (Eph. 4:4-6).

Seven is more than bare enumeration. Practiced readers of Scripture detect a symbolic sense here: the completeness of the seven days of creation, the seven "thunders" of the voice of the Lord in Psalm 29, the seven "sevens" that structure the comprehensive finality of the book of Revelation. And so here: the seven items do not indicate that each item is a unity unto itself but that each measures the basic unity of God and church, the Christian calling in its many dimensions.

Henry Adams in his brilliant study of the marvels — theological, spiritual, architectural — of two medieval churches, Mont-Saint-Michel and Chartres, takes his readers on pilgrimage through these elaborate places of worship and the men and women who lived and prayed in them. He coined the word *deometry* to name his subject: taking the measure of God as the unity that produces diversity.[6] This is essentially what Paul is doing, but with this difference: Henry Adams is writing a historical and aesthetic study of the church in the twelfth century; Paul is writing to a church (or churches) in the first century who are actually experiencing the calling that was simultaneously unity and diversity, the one and the all. For Paul, deometry is not a sub-

---

6. Henry Adams, *Mont-Saint-Michel and Chartres* (Garden City, NY: Doubleday Anchor Books, 1959), p. 338.

ject out of the past to study. It involves observing the practice of what he and his readers are engaged in as they are being built together into church.

There is more to be observed. Each part of the creed is grouped in two triads of similar length: body-Spirit-hope followed by Lord-faith-baptism. The second triad contains three genders of "one" in a grammatically precise sequence of masculine, feminine, and neuter *(heis, mia, hen)*. The seventh item, "God and Father of us all," is finished off with a concluding triad of prepositions — "above all and through all and in all."[7]

The symmetries and repetitions develop a kind of liturgical rhythm that has the effect of harmonizing "all" into "one." The many dimensions to this called life, this Christ life, this church life of All, take the measure of the One. The more we live this creed, the more life coheres. The more we enter the unity, the more we find ourselves "put together."

As we "lead a life worthy of the calling," we gradually assimilate the creedal rhythm set down by the tympanic variations on the one: one body, one Spirit, one hope, one Lord, one faith, one baptism, one God and Father of us all. The crescendo flourish of prepositions at the end — "above all and through all and in all" — brings every conceivable "all" into the unity.

*　　*　　*

Some years ago, Jan and I spent a year in Pittsburgh. We were in a new place where the streets and the people and the work were all unfamiliar. We had left the routines and rituals of thirty years behind us. We felt the strangeness, missed the familiar, and deliberately set out to make ourselves at home in this new calling, to fit in. One of the things we did was to take a walk each day at noon to a park a mile or so away, strolling around a large pond, observing the birds and plant life, and

---

7. Markus Barth, *Ephesians 4–6*, The Anchor Bible, vol. 34A (Garden City, NY: Doubleday, 1974), pp. 429 and 467.

reflecting on the meaning of this abrupt change in our lives and how it might play out in the years ahead.

One day as we were walking to our meditation pond, a man on a bicycle passed us, then suddenly braked and waited for us to catch up with him. Without introduction or preface he asked, "How long have you been married?" We were startled by the out-of-the-blue abruptness, but managed a puzzled but courteous "Thirty-three years."

"I knew it," he said. "Do you realize that you walk in perfect step with one another? I mean absolutely synchronized perfect. My wife and I have been married five years and we haven't got it down yet. We are always just micro-seconds off." That was it. He was back on his bicycle and on his way.

We resumed our walk, pleased with ourselves that across thirty-three years of marriage we had mastered this miracle of walking together in perfect rhythm. We had no idea that we had achieved something in our marriage that could stop a bicyclist in his tracks. This required comment and further conversation. But the moment we became self-conscious about it, we couldn't do it. We felt clumsy, uncoordinated. The harder we tried to recover our marital rhythm, the worse it got. Eventually we quit trying and went back to just walking. We did observe, though, that "walking in perfect step" doesn't come from setting that as a marital goal and disciplining ourselves to an hour of practice each day.

Later it occurred to us that living a coherent, mature life in Christ cannot be accomplished self-consciously — there are too many details involved across too many conditions. Maybe this was something of what Jesus was getting at when he said, "The kingdom of God cometh not with observation" (Luke 17:20 KJV).

## Baron von Hugel

America in the twenty-first century does not offer propitious conditions for growing up. Maturity is not the hallmark of our culture. Our culture is conspicuous for its obsession with "getting and spending." Instead of becoming more, we either get more or do more. So it is not surprising that many people are offering to sell us maps for living better than we are without having to grow up: maps to financial security, sexual gratification, music appreciation, athletic prowess, a better car, a better job, a better education, a better vacation.

As it turns out, the maps never get us to where we wanted to go: the more we get and do, the less we are. We regress to the condition of "children, tossed to and fro and blown about by every wind of doctrine, by people's trickery, by their craftiness in deceitful scheming" (Eph. 4:14). It is hard to know whether things have gotten worse since Paul wrote, but with the multi-billion dollars spent every year in America to fund "trickery" and "craftiness in deceitful scheming" in business and entertainment and government, and, most distressingly, church, it certainly is not getting any better. Paul has something quite different in mind for us.

A friend of mine recently spent a few days on retreat in a Benedictine monastery. Their founder, Benedict, had instructed his first monks at Monte Cassino in the sixth century to "Receive each guest as Christ himself." For over fifteen hundred years now, Benedictine monks have been doing this. Their reputation for hospitality grows by the century. My friend reported that on the first evening after supper the guest master gathered the guests together and said, "If you find that there is something that you need, come to one of the brothers and he will tell you how to get along without it."

There are no maps to the mature life, and certainly not to the mature life in Christ. Growing up involves an assimilation of nothing less than everything, the "all," to the "one." The "all" of parents, biology, schooling, neighborhood, worship, Scripture, friends, prayers, disappointments, accidents, injuries, songs, depression, politics, money, sin, forgiveness, occupations, play, novels, children, poems, marriage, suicides — and the "one" of God, also referred to four times in Ephesians as "the fullness" *(pleroma):*[8] Father, Son, and Holy Spirit.

*       *       *

8. Ephesians 1:10, 23; 3:19; 4:13.

So if there are no maps, what do we do? We forget about getting a map. We dismiss the expertise of "answers." We quit defining our lives by what we think we need. There are no shortcuts to the unity, to the one, to the center. When life is bewildering and we are faced with competing voices, simplistic, one-answer solutions are enormously attractive. But they are also routinely deceptive and will mire our lives in a cul-de-sac of continuing immaturity.

The gospel alternative to this cultural welter of one-answer advice and crafty deceit, seduction and empty promises to a better life, is church. Church just as it is, revealed to us in Paul's One and All: the One circulating all the particular blood cells through the body of Christ. We immerse ourselves in this community that provides conditions congenial to growing up to "the measure of the full stature of Christ." Informed by Paul's Ephesian orientation, we make ourselves at home in the verbs of God and his glory, in the company of Paul and all saints, in the world of grace and good works, in the work of Christ making peace and creating church, in God's manifold wisdom and prayer, playful as children in the diversity of the "all" and content to slowly mature in the "One."

*   *   *

But with this caveat: the church is not ideal. It is not, nor was it ever intended to be, a gathering of the nicer people in town. God is not fastidious in the company he keeps. There are sinners aplenty, hypocrites in droves, the ill-mannered and unwashed. We will be mightily disappointed if we look around expecting to meet men and women who measure up to "the full stature of Christ." These are men and women who are *on the way to growing up* to the stature of Christ. Not many of them are there yet. We find ourselves among Christians of all ages in all stages of growth: toddlers not yet out of diapers; children innocent and pure in the discovery of what it means to be a child of God; adolescents who are in turns contagiously enthusiastic and sullenly rebellious; young mothers and fathers who are struggling to come to terms with the demands and responsibilities of parenthood;

mid-lifers who got distracted years ago by job and family and are now looking again for what they feel they missed, hoping it's not too late; the elderly who are facing death in a culture that denies death and uses every ruse it can come up with to delay it medically and avoid it emotionally.

Occasionally — and it is not as rare as one might think — we come across a man or woman who seems to measure up to "the full stature of Christ." American church culture has been infiltrated to an alarming degree by the secular glorification of the infantile and the celebration of the adolescent, so if we don't know what we are looking for we will almost certainly miss noticing them. But the men and women of mature stature are there.

I grew up around people who identified the Christian life with inflated emotional states. Grandiosity was epidemic. The ordinary was for people "without Christ." We were in training for ecstasy. I soon tired of it. I began looking for men and women who had somehow managed to grow up. Locating them wasn't always easy or immediate. But patience paid off. I have never been in a congregation in which I have not found them. Some became friends and guides. For others it was enough to know and observe them from a distance.

I soon learned that the way to maturity is through the commonplace. I had to unlearn much — learn not to overreach, not to strain for high-flown epithets or resolutions, learn to stay as true as I could to the grain of life as I found it in the lives around me in the congregation and Scriptures that formed my identity.

*     *     *

The most formative of these guides for me, though, is a man I never met. Baron Friedrich von Hugel died seven years before I was born. As measured by an annual physical exam and my academic degrees I was certified as an adult, but as measured by Paul's standard of maturity I was still a child "tossed to and fro . . . by every wind of doctrine" (4:14) — far from being mature vocationally or spiritually. One of my guides, the Quaker philosopher Douglas Steere, recommended that I read von Hugel's books. I hadn't read many pages before realizing that I was in the presence of a mature man who knew what it meant to measure up to the "full stature of Christ." I've been reading him ever since.

Von Hugel supplied me with an image that came at just the right time for me. I was no stranger to the Christian faith. But church as an institution in time and place, theology as critical thinking about God, and prayer as the practice of resurrection were like separate planets in orbit around the wobbly center that was me. Von Hugel used the analogy of physical growth — infancy, adolescence, adulthood — to elaborate on the integration of the Christian life. Infancy corresponds to the institutional; adolescence corresponds to the intellectual; adulthood is analogous to prayer as everything we live through coheres in a resurrection life. The three stages are ages through which we develop into maturity. No stage can be omitted. And no stage can be left behind — maturity develops as each is assimilated into the next, resulting in a single coherent life.

This summary doesn't do justice to the richly textured treatment von Hugel provides. I only intend here to give witness to the shaping influence he has had on my life, second only in these matters of maturity to St. Paul in Ephesians. The Baron cannot be summarized any more than the Apostle can be summarized. The intricate complexities that result in his lucid clarities can only, I am convinced, be received firsthand from his own writing.[9]

\* \* \*

Much of von Hugel's deeply lived and extensively pondered experience as a Christian layperson, rooted and grounded in the life of Christ and at the same time in the earthly and domestic realities of a wife, three daughters, and dog Puck, comes to us via letters written in his own

9. See Baron Friedrich von Hugel, *The Mystical Element of Religion as Studied in Saint Catherine of Genoa and Her Friends* (London: J. M. Dent & Sons, 1961 [first edition, 1907]), vol. 1, pp. 3-82.

hand to an astonishing number of correspondents. A constant note in his counsel, insistently sounded, is that the road to a life of maturity is not a "yellow brick road," but involves considerable difficulties that cannot be bulldozed away. This portion of a letter written to his niece is thematic:

> When at eighteen, I made up my mind to go into moral and religious training, the great soul and mind who took me in hand — a noble Dominican — warned me — "You want to grow in virtue, to serve God, to love Christ? Well, you will grow in and attain these things if you will make them a slow and sure, an utterly real, mountain step-plod and ascent, willing to have to camp for weeks or months in spiritual desolation, darkness and emptiness at different stages in your march and growth. All demand for constant light ... all attempt at eliminating or minimizing the cross and trial, is so much soft folly and puerile trifling."[10]

Magnificent as the Christian life is, when it comes to growing up in Christ in the practice of resurrection, von Hugel will permit no shortcuts, no romanticizing that depreciates the ordinary, "no cutting of knots however difficult, no revolt against, no evasion of abuses however irritating or benumbing,"[11] but an insistence that the road to maturity necessarily follows a route that, in his words, often is "obtuse-seeming, costingly wise, not brilliantly clever, ruminant, slow, if you will, stupid, ignored, defeated, yet life-creating."[12]

It is a well-documented axiom in the practice of resurrection that we can know this life only by *becoming* it, growing in every way into a maturity that is sane, stable, and robust. The Apostle, with the Baron seconding the motion, would have us settle for nothing less than the "full stature of Christ."

10. Friedrich von Hugel, *Selected Letters 1896-1924*, ed. Bernard Holland (New York: E. P. Dutton & Co., 1933), p. 266.

11. Von Hugel, *Selected Letters*, p. 38.

12. Von Hugel, *Selected Letters*, p. 137.

# IV

# THE CONGREGATION AT WORK

*To be a witness does not consist in engaging in propaganda nor even in stirring people up, but in being a living mystery. It means to live in such a way that one's life would not make sense if God did not exist.*

CARDINAL SUHARD

## CHAPTER 10

# Holiness and the Holy Spirit: Ephesians 4:17-32

*You were taught to put away your former way of life . . . and to be renewed in the spirit of your minds, and to clothe yourselves with the new self, created according to the likeness of God in true righteousness and holiness. . . . And do not grieve the Holy Spirit of God, with which you were marked with a seal for the day of redemption.*

EPHESIANS 4:22-24, 30

*. . . a big piercing fact, that you have all the materials ready to your hand of downright holiness.*

FRIEDRICH VON HUGEL,
*Letters from Baron Friedrich
von Hugel to a Niece*

Sometimes a single word can mask itself in seeming insignificance, and yet that very word serves as the pivot point for the more "exciting" words all around it. Paul's "therefore" marked the beginning of the transition at Ephesians 4:1, the transition from the ways in which God creates and inhabits church to the ways in which we now live appropriately as the church that God creates and inhabits: "I *therefore*, the prisoner in the Lord, beg you to lead a life worthy of the calling. . . ." Paul's "therefore" connects everything that God is and does (the subject of the letter to this point) to everything that we are and do (the subject of the rest of the letter). The transitional passage, Ephesians 4:1-16, takes us from church as God creates and inhabits it, to the church as we inhabit and participate in it, the country in which we grow up to maturity, to "the measure of the full stature of Christ." The Christian life, a *church*-conditioned way of life, must be congruent with who God is and the way he works in church, in *us*. And not just in bits and pieces, but maturely.

Paul posts a second "therefore" (4:17) to mark the completion of the transition.[1] He now gives us his full attention. For the rest of the letter the spotlight is on us: what we do and the way we do it.

"Spotlight" might not be the best word, for we are never the center of what is going on in church. God is. Paul's "therefores" keep us mindful of our connection to everything that has gone before. We are not on our own. Church is not a job in which we are given the responsibility of managing and adapting to whatever we see that needs doing. Church is already complete, in the words of the Nicene Creed: "one, holy, catholic, and apostolic."

So to make sure we do not go off on our own in matters of church, Paul throughout these chapters 4–6 repeatedly uses the connecting conjunction "therefore" to keep our place and behavior in church, our calling, organically joined to the one who calls us. He uses the word nine times.[2] When the connection is maintained intact, the lives that we live are representative of righteousness and holiness, freshly created in us by the Holy Spirit.

The term "spirit" comes into its own at this point in the letter in a phrase in which Paul lays out his agenda for us, namely, that we are to be "renewed in the spirit of [our] minds . . . [a] new self, created accord-

---

1. It is the same word as in 4:1. But the NRSV translates it "Now this I affirm . . . ," an excellent translation except that it obscures the repetition of the first "therefore" in 4:1. The KJV translates it "therefore," preserving the repetition.

2. His usual term is *oun*: Eph. 4:1, 17; 5:1, 7, 15; 6:14 — six times. Its synonyms, *dio* (4:25; 5:14) and *dia touto* (6:13), account for the other three.

ing to the likeness of God in true righteousness and holiness" (Eph. 4:23-24). That is the usual translation, with "spirit" taken to be a straightforward reference to the human spirit, the inner person. But Gordon Fee, one of our finest exegetes of Pauline texts, translates quite differently, taking "spirit" to refer not to the human spirit but to the Holy Spirit: "be renewed in your minds by the Spirit." The overall emphasis of Ephesians on the work of the Holy Spirit to live the life of God in us is maintained. Fee's exegetical work on this text, backed up by the work of several other scholars, both ancient and modern, is (for me) compelling.[3] It means that it is the Spirit's renewal of our minds that results in the Spirit's creation of righteousness and holiness in us, a God-fashioned life as God re-creates his character in us. Paul will pick up this role of the Holy Spirit a few verses later in 4:30.

## Stalamus Chief

Sixty miles north of where I once lived in western Canada, there is a mountain popular among rock climbers named Stalamus Chief. It is a vertical slab of smooth granite, two thousand feet high. On summer days rock climbers are spread out in varying levels of ascent on its face. Occasionally climbers spend the night in hammocks (they call it bivouacking), hanging like cocoons attached to barn siding. It struck me as a mighty dangerous way to have fun.

I was always fascinated by the sight. Whenever I was in the vicinity I pulled off the road and watched for a while with my binoculars. It was not the action that held my attention, for there was not much in the way of action up there. The climbers move slowly, cautiously, every move tested, calculated. There is no daredevil spontaneity in this sport, no rash thrills. Except perhaps the ultimate thrill of not falling — not dying. Maybe what gripped my attention was death, the risk of death — life dangling by a thread.

3. Gordon D. Fee, *God's Empowering Presence* (Peabody, MA: Hendrickson, 1994), pp. 709-10.

Still, dangerous as it was, I knew that it was not as dangerous as it looked. When I watched from the valley floor with my naked eye, the climbers appeared to be improbably exempt from gravity, but with my binoculars I could see that each climber was equipped with ropes and carabiners and pitons (or chocks, wedges, and camming devices). The pitons, sturdy pegs constructed from a light metal, are basic. I have two sons who are rock climbers, and I have listened to them plan their ascents. They spend far more time planning their climbs than in the actual climbing. They meticulously plot their route and then, as they climb, put in what they call "protection" — pitons hammered into small crevices in the rock face, with attached ropes that will arrest a quick descent to death. Rock climbers who fail to put in protection have short climbing careers.

One day while I was watching the climbers on Stalamus Chief, it occurred to me (I was mentally preparing a lecture on this passage of Ephesians at the time) that Paul's "therefores" function very much as pitons, pegs driven into the vertical rock face of *church* (stretching between heaven and earth), on which the Christian calling is played out. A "therefore" is a peg, protection against moods and weather, miscalculation and fatigue. Vision ("you are the Christ!") and risk ("deny yourself and take up your cross") and inspiration ("the praise of his glory") are what we are most aware of when we set out to grow to the full stature of Christ. But if there is no "protection," survival is precarious.

Life in the church is dangerous. Much of the danger comes from becoming so cozily familiar with the way of faith that we feel set apart or above our early status of what we sometimes think of as a mere Christian. We become so diligent in learning about and working for Jesus that our relationship *with* Jesus erodes. The constant danger — and this has been going on a long time in church — is that we take on a role, a religious role, that gradually obliterates the life of the soul.[4]

But our participation in the life of church does not bring us into

---

4. Aldous Huxley's novel, *Grey Eminence*, is a sober warning of this descent from a devout and supple love of Jesus and church to a harsh and arthritic political role (New York: Harper & Brothers, 1941, first edition).

an advanced level of gospel living. Faith is life at risk. Love is life at risk. Worship is life at risk. Familiarity with God and church and congregation can dull awareness of the stakes involved so that we forget to put in protection. Each "therefore" is a piton hammered into the rock to keep us connected to the granite face. Paul is liberal in supplying us with pitons. We will need every one of them.

Karl Barth is eloquent in his insistence that we are always and ever beginners in this Christian life. No matter how much we know, no matter how diligent we are, we never graduate from being "Christian" and go on to advanced levels. Neither Christian living nor Christian service, whether as layperson or pastor, can ever "be anything but the work of beginners. . . . What Christians do becomes a self-contradiction when it takes the form of a trained and mastered routine, of a learned and practiced art. They may and can be masters and even virtuosos in many things, but never in what makes them Christians, God's children."[5]

There is a huge irony here. Christians who keep their distance from the church, who hang around the fringes, who dabble from time to time, are ordinarily exempt from these dangers. But those of us who make a strong identification with church and take up its responsibilities quite naturally get the attention of others. We are the rock climbers on Stalamus Chief. Some people criticize us, others admire us, but either way we are aware that we are being treated as a class apart. We are seasoned Christians. We have it made — we are mature. We gradually take on airs as insiders.

Jesus' words "Except ye . . . become as little children . . ." (Matt. 18:3 KJV) maintain their pertinence whatever our place or reputation in the Christian church. But when we have spent a number of years getting to know the ropes in the culture of church, with others looking up to us as mature or leaders or, God help us, even "saints," it is astonishingly difficult to think of ourselves as children. Humility recedes as competence increases.

---

5. Karl Barth, *Church Dogmatics*, IV/4: *The Christian Life* (Grand Rapids: Eerdmans, 1981), p. 79.

It is a subtle thing and usually takes years to accomplish, but without "protection," without the connective tissue of the "therefores" keeping us who are parts of the body organically related to the head, it not infrequently happens that instead of living as we started out — child followers of Jesus — we become bosses on behalf of Jesus. Sometimes we are very good bosses, looking out for the welfare of others; other times we are barely disguised pious bullies.

## Negative Space

The change of emphasis from church as the being and work of God to church as our participation in the being and work of God begins with a negative command: "you must no longer live as the Gentiles live" (Eph. 4:17). As familiar as I am with this letter, every time I come to this, it feels like a bump in the road. Up until now, virtually everything has been stated with glowing affirmation. Paul is extravagant in his enthusiasm, unstoppable in his praise. It is as if nothing were ever praised enough and he can't wait to make up the deficit — if necessary, single-handedly. The energy of his language overflows with metaphor and simile, stretching the sinews of syntax to the breaking point.

The colorless, austere, negative words, "you must no longer live as Gentiles," seem out of character. Why doesn't Paul just transfer his enthusiasm for what God does to an equivalent enthusiasm for what this congregation can now do with and for God? Why doesn't he challenge them to "do great things for God"? The momentum is up. Why doesn't he bring them into the action? Why this "no" just when they are ready to get involved in every "yes" God is doing in and for them?

I'm wondering if it's because he doesn't trust their maturity. These newly Christian men and women grew up in a non-Jewish culture. They came into the church without the rich centuries of stories and worship and moral practice that were deeply embedded in anyone growing up Jewish. These Ephesian Gentiles are newcomers to all this. As Gentiles they come from a world in which Greek and Roman gods and goddesses provide the stories that are background to everyday life. These stories, while they are certainly religious, have no moral content to them. Sexual immorality and violence permeated the supernatural in that culture.

In the Gentile imagination of that age, religion and morality didn't mix. Not that morals were absent from their culture. They had philosophers who had many wise things to say about the moral life that continue to stand the test of centuries. Their literate intelligentsia took second place to no one in providing moral guidance. But the men and women in the street, mostly unschooled, along with a considerable slave population, wouldn't have been much affected by the philosophers. In the imagination of the common people, Zeus and Hera presided over a pantheon of sexually profligate and murderously rapacious deities. The stories the Gentiles told about their gods and goddesses sometimes showed remarkable psychological insights and were endlessly entertaining, but they were also devoid of righteous moral content. Artemis, the reigning goddess of the city of Ephesus, was a fertility figure on public pornographic display, an idol carved with a thousand breasts.

So that is the world that seems most likely to be behind the term "Gentile" here — not so much an ethnic designation in contrast to Jew but a reference to this culture that was rich in religious imagination and so impoverished morally.

So as Paul moves his attention into the daily world of the work and behavior of these Gentile Christians as they live out this resurrection life to "the praise of his glory," he is pastorally alert to how easy it would be for them to unconsciously take on this wonderful new gospel but unthinkingly fail to remove the trappings of the old culture. Out of long Gentile habit they well might continue to assume that religion has nothing to do with morals. When Paul characterizes this old Gentile way of life, he describes it as "darkened" understanding, "alienated from the life of God . . . , abandoned . . . to licentiousness, greedy to practice every kind of impurity" (4:18-19).

If Paul were writing to a mostly Jewish congregation, I doubt very much if he would be going over the moral basics in so much detail. Jews were raised from the cradle on the Ten Commandments. They prayed Psalm 15: "O LORD, who may abide in your tent? Who may dwell on your holy hill?" (v. 1). They answered the questions with a list of ten simple actions about which there is no ambiguity — straightforward moral acts. They also prayed Psalm 24, which asks a similar double question: "Who shall ascend the hill of the LORD? And who shall stand in his holy place?" (v. 3), answered this time with three obvious straightforward moral acts. Jews had centuries of thorough schooling in moral behavior that tilled the soil of the heart for receiving the gifts of God and growing in righteousness and holiness, the two summarizing words that Paul uses to designate life lived appropriately in church in response to God.

But Gentiles didn't grow up under the tutelage of Moses or the prayers of David. They grew up on the stories of Artemis and Helen, Odysseus and Achilles, Orpheus and Euridice, Oedipus and Jocasta. And so Paul, as he leads them into the world of faithful living, cultivating a life that is responsive to the gifts of grace, a life that can flourish as it grows in righteousness and holiness, sets some negations in place. Nothing complex or difficult, just a few simple guidelines, giving the Gentiles a helping hand on their way to developing a moral life that provides good soil for growing up in Christ.

The Christian life does not start with moral behavior. We don't become good in order to get God. But having been brought into the operations of God, moral behavior provides forms for maturing in a resurrection life. Moral acts are forms in the sense that a pottery vase gives form to a bouquet of flowers, in the sense that a bucket provides a container for getting water from the well to the kitchen, in the sense that a bugle gives form to a compressed column of air so that taps can be played. Moral acts are art forms for arranging and giving expression to resurrection.

*　　*　　*

A woman in her late twenties began attending my congregation at the invitation of some friends. After a few weeks she asked if she could have a conversation with me. She wanted to become a Christian. She knew virtually nothing about the Christian faith, had no idea of what "becoming a Christian" involved. We talked and prayed. She was ready. She made the commitment to follow Jesus. She presented herself for baptism.

But she didn't know much about the faith. She had never gone to church, never read the Bible, had just more or less gone along with the culture she had grown up in and did what her friends did. She asked for more conversations. So we met every two or three weeks in my study, talked and prayed together, explored the meaning and implications of this new life on which she had embarked. It was all so fresh and new, an interior life that she had never even known she had, a community that she never knew existed. She was a "Gentile," American style, and knew nothing of church.

Conversations like this are always interesting, listening and observing as the Christian faith, this practice of resurrection, comes alive in a person for the first time. She took everything in, embraced everything readily and gladly. But one thing puzzled me. She lived with her boyfriend. Eventually I learned that she had always lived with her boyfriends, beginning when she was twenty. The living together rarely lasted more than six months or so. She wasn't interested in marriage. She told me all this without apology and not as a confession but quite casually, as we were getting acquainted with one another. I wondered if I should say anything. Surely she knew that the Christian way had some sexual implications for the way you lived. She was in church each Sunday. She was becoming acclimated to church, this Christian community. I assumed that she would eventually notice. I waited for her to bring up the subject.

One day on impulse I said, "We have been having these conversations for seven months. Astrid, would you do something for me?"

"Sure. What is it?"

"Live celibate for the next six months."

Surprised, she said, "Why would I do that?"

"Just because I asked you. Trust me. I think it's important."

I learned later that her boyfriend moved out before the week was over. A month later when she came to see me, she didn't mention it. But the following month she brought it up: "When you asked me to live celibate for six months, I had no idea what you were up to. You asked me to trust you, and so I did. It's been two months now and I think I understand what you were doing. I feel so free. I've never felt so 'myself' before, never felt so at home with myself. I thought everybody did what I was doing — all my friends did. I just thought this was the American way. And now I am noticing so many other things about my relations with others — they seem so much more clean and whole. So uncluttered. And do you know what? I have been thinking that I might want to get married someday. Thank you."

The celibacy decision survived the six-month mark and continued for two more years, at which time she and her fiancé exchanged vows and I blessed their Christian marriage.

*     *     *

Artists use the term "negative space" to name the importance of what is not there in a sculpture or painting. An artist has to know what to leave out as well as what to put in. Openness, emptiness, breathing space — what you don't see provides adequate room to see the created work. Negative space is as much a part of a work of art as what you do see.

The negatives are important as we find our way into the practice of resurrection. They keep the clutter down. As Paul brings us into the church picture, he is cautious. He doesn't pepper us with imperatives of what needs to be done, what opportunities are out there just waiting for us to accomplish. He is careful not to give us any encouragement to take charge of this kingdom business. He lays a groundwork consisting of what we don't do. None of Paul's negatives require anything heroic. Modest self-restraint, minimum effort: put away falsehood, don't let the sun go down on your anger, no stealing, no evil talk, don't grieve the Holy Spirit, no wrangling, no slander, no malice, no fornication. These negatives name actions or attitudes that were accepted as commonplace, some even sanctioned, in the Gentile culture of the Ephesians. Also in the Gentile culture of Americans. Things haven't changed all that much.

Most of the Christian life is a response to what God says and does. The negatives don't define our lives. God's positives define us. What the negatives do is leave room for the main action, God's action.

When we talk too much or do too much, we get in the way of what God is doing. We become a distraction. As we immerse ourselves in church, we realize that there are culturally accepted practices, Gentile ways of life, that we must set aside. We realize that there are things in this Gentile culture that we grew up in that are extravagantly admired and rewarded by our secularized society but that we must not do. A good thing, said or done in the wrong place or at the wrong time, is a bad thing. Becoming mature "to the measure of the full stature of Christ," the practice of resurrection, requires a lot of negative space — a lot of not saying, a lot of not doing.

## Shy Member of the Trinity

The premise behind all these negatives — "you must no longer live as the Gentiles live" — is a huge positive: God is active, incredibly active, active beyond our imagining. By this time it will not have escaped notice in our reading of Ephesians that God is referred to sometimes as Father, sometimes as Son (or Jesus or Christ) and sometimes as Holy Spirit. All three Persons have a way of being over us, creating and providing; a way of being with us, revealing and saving; a way of being present in us, blessing and sanctifying.

In the three Persons, there is a versatile and dynamic oneness, yet there are also roles and primary actions that proceed uniquely from Father, Son, and Spirit. God the Father: God bringing everything into being and holding everything together by his word. God the Son: God entering our history, showing us God in action in human terms that we can recognize, accomplishing salvation for all. God the Spirit: God present with and in us, inviting us, guiding and counseling us, wooing us into participation in all of God's ways of being God. All these operations of God are in evidence as Paul directs and accompanies us in the process of growing up in Christ. The doctrine of Trinity is the church's way of thinking about God that keeps all of these operations of God together and in relation to one another.

As we assimilate and participate in all the ways that God is God, it is essential that we acquire a Trinitarian way of looking at God — understanding that whenever one of the Persons of God is in the forefront the other two Persons are at the same time implicitly involved. Father is never isolated from Son and Spirit; Son is never present apart from Father and Spirit; Spirit is never experienced apart from Father and Son. There is one God, but this God can never be understood as an abstraction, as an idea, as a principle, as a truth, as a force. All God's ways of being God are thoroughly personal, not impersonal; relational, not disparate; particular, not general — and *only* personal, relational, and particular.

A Trinitarian vision prevents the "one" God from being defined mathematically, the living God from being reduced to a lifeless number. Numbers are language at its most abstract and impersonal. Numbers are unsurpassed in dealing with anything impersonal — machines and planets and money markets — but virtually useless in dealing with persons, and less than useless as a language with and about God. So we don't understand Trinity by working with numbers, puzzling over how one equals three or three equals one. Trinity has nothing to do with arithmetic. Trinity is the church's way of learning to think and respond relationally to God as he reveals himself to us as Father, Son, and Holy Spirit. God is triply personal, emphatically personal, unrelentingly personal. Growing up in the practice of resurrection must also be unrelentingly and emphatically personal.

Up until now Paul has referred to God mostly as Father and Son, which is to be expected since what Paul is doing is expanding our understanding of everything that God is doing on two fronts: making us who we are (children of God, redeemed, chosen to live to the praise of his glory), and making the church what it is (the body of Christ, a resurrection community, a congregation of Christians growing up to maturity in Christ).

Paul's citations of God's presence with us as Holy Spirit are not nearly as frequent as those of Father and Son,[6] but the first occurrence

---

6. In this Ephesian letter, Father (or God and Father, or God), 33 times; Jesus (or Jesus Christ, or Christ Jesus, or Son), 21 times; Holy Spirit (or Spirit), 14 times.

is strategically prominent in that it provides the conclusion to that long opening sentence that brings all "the spiritual blessings in heavenly places" home to us "on earth as it is in heaven." We are in on all of it. We are not spectators to all that God is doing but insiders, "marked with the seal of the promised Holy Spirit; this is the pledge of our inheritance toward redemption as God's own people, to the praise of his glory" (Eph. 1:13-14). Paul is about to repeat this text as he orients us in behavior appropriate to a resurrection life.

Holy Spirit is God present with us, making us personal participants in all his work, empowering us to be present in all his work. Nothing in creation, nothing in reconciliation, is "out there" to be admired or "on hold" for special occasions, or reserved for God's favorites. Everything in Scripture is livable. But not in the sense of a commodity that we can get and then use as we like, and not in the sense of a skill that we can acquire and then do with as we please. Holy Spirit is God's active presence, making us full-blooded participants, Spirit-breathing (God's breath — "spirit") God's creation and salvation in our resurrection lives.

This livability, living this resurrection life in our bodies, in our homes, in our neighborhoods, in our workplaces, is the work of God localized and personalized in church and in us. But it also has a certain quality of divine anonymity to it. It is important to notice this quiet anonymity. When God brings us into this Holy Spirit life of participation, he doesn't make a show out of it. Righteousness and holiness do not consist in walking on our hands or executing a somersault dive off the high board. God uses us just as we are to give witness to him: to serve, to praise, to help, to heal, to care, to love. He doesn't put a halo on us so that everyone will notice that God is present and alive to make sure God will get proper credit. And God doesn't seem to be embarrassed to be mixed up with lives such as ours, sometimes indolent, not infrequently faithless. He doesn't keep his distance from us to protect his reputation.

*       *       *

Yesterday my wife and I were walking in the woods and were startled as a bald eagle only twenty feet away exploded into flight. The eagle had been feeding on the carcass of a deer and was forced to retreat at our approach. We rarely get this close to a bald eagle. We stood there in awe — its huge seven-foot wingspread took our breath away. It flew up to a tree branch at what it must have considered a safe distance and watched us suspiciously as it kept a protective watch over its supper. We felt honored to be included as insiders to this fierce beauty of creation in action.

This morning I spent an hour or so reading and pondering St. John's account of the crucifixion and resurrection of Jesus, the story of my salvation. I was in a nostalgic mood and reminisced on a few of the many people that I have known, some dead, some alive, who are in this same story. Not for the first time I was overwhelmed in realizing that I am an insider to this radically hopeful way of understanding the salvation action that is at the heart of history.

After lunch I drove three miles to our village. I picked up the mail at the post office, stopped by Blacktail Grocery and bought a red onion and some yogurt, makings for a salad for this evening's supper, and filled up the car with gas at the Exxon station. I saw and spoke to maybe fifteen people. I knew about half of them by name and something of their stories. Three or four of them I worship with each Sunday. Nothing "happened." I heard nothing memorable spoken. But I know differently. I know that holiness and righteousness are being worked out in some of those lives, maybe all of them for all I know. I know the details in a few of them: lived creation, lived salvation.

This is the context in which God the Holy Spirit lives the creation, living salvation in us, body and soul, as we go to work, run errands, greet friends and strangers. This Holy Spirit work often goes unnoticed and unremarked. Other times it is very much noticed and enthusiastically remarked. But not for the most part.

A friend, New Testament scholar F. Dale Bruner, calls the Holy Spirit "the shy member of the Trinity." That seems right to me. The Spirit is a quiet but powerful nurturing presence. There is a kerygmatic, attention-getting, dramatic quality to the Father's work in creation and the Son's work in salvation that makes the public square an appropriate venue for consideration. When creation and salvation are embodied by the Holy Spirit in ordinary men and women and in ordinary circumstances, these ordinary men and women and circumstances don't ordinarily make headlines, but they are no less powerfully and effectively the work of God. The adjective "shy" in this Trinitarian context has nothing to do with timidity or hesitancy, but is a well-placed caution against expecting flamboyance as evidence of the Spirit.

*   *   *

The first mention of God the Holy Spirit in Ephesians 1:13-14 is now picked up and repeated by Paul in 4:30. But here the setting is different. In chapter one the Holy Spirit is the promise that all this work of God will be worked out in our lives, the Holy Spirit a guarantee that this great work of redemption will take place in "God's own people" — *us*.

This second mention in chapter four repeats from chapter one the nature of the Spirit's work, that the Holy Spirit is the guarantee that we will receive this redemption inheritance, but it is prefaced this time by a negative: "Do not grieve the Holy Spirit of God." That catches our attention.

So far all the moral and ethical imperatives Paul has set down have to do with the way we conduct our lives with one another. And all of them come in the form, Don't do this, *but* do this. First a negative, then a positive. But this imperative stands alone. All the other imperatives are directed to how we behave with others; this one is directed to our behavior toward God. And it is the only one that is not complemented by a positive.

This is worth pondering: "Do not grieve the Holy Spirit of God." "Grieve" is a personal, relational verb. We are being oriented in behaviors that provide appropriate conditions for growing up in Christ, for developing a mature life. These behaviors are forms that the Holy Spirit uses to give witness to the ways that God is God in Father and Son, through church, to the world. The forms in themselves are just forms, empty forms. It is the Holy Spirit that provides the content and energy that fills the forms so that they become vessels of righteousness and holiness.

201

If we understand the forms as impersonal rules that we can keep or break with no consequences other than what happens to us, then we show ourselves to be oblivious to the reality that there are deeply personal consequences in the Godhead: the Spirit of God suffers — *grieves*. If we take the forms and use them on our own terms (truth-telling, working honestly, sharing with the needy, being kind, loving, etc.), take them over and use them as scripts for a personal performance, we, in effect, reject or ignore or dismiss the Spirit. We "grieve" the Spirit. At the very least we are rude. At worst we are blasphemous, turning our back on the Spirit, taking charge of our own lives and concocting our own version of righteousness and holiness.

What we must realize in all of this is that the Holy Spirit is above all courteous. There is no coercion, no manipulation, no forcing. The Holy Spirit treats us with dignity, respects our freedom. The Holy Spirit is God's empowering presence, and what he empowers in us is a life of blessing and salvation, a life of resurrection. It is most definitely not a life of self-will, a life of self-righteousness, a life of using God to get what we want. If we live on those terms and with that mind-set we will certainly be grieving the Spirit.

One more thing. In some places in the church there is considerable complaint about the absence of the Spirit. These critics are confident that they know what the presence of the Spirit should look like and are loud in protesting his alleged absence. They are also ready with strategies to recruit the Spirit. But given what we know from Scripture and church about the Spirit's well-known penchant for anonymity, and Paul's guarantees that we are already "marked with the seal of the promised Holy Spirit" (1:13 and 4:30), wouldn't it be wiser to look around for what is being given right now and enter into it with praise? Some have suggested that this habit of protesting the absence of the Spirit and working up a revival sweat may very well be one more form of "grieving the Holy Spirit of God."[7] God's Spirit is the essential Guide to our spirit.

---

7. See Markus Barth, *The Broken Wall* (Chicago: Judson Press, 1959), p. 70.

## CHAPTER 11

# Love and Worship: Ephesians 5:1-20

*Therefore be imitators of God, as beloved children, and live in love, as Christ loved us and gave himself up for us, a fragrant offering and sacrifice to God.*

EPHESIANS 5:1-2

*The resurrection sets me in a world that is not self-contained, but open, and draughty, with the winds of eternity blowing through it.* . . .

PAUL SCHERER, *The Word God Sent*

We are by now well on our way to entering into a deep Trinitarian rhythm in our lives, a lived awareness of all the ways of God being God and then *participating* in these ways, which is practicing resurrection. Paul started us off by bringing us into a participating understanding of righteousness and holiness (Eph. 4:17-32). Now in chapter five it is love and worship.

˙ We are well launched, launched into a life of participation in the being and work of God the Father and God the Son. Not application, mind you, the common American word for getting in on what God is doing. "Application" seems to suggest that once we know who God is and what he does, it is up to us to take charge and get it put into action. Nothing could be more misleading. God is as thoroughly involved in our participation as in his Revelation and Incarnation. And his way of doing this is the way of the Holy Spirit.

Paul has built a strong foundation for understanding and entering into the comprehensive ways in which God is God: the ways in which God reveals himself as Father (the glories of creation and covenant); the ways in which God makes himself known as Son (the salvation accomplished in Jesus and the salvation community that is the church); the ways in which God is present with us as Spirit (the very life of God given to us in a profusion of gifts empowering us to live the life of God). God's ways of being God as Father and Son filled the horizon in Ephesians chapters 1–3. The Spirit was not absent — how could he be? All the ways that God is God are implicit in all that God is and speaks and does.

But in 4:1-16, Paul makes a very artful transition from dealing with God as he is and does to our participation in who he is and what he does. It is not a black-and-white transition — the first part all about God, the second part all about us. No, we have been in on this with God from the beginning, and God will be in on this with us to the very end. The life of God and human life are not separate subjects. The primary way in which we participate in who God is in all the particularities of our actual living, deeply, personally, and inextricably in relationship, is the way of the Holy Spirit.

It is because of God's way with us as Spirit that we know that everything in and about God is *livable* — God bringing us into participation with God. Father, Son, and Holy Spirit are not merely truths to be learned and believed. They are to be lived. The church is not primarily a place for education. It is a place, a playing field if you will, to practice God, practice resurrection.

*       *       *

But first another "therefore," putting in protection (Eph. 5:1). As familiar as we are with what is involved in living out God's calling, as often as we have engaged in these actions, we must maintain an alert watchfulness, continuously nurturing a live, organic connection between the being and work of *God* in church and world and the being and work of *us* in church and world. Nothing can be taken for granted. Everything involved in the practice of resurrection requires vigilance lest we wander off on our own. Not a worried, anxious, paranoid vigilance, to be sure, but vigilance nevertheless. There will be yet another "therefore" in this section (5:7) before we are finished dealing with this pair of resurrection practices, love and worship.

Protection here consists in deliberately and unhurriedly immersing ourselves in God's ways before we go off on our own: "Therefore be imitators of God. . . ." We are not cramming for an exam that will provide us a certificate for good resurrection behavior or admission to heaven; we are absorbing into our praying imaginations a way of being. Watch what God does, and then do it his way. Like children who learn proper behavior from hanging around their parents, be imitators of God, keep company with God. Read the stories of Abraham and Moses, Joshua and Caleb, Deborah and Ruth, David and Jonathan, Elijah and the widow of Zarephath, Jeremiah and Pashur, Isaiah and Ahaz, Amos and Amaziah, Hosea and Gomer. And Jesus. Most of all Jesus: Jesus and his mother, Jesus and Herod, Jesus and Zacchaeus, Jesus and Peter, Jesus and Judas, Jesus and Mary Magdalene, Jesus and Cleopas. We marinate our prayers and our behavior in these stories that reveal God and his ways to us.

Left to ourselves, most of what we imagine God to be and do is wrong. Nearly all of what our culture tells us that God is and does is wrong. Not dead wrong, mind you — there is an astonishing amount of truth and goodness and beauty mixed into it — but enough wrong that if we swallow it whole we risk a "sickness unto death" (Kierkegaard's diagnosis). Revelation is a radical reorientation of reality — God reality, church reality, soul reality, *resurrection* reality. We require a continuously repeated immersion in the revelation of God in the Scriptures and Jesus as protection against the lies of the devil. They are such affable lies: lies that smilingly seduce and distract us from the cross of Christ, lies that genially offer to show us how to depersonalize the living God into an idol customized to our use and control.

Therefore, *therefore*, "be imitators of God." Observe carefully the ways of God in love, "as Christ loved us," and the ways of God in worship, as Christ "gave himself up for us, a fragrant offering and sacrifice to God" (5:1-2).

## "Things fall apart; the centre cannot hold . . ."

A formidable difficulty in practicing love and worship is placed in our way by the ways of this world. It is a world in which neither love nor worship has a high profile of credibility. To love and worship in contemporary America — and it was no different in ancient Ephesus and Rome and Athens — is to be dismissed by the culture to a dustbin of irrelevance. Love and worship are well and good if all you want to do is take care of your soul. But if you want to make a difference in the world, bring prosperity to the poor, bring peace to nations, bring food to the hungry, bring healing to the sick, bring health to the environment, forget about love and worship as ways to get anything done. If you are serious about doing something about what's wrong with the world, you must adopt ways that have a proven track record, do something that *works*, something that is effective.

The approved means of doing good in the world, accredited by the "powers that be" and sanctioned by popular practice, are education, technology, propaganda and advertising, legislation, and money. And, as a last resort, war. If problems can't be solved any other way, we go to war. It is alarming the way war language infiltrates our vocabulary and imagination. We fight cancer and fight for freedom; we launch wars on drugs, wars on poverty, wars for peace. This last is the greatest of ironies, a policy of killing people who are against peace.

The Irish poet William Butler Yeats wrote his much-quoted poem "The Second Coming" in 1919 in prophetic response to a world raging with hate and bloody with war. It was a world impressively educated, highly technologized, relatively prosperous. He watched as it sank into a sump of lies and violence:

Things fall apart; the centre cannot hold;
Mere anarchy is loosed upon the world,
The blood-dimmed tide is loosed, and everywhere
The ceremony of innocence is drowned.[1]

His poem prophesies the destruction of the two-thousand-year Christian cycle and the birth of a new, violent, bestial anti-civilization, a birth in total contrast to the birth of Jesus. This is Yeats's "Second Coming." Instead of "'the Son of Man coming on the clouds of heaven' with power and great glory" (Matt. 24:30) that Jesus promised, Yeats's revelation of the second coming is of the beast of the Apocalypse, a "rough beast, its hour come round at last,/[that] Slouches towards Bethlehem to be born."

"The Second Coming" has for many become *the* prophetic text for a society that like the judge in Jesus' parable has "no fear of God and no respect for anyone" (Luke 18:4). In the years since Yeats wrote those words, the "blood-dimmed tide" has swelled to a tsunami of social, political, and sexual violence. This is the world in which the church practices love and worship? The sheer enormity of the corruption in morals and the degradation of language leads many to put love and worship at the periphery of their lives and try to make the best of things by taking on the world's agenda.

But this is what I find interesting. A month after Yeats had written "The Second Coming," his daughter Anne was born into this very uncentered world of "mere anarchy" that he had painted ominous with doom. Three years later he wrote another poem, "A Prayer for My Daughter," which, despite all the evidence to the contrary that he set down in "The Second Coming," is full of poignant hope. In his prayer he acknowledges that his daughter will grow up in desperate times. But if "the centre cannot hold," how can this birth, his daughter in her cradle, escape the nightmare imaged in the rough beast rocking where Christ had once been cradled? He now prays with a most tender love and sense of reverence and ceremony that is worship. When he later

---

1. W. B. Yeats, *The Collected Poems* (New York: Macmillan, 1959), p. 184.

arranged the poems for publication, he placed the prayer for his daughter directly following the prophecy of the rough beast slouching toward Bethlehem to be born.[2] His prayer of love trumps his prophecy of doom. The seemingly frail ways of love and worship that Yeats articulated in "A Prayer for My Daughter" provided hope that the "arrogance and hatred" of his contemporaries who were making all the noise — "an old bellows full of angry wind" — would not prevail over the "radical innocence" he was praying for on behalf of his infant daughter.

I am not calling Yeats in as an expert witness in a courtroom defending love and worship against its detractors. He didn't identify himself as a Christian. His spirituality was in large part a self-creation that he composed out of a storehouse of occult ideas and myths. But I find him useful as a voice in the public square, one who testifies to the indestructibility of love and worship, outlasting and outperforming the worst that a world opting for hate and war throws in our way as we practice love and worship. Men and women who practice resurrection are not naïve. The practice came to its fullest expression, after all, in the "blood-dimmed tide" loosed by the crucifixion. Conditions, at least the conditions reported in the media, are never propitious for the practice of resurrection.

Three thousand years before Yeats, a Hebrew poet, after detailing the unpromising conditions that left him reeling, records how he recovered his balance. He concludes his prayer with a couplet of reconnection:

> With God we shall do valiantly;
>    it is he who will tread down our foes.
>
> (Ps. 108:13)

So. Love and worship in the practice of resurrection. No one I know questions the desirability of love and worship. Very few, at least in the

---

2. John Unterecker, *A Reader's Guide to William Butler Yeats* (New York: Noonday Press, 1959), pp. 166-68.

Christian way, deny their place somewhere or other in our lives. But *practice?* Here the consensus begins to fray at the edges. We need to get this right.

## The Language of Love

The imperative to imitate God, to love after the manner in which God loves, is filled out with three grammatical forms of the word "love" — as an adjective, as a noun, and as a verb. We are defined as loved, *beloved children*. We are commanded to live *in love*. Paul's action word is "walk" *(peripateo)*, a feet-on-the-ground kind of love. And this love is the kind we see acted out on actual streets and sidewalks, in real history, and told in the story (the revelation) of Jesus, the kind of love that we experience firsthand in Jesus, who *loved us*. These grammatical forms cover all the bases: our baptismal identity as beloved, the country of love that we live in, our experience of being loved by Jesus.

These are not the ways in which we have grown up using the word "love." If we are fortunate (and not all of us are), we hear the word first from our parents. Later we use it ourselves with childhood friends, still later as adolescents in fumbling attempts at intimacy. A few of us — by no means the majority — bring more serious considerations into the word when we use it in marriage vows. But it isn't long before we are using the word at random, cheapening it to the flatness of a synonym for "like": "I love the outdoors . . . that dress . . . this movie . . . those Yankees. . . ." "Love" is probably the most frequently used word in our vocabulary for saying what we like, what attracts us, what we hunger for. In common use it is stripped of theological connotations and personal reciprocities.

If we are going to recover the word for use in the practice of resurrection, we have a lot of work to do.

The love that we practice in this resurrection life originates in God and only in God. All love originates in God's love. God's love permeates all expressions of grace from Father, Son, and Holy Spirit. It is always personal, never impersonal; it is always "on earth as it is in heaven," never an abstraction or idea; it is always particular in person and place, never a misty generality.

\* \* \*

This has to be repeatedly insisted upon, for there is probably no word in the language that has been more eviscerated of its Father origins, Jesus content, and Spirit dynamic than this one. More lies are told using the name "love" to give the lies credibility than perhaps any other. And without question more silliness is perpetrated under the banner of love than any other.

"I love you" is a life-transforming, life-deepening, life-saving sentence. Spoken by God it is. And spoken in God's name it is. But with its God-origins and God-content removed, it is a hollow word, hopelessly trivialized, endlessly banalized. Every year Valentine's Day makes a parade of the banality, puts it on public display. Men and women by the millions buy Valentine cards clotted with insipid clichés, tons of boxes of chocolates, and vast fields of roses in vain and futile cover-up attempts to say "I love you" without actually having to take the trouble to do it.

But things are worse than that. The word has been so relentlessly eroticized that even when it *is* used with the best of intentions and a pure heart, it says the exact opposite of what it means. Here is one of our very best words, redolent with all the operations of the Trinity, comprehensive in its implications for every man and woman on earth, fundamental in the practice of resurrection — trashed. The eroticization of love empties it of everything except genitals and lust, reduces the person who loves and the person loved to consumers of ecstasy. And as with any life dominated by getting some *thing*, it finally incapacitates him or her from being some *one*. The more a person *gets* the less he or she *is*. "Love," the best and most complex relational word we have, is abused in such a way that it turns people into objects to be used. The word itself is ruined, and the more we use it the more it ruins us and others. Words matter: words kill and words give life. Which will it be for "love"?

It is significant that immediately after introducing the practice of love Paul warns against the corruption of love by fornication (Eph. 5:3-5). Fornication is love reduced to sex, love without relationship, "love" without love. The corruption of the best is the worst. "Lilies that fester smell far worse than weeds" is Shakespeare's acerbic comment. Not that there is anything wrong with sex. The prominence of the Song of Songs in our Scriptures, a most exuberant celebration of love that embraces the sexual in a mature, holy intimacy of dignity and goodness, is adequate refutation of any attempts, however "spiritual," at de-sexed love. But love *reduced* to sex, depersonalized for mere consumption, whatever the initial pleasures experienced, soon turns ugly, degrades and eventually destroys intimacies. When loveless "love" becomes epidemic, we find ourselves, even as Jesus did, living in an "adulterous generation" (Matt. 12:39), and we know that we need to prepare ourselves for a strenuous reorientation in the ways that God is love, the ways that God loves, and the ways that we practice love in company with God.[3]

\* \* \*

Bernard of Clairvaux, a twelfth-century Christian, wrote a treatise called "On Loving God" in which he provided sane and holy counsel in the understanding and practice of love in his own culture, which was also mightily confused on the subject. This was the century in which the eroticization of love became epidemic in the western world. The epidemic continues unchecked into our own times. Any love worth the name came to be identified as passion-love and developed into a cult of courtly love. It was pursued by knights and sung by troubadours who succeeded in redefining all "real" love as adulterous love,

---

3. Paul precedes his love imperative in Ephesians 5:2 — gives us a running start in this reorientation — by using the word eight times in its God-originating context: "holy and blameless before him in love" (1:4), "Beloved" (1:6), "love toward all the saints" (1:15), "the great love with which he loved us" (2:4), "rooted and grounded in love" (3:17), "know the love" (3:19), "speaking the truth in love" (4:15), "building itself up in love" (4:16).

that is, love conceived as idealized conquest, not mutually relational and personal, and, of course, quite outside anything that included God, Jesus, the Spirit. It also found a religious expression in the love heresy of the Cathars that poisoned the understanding and practice of love in the Christian church.[4]

Bernard of Clairvaux knew this culture well. He recognized the deadly threat it posed to the Christian revelation of love in Jesus and the Scriptures. He made it a major theme in his writing, preaching, and pastoral work to counter the seepage of this toxic expression of love into both society and church. His most extensive work was a magnificent sustained commentary on the Song of Songs. Given the adulterous, romantic love culture of the times, this is significant, for the Song is the most sexually explicit scriptural witness to the beauty, dignity, and thoroughly relational mutuality involved in God-created, God-blessed love.

In his more succinct treatise Bernard described the four degrees of love. In the first degree, "loving one's self for one's own sake," we try to handle things on our own. We develop competence in living, what we moderns call "self-esteem." It sounds like a good thing to do and gets a good deal of affirmation from others. But life is too complex and throws too much at us that we don't know what to do with. Limited to the inadequate competence acquired in self-love, we sooner or later find ourselves out of our depth. We turn to God for help.

This brings us to a transition to the second degree: "loving God for one's own sake." We turn to God for what God can do for us. We pray. We search the Scriptures. Even though our prayers are seldom answered on the terms we expected, and even though the Scriptures don't turn out to be the manual for problem-solving that we had hoped for, good things do happen. This stage can last a long time. But gradually as we get acquainted with the ways of God, our immature,

---

4. A thorough treatment of this century of "romantic love" and the detailed ways in which it continues as a major rival to Christian love is given by the French theologian Denis de Rougement in his magisterial study, *Love in the Western World* (Garden City, NY: Doubleday, 1957).

self-centered preoccupations recede and we begin to recognize and understand God as he is, not as we imagined him to be, and we are attracted to what we are finding: God's essential goodness. The margins of the daily lists of what we want God to do for us begin to accumulate scrawls and notations in the margins of who God is for us. The God agenda is still there, but it is not the only thing there.

We are now well on our way into the third stage, "the love of God for God's sake." Love develops into the intimacies of adoration. We love not for what we can get out of God but for who God is in himself. It is a self-forgetful love. It is the Virgin saying to God, "Let it be with me according to your word" (Luke 1:38). It is Simeon praying, "Lord, now lettest thou thy servant depart in peace" (2:29 RSV). It is Mary sitting at Jesus' feet giving herself to the "one thing needful" (10:42 RSV). It is Isaiah in the temple saying, "Here am I; send me" (Isa. 6:8).

The fourth stage is now only a few steps away: "loving one's self for God's sake." We do not become less human as we love God more. God's love makes more of us. God's love does not condescend to us. God's love does not patronize us. God's love for us permeates our love for God. There is a mutuality in mature love. Not that we are ever equal or on a par with God, but we find our own human wholeness affirmed in the love of God. The three early stages of love are not replaced. They are completed.

\*     \*     \*

God is love. Love is the core of God's being. Man and woman, made in the image of God, are also, at that core, love. This is who we were created to be, persons who love, persons who receive love. When we love we are most ourselves, living at our very best, mature. Everyone, I venture to say, feels at some deep level this primary core identity.

But here is the supreme irony: love is who we are, love is what we want, love is what we want to practice, but it is in loving and being loved that we accumulate the most failures. We are repeatedly disappointed in love. We realize that we are hopelessly inadequate in love.

We can become competent in school, get excellent grades, and put our diplomas on display to certify our intellectual achievements. We can become competent at our work, get promotions, receive raises in salary, and acquire a reputation as an excellent physician, a trustworthy mechanic, a skilled attorney, a wise and diligent farmer. We can become a competent politician, win elections, work for the public good, enact legislation, inspire good citizenship.

But competence in love eludes us. There are no awards given in the practice of love. There are no levels of achievement. There are no graduate degrees to affirm our accomplishments. What so often happens then is that we give up. "Yes, I would love to love, love well, love faithfully, love steadfastly, love with my whole heart and mind and strength, but face it, I am not much good at it. So why not leave it to the natural lovers and the saints? I'll do what I am good at: work or hospitality or gardening or writing or teaching. I will certainly try to do whatever I can to love, but it's not my gift. I'll just cultivate this plot of ground that I have been given."

This is certainly understandable. But it doesn't feel right. What doesn't feel right about it is that love is understood and interpreted as something that I do, and the more I give myself to doing it, the better I will get at it. And when I don't get better at it, I go back to doing the things that I *am* good at and get some affirmation for being good at. In other words, I understand love on a continuum with everything else that I am given to do to keep my job, support my family, stay out of jail, and enjoy myself as I have opportunity on weekends and vacations.

There are two obvious things wrong with that. One, love is understood as a skill that I can improve or even perfect, like a golf game. Two, love is understood without any context in the operations of God.

We misunderstand love when we suppose that it has to do with saying the right things at the right times. No. It has to do with being in relation with God and our neighbors, regardless of what we are saying and doing and wherever we are. Love is the relational language *par excellence*. We also misunderstand love if we are ignorant of its origin in God. It begins as theological language. It is a language used in a listening, attentive relationship with God in all the revealed operations of the Trinity *and* a way of being in a listening, attentive, affectionate relationship with another person just as she or he is before us.

\*      \*      \*

Years ago in graduate school I had to pass an examination in German but didn't have time to take a course and get proper instruction. So I got some grammars and reading books and tried to learn the language on my own. When I thought I was prepared for the examination I went to my professor and told him that I was ready to be examined. Language examinations were conducted informally in that university department. My professor took me to his study, took a book off the shelf, and said, "Read it in German." I read. Then, "Translate." I translated. It was a Syriac grammar. Grammars have a limited vocabulary, so the translation was easy. He took another book, handed it to me, and we went through the same process. I thought I was doing all right. I was understanding what I was reading and seemed to be translating satisfactorily. But a frown was developing on his face that made me apprehensive. Then a third book, this one an Egyptian history. I opened it at random and started to read from the top of the page. And read and read and read. It was one of those interminable German sentences. Halfway down the page I hadn't yet come to a period, had lost all connection between the subject and the verb, and finally stuttered to a stop. He interrupted, "Mr. Peterson, where did you learn your German?" I was reluctant to tell him that I had done it privately, fearing he would probe for areas of ignorance. I hesitated. He continued, "What language did they speak in your home?" I told him, "A little Norwegian." ("Little" is an exaggeration — it was spoken once a year at Christmas dinner by my uncles and aunts and mother.) He went on, "You have a most unusual accent. I can't place it. I am intrigued by it." He then went on to talk at some length about accents — and forgot to ask me to translate. I passed. I later learned that he took great pride in being able to identify accents, a pride that saved me from a fall.

This kind of thing happens all the time. We hear the command, "Live in love." In a hurry to get on with it, we read some books and ask a few questions. When we think we have the hang of it, we start putting our knowledge into action. We are feeling pretty good. We think we are doing all right. God listens in. Then there is some slight sense of things not going so well: "Where did you learn your love language?" It turns out that we did it privately, alone — not so we could be in living relation with other people or with God but just to pass an examination. But God picks up on what we are doing. We are using the right words in the right order, but something is wrong with the inflections, the accent, the rhythms. It is not authentic. It is not personal. It is not a living language, but "book" language.

Church is the primary place we have for learning this language of love. The conditions here in church, unlike the conditions in the world, *are* propitious — not the endless variations on eroticized fornication and adultery posing as love in the world, nor, to take a de-eroticized alternative, a classroom with a distinguished professor giving lectures on love, assigning papers, our desks strewn with grammars and concordances and dictionaries. Rather, in church we find a gathering of people who are committed to learning the language in the company of the Trinity and in company with one another. We don't learn it out of a book.

## "Sleeper, awake!"

Love. And worship. The imperative "live in love" is backed up by the way Christ loved us *and* by the way he "gave himself up for us" (Eph. 5:2). We mature in love by entering a protected time and place where we can be told again the "old, old story of Jesus and his love," rub shoulders with men and women who are serious about the practice of love the way Christ loves. The church at worship is that time and place. The church at worship immerses itself in Jesus' "fragrant offering and sacrifice to God" (5:2). When we worship we become participants in that offering and sacrifice, and over time that participation permeates our lives with the same love in which Christ loves. In the act of worship we cultivate a life of love in company with the Trinity of love, and in company with men and women and children who are there with us, all of us practicing resurrection.

I want to use the term "worship" here in this Ephesian context for the worship that Christians engage in together when we assemble in a place of worship in response to the invitation, "Let us worship God." Worship is also used to name an interior attitude or response of adoration before God. As such it can take place under any circumstances, in any place, in solitude or surrounded by others, while listening to a string quartet, standing on a crowded beach watching a sunset, being present with a few others in a birthing room in sacred awe as an infant miraculously enters the world. But in the present Ephesian context, as we nurture the practice of resurrection in which we grow to maturity in Christ, I want to insist on *common* worship, worship in common with others — taking our place sitting or standing with others in a congregation under conditions that do not cater to our personal needs or preferences but honor the priority of God: God speaking to us, Christ giving himself for us, the Spirit empowering us in our lives. Every man, woman, and child in that congregation is being treated with the dignity that comes with being a son and daughter of God, who first loved us.

\*     \*     \*

The call to worship to the church in Ephesus is succinct and commanding:

> "Sleeper, awake!
>    Rise from the dead,
> and Christ will shine on you."
>
> (Eph. 5:14)

Worship requires our full attention. Growing up in Christ involves everything that is in us and in all our relationships. In the practice of resurrection we become awake to all that Christ is and does. As we stay with it, we become mature. We need all the help we can get. Congregational worship is the appointed place to get the help. It is not the only place, but it is the place where most Christians, in most centuries, in most countries, have received the most help.

Jesus' "fragrant offering and sacrifice to God" anchors worship in the ocean depths of God's love. For centuries Hebrew men and women had been bringing fragrant offerings of meal and lambs, incense and bulls, and sacrificing them on altars at Shechem and Hebron, Bethel and Beersheba, altars in the wilderness tabernacle and the Jerusalem temple, offerings freely given to God in thanksgiving and atonement, in expiation and reparation, for sin and forgiveness. Worship was an act of a people, a congregation, gathering before God offering sacrifices, various sacrifices providing a kind of sign language for all the ways in which they brought their failed or needy or grateful lives to God.

The centerpiece of all those centuries of worship, the act of worship that held all of those altars and sacrifices and prayers together, was Passover Week with its climax in the Passover Supper. That annual Passover meal was the act of worship that kept alive and intact the Hebrew memory of God's deliverance from Egyptian tyranny and his salvation gift of new life. For well over a thousand years that worship had been formative in maintaining the Hebrew people's identity as a people-of-God. Passover worship was their salvation story, but not just a story told; it was a story re-lived as they participated in a dramatic re-enactment of their salvation, eating and drinking death and resurrection.

Jesus gathered those centuries of worship — "a fragrant offering and sacrifice" — to completion when he called his twelve disciples together to eat the annual Passover feast in Jerusalem. Jesus was the host. What he did and said at the table — "this is my body broken for you . . . this is my blood poured out for you" — transformed the Passover Supper into the Lord's Supper. The next day he himself became the sacrificial Passover lamb as he was crucified on the Golgotha cross.

It wasn't long before that Lord's Supper had become the defining act of worship in the Christian church.

\*     \*     \*

The church does other things besides eat and drink the Lord's Supper when we come together and worship. We sing "psalms and hymns and spiritual songs . . . making melody to the Lord" (Eph. 5:19); we give "thanks to God the Father at all times and for everything" (5:20); we baptize; we read and preach and teach God's Word from the Scriptures; we bring offerings; we bless our dead in services of witness to the resurrection; we bless men and women as they exchange vows of fidelity in ceremonies of marriage. But the Supper is the center that holds everything in worship together. If there is no center, "things fall apart." Worship deteriorates into "mere anarchy."

In the practice of resurrection, worship is fundamental to the practice of love. Love is not a solitary act; it is relational. Love is not a general act; it is always local. Love is not self-starting or self-defined; it is always "as Christ loved us." So how do we acquire maturity in the practice of love that respects the relational, the local, and the way of Christ? We go to church and worship God who "first loved us."

Christians have always done this. Forms and orders of worship have proliferated throughout the church on every continent over our twenty centuries of worshiping God. No single form or order is mandated in our Scriptures. Still, it is not as if it is "anything goes," with every congregation for itself — "and the devil take the hindmost."

We know that love is continuously at risk of being pulled up by its roots from its grounding in Christ (Eph. 3:17) and then eroticized past recognition for anything that might develop into a mature human life. Romantic illusions depersonalize. Worship is also continuously at risk, but with worship the danger is commodification, being debased into a commodity for consumers who are shopping for the best buy in God or the latest in spiritual fashions. But the moment that God or the things of God are packaged and then advertised as programs or principles or satisfaction, we are depersonalized, diminishing our capacity to love. There is not much chance of growing to the measure of the stature of Christ in a place of worship that markets goods and services stamped with a God logo. The very place and time given us to cultivate conditions congenial for acquiring an understanding of and companionship in the practice of love is no longer available.

The extensive commodification of worship in America has marginalized far too many churches as orienting centers for how to live a more effective life for God. What the secular culture has done to love by romanticizing it into fornication and the practice of adultery, the ecclesial culture has done by promoting ways of worship calculated to appeal to consumer tastes in which love is redefined as "Oh, I like that," or "I have to have that," or negatively as "I don't get anything out of that."

*   *   *

Some think that it is a scandal that love and worship, the two most important things that Christians do, are done so badly by so many of us. No wonder the church has such a murky reputation among its cultured despisers. If banks were as inept at handling money as the church is in handling love and worship, they would be out of business within a week. If hospitals were as amateurish in caring for the sick, treating emergencies, administering anesthesia, and overseeing childbirth as the church is in love and worship, they would be bankrupt in short order. If professional baseball teams made as many errors in fielding, batting, and pitching as the church does in love and worship, they would be playing to empty stadiums.

But there is another way to look at this. It is true that love and worship demand our very best, our created and redeemed best. But this created and redeemed best cannot be achieved by determined individual effort. There is God in all the operations of the Trinity; accordingly there is church in all the particularities of its members. Every detail involved in love and worship requires personal relationship with others, with family and friends and neighbors — responding, receiving, giving — and with Father, Son, and Holy Spirit — also responding, receiving, giving. No part of love and worship can be isolated, removed from the complexities of relationships to a laboratory, studied, mastered, and then, having been clarified with all the contaminants and ambiguities removed, returned to daily life and put to use. I am never in charge of love and worship, but always participating in many-dimensioned relationships.

It takes a lot of growing up to become even moderately at home in these practices. To achieve anything like competence is out of the question. They are not practices in which we can specialize and by training and discipline become experts, some of us maybe even achieving world-class status. There are no Olympic events in love and worship.

There is also this. The church has men, women, and children in its community at all levels of immaturity and maturity. It is as if a symphony orchestra had beginners and masters playing alongside one another, the first violinist seated next to a ten-year-old who hasn't yet learned how to tune her strings. Church is not a performing arts center for love and worship.

And then there is this. Every detail in the practice of love and worship is susceptible to perversion and sacrilege. There are no flu shots against sin. There are many more ways to sin against love than by going to bed with Bathsheba. There are many more ways to sin against worship than by dancing around a golden calf.

In writing all this I have no intention of putting an imprimatur on mediocrity or shrugging my shoulders at sloppiness. All I am insisting on is that if we want to embrace a truly Spirit-formed church, we must embrace the messy conditions — the complexity of relationships both interpersonal and Trinitarian, the many levels of maturity and immaturity, the ever-present vulnerability of everyone to sin — out of which it is being formed. These are the conditions in which the Holy Spirit is working. If we are serious about church and want to participate in what the Holy Spirit is doing, these are the conditions. Get used to it.

*       *       *

The usual place where we are called to worship is in a church sanctuary — a place consecrated for the worship of God and designed to immerse us in the world of God's revelation by what we hear and what we see in word and sacrament. The usual time set aside is Sunday, the day that fuses the Hebrew seventh creation day of Sabbath rest with the Christian first day of Jesus' resurrection. The usual frequency is week by week.

Christian worship orients us in a comprehensive reality given form by God the Father, God the Son, and God the Holy Spirit. It is an all-inclusive reality comprising all that has taken place in the previous six days and all that will take place in the next six days. All that we see and all that we don't see. All the operations of God that make us who we are, that day by day form an eternal salvation life in us, that place our workweek in the larger context of God's workweek, that make it possible for us to participate in a life of holiness and love at the same time that we are doing the laundry, repairing machines, selling groceries, teaching quantum physics, and planting wheat. It is a big order. No congregation does it perfectly. Some don't even try. But for all the failures and semi-failures, I am convinced that anyone who pays attention and discerns the work of the Spirit in the congregation — dare I say *any* congregation? — will get at least a glimpse of worship that gives witness to "the praise of his glory."

The call to worship wakes us up to what is going on in and all around us: "Sleeper, awake! Rise from the dead, and Christ will shine on you!" The world is alive with God: Look! Listen! Lift up your hearts! Come and eat!

In acts of worship, the Holy Spirit internalizes himself in us and makes us "insider" participants in the Father's work of creation and the Son's work of salvation. In the act of worship, we deliberately remove ourselves from our workaday world of assignments and responsibilities and relationships, we assume a posture of not-doing — sitting, kneeling, folding our hands in prayer, lifting our arms in praise — and we invite the Holy Spirit to form in us the life of love and holiness that makes us one with the Father and the Son, which, we are assured, the Spirit is more than ready to do. We don't have to do anything, at least not in the way we are accustomed to doing things. But we do need to be present, attentive, receptive. We want to be in on what God is doing. We want God to be in on what we are doing: "Come, Holy Spirit." We want to walk out of the place of worship with a lighter step — still present, attentive, receptive — with a blessing on our heads and obedience in our steps.

Christian maturity is not a matter of doing more for God; it is

God doing more in and through us. Immaturity is noisy with anxiety-fueled self-importance. Maturity is quietly content to pursue a life of obedient humility. Christian worship is an intentional act of redressing the proportions, the priorities — from me working for God to God working in me, which is the Holy Spirit.

Evelyn Underhill was a deeply learned and deeply devout English layperson who, as so many of us do, had difficulty with church. But after long pondering and reflection she wrote this: "The Church is 'essential service' like the Post Office but there will always be some narrow, irritating and inadequate officials behind the counter and you will always be tempted to exasperation by them." But she eventually got over the "irritating" officials and arrived at this: "I feel the regular, steady, docile practice of corporate worship is of the utmost importance for building-up of your spiritual life. . . . no amount of solitary reading or prayer makes up for humble immersion in the life and worship of the church."[5]

\*     \*     \*

Paul uses a pair of strikingly contrasting imperatives to focus our attention on just what is and what is not involved in worship: "Do not get drunk with wine . . . but be filled with the Spirit" (Eph. 5:18). Wine and Spirit are set in contrast as ways of worship. In the Asiatic world of Ephesus one of the most prevalent forms of worship centered around the god Dionysius. Dionysiac worship employed dances and exciting music to produce ecstatic rapture. Dionysius was the god of wine. Intoxication with wine combined with dancing and music was the method of choice for getting to the desired state of enthusiasm (literally, "the god within"). Paul points to these riotous, drunken orgies on display all around the people of Ephesus and contrasts them with what takes place in worship as Christians come to be "filled with the Spirit." Not the "mere anarchy" of drunken dances, but rather the sweet harmony of "singing and making melody to the Lord in your hearts" (5:19).

5. Quoted in Douglas V. Steere, *Dimensions of Prayer* (New York: Harper and Row, 1962), p. 115.

The manic debauchery associated with Dionysiac worship sets a sharp and unforgettable contrast to the beauty of the singing, the melodic harmonies, that it is the work of the Spirit to bring to expression in each worshiping congregation. This is the church at worship as we drink our fill of God's Spirit. We listen to God's Word read and preached, and once again get our story straight; we receive the life of salvation eating and drinking the Lord's Supper, his "fragrant offering and sacrifice to God," and recover our Jesus focus; we find ourselves in the singing and giving thanks, in the greetings and the prayers, freshly renewed by the Spirit to practice resurrection in the company of the Trinity.

We are not adequate to live a life of love out of our own will or resources. Trying harder doesn't do it. Enter the Spirit. God provides his Spirit to live the life of God in us, and we are reoriented around the center that holds. When we leave church, dismissed by the benediction, we are far less likely to be intimidated by the "rough beast slouching towards Bethlehem to be born."

## CHAPTER 12

# Household and Workplace: Ephesians 5:21–6:9

*Be subject to one another out of reverence for Christ.*

EPHESIANS 5:21

*Heaven in ordinary. . . .*

GEORGE HERBERT, "PRAYER," IN The Temple

Now Paul moves us onto home ground, the most immediate places where we practice resurrection. First, the place where we live together intimately in our homes as husbands and wives, as parents and children — our kitchens where we cook food and eat our meals, our bedrooms where we sleep and make love, our living quarters where we receive guests and enjoy one another's company (Eph. 5:21–6:4). He then moves on to the places where we rub shoulders day after day working together as masters and servants, employers and employed, owners and workers — our farms and markets, schools and quarries, building roads and laying bricks (6:5-9).

He has already laid an extensive groundwork for understanding the thoroughness with which the Holy Spirit penetrates our being with the very life and presence of God, into every detail of our lives. There is nothing of God that is not livable by us. Nothing in creation, nothing in salvation is remote from or irrelevant to who we are, the people we live with, and the people we work with. Every jot and tittle in the gospel of Jesus Christ is here for *living*, for embodiment in each and every one of *our* bodies, for working into the muscle and bone of our ordinary lives.

If we once thought that the world around us was divided into secular and sacred and that it is the Christian's assignment to specialize in the sacred but just put up with the secular, we can think that no longer: "God so loved the *world* . . ." (John 3:16). And if we once thought that the ideas and actions available to us each day are arranged in a hierarchy upwards from incidental housework and working for a paycheck to an apex of strategically important kingdom work where "real" Christians prioritize the strategic, we can think that no longer. Jesus turned that concept on its head when he said, "Whoever becomes humble like this child is the greatest in the kingdom of heaven. . . . If any of you put a stumbling block before one of these little ones who believe in me, it would be better for you if a great millstone were fastened around your neck and you were drowned in the depth of the sea" (Matt. 18:4, 6).

*       *       *

Still, despite the unambiguous clarity of our Scriptures and Jesus in these matters, we often let the big ideas, the majestic vistas of salvation, the grand visions of God's work in the world, and the great opportunities for making an impact in the name of Jesus distract us from taking with gospel seriousness the unglamorous ordinary. A person who is endowed with charisma, extraordinary motivational gifts, and organizational energy may tend to pull away from the tedium of dailiness to the large, the visionary, the influential — the eternal verities — in a way that is magnetic and virtually irresistible.

But when that pull is indulged, the consequences are disastrous and virtually guarantee perpetual adolescence. And the people we spend most of our time with, our family members and fellow workers, bear the brunt of suffering our immaturity. Men and women who achieve public acclaim are especially vulnerable. Too many prominent leaders in church and government, in business and university, writers and entertainers, are infamously infantile and disappointing in intimate relationships. They never seem to notice "a bruised reed . . . and a dimly burning wick" (Isa. 42:3).

So it is understandable that Paul, as he leads us into the home stretch in this comprehensive Ephesian presentation of what is involved in the mature life in Christ, takes up the less glamorous aspects of practicing resurrection in our homes and workplaces. Great things for God are quite wonderful. Little things for God are in one sense even more wonderful. Kathleen Norris in her poems and memoirs insistently keeps our attention on the local: "it is the daily tasks, daily acts of love and worship that serve to remind us that religion is not strictly an intellectual pursuit. . . . Christian faith is a way of life, not an impregnable fortress made up of ideas; not a philosophy; not a grocery list of beliefs."[1]

## Borrioboola-Gha

Charles Dickens in his novel *Bleak House* wrote a long, detailed, devastating exposure of a cast of people who spent their lives engrossed in great ideas and causes, primarily in the pursuit of justice and attendant legal affairs, all the time living in pig-headed ignorance or indifference to the actual people involved. Early in the novel he presents us with Mrs. Jellyby, an unforgettable reincarnation of the men and women through the centuries who, so to speak, made a good start in reading Ephesians but never completed the letter, never got to chapter five.

Mrs. Jellyby is a tragicomic representative of the not inconsiderable number of Christians who open their Bibles and start reading Paul's Ephesians. By the time they pause to catch their breath at the end of that first long sentence (Eph. 1:3-14) — that 201-word, in Greek, nonstop sentence of stunning theological poetry! — they are hooked.

1. Kathleen Norris, *The Quotidian Mysteries* (New York: Paulist Press, 1998), p. 77.

Paul's eloquence, the kaleidoscopic dazzle of the Trinitarian permutations of creation and Christ and church, has them energized. But by the end of chapter four, they begin to get restless. They notice that the marvelous metaphors are being replaced by plain Jane imperatives. They sense that the poetry is tailing off into pedestrian prose. They know that by now they have the meat of Paul's message and are impatient to get started in the glorious practice of resurrection. Compelling. They had never heard it put quite like this — living "to the praise of his glory!"

They shut the book. They never read chapters five and six. But they have quit too soon.

*    *    *

We learn about Mrs. Jellyby through the eyes and ears of a young girl, Esther Summerson. She is a companion to two cousins, Richard and Ada. They have been delivered to the care of Mrs. Jellyby in London for the hospitality of a night's bed and board. The next day the cousins are to meet with the law firm of Jarndyce and Jarndyce, which is handling their complex legal affairs.

Mrs. Jellyby is not there to meet the young people, so they let themselves in. They make their way as best they can through a household teeming with Jellyby children, unwashed and scantily clothed, in a chaos of dirt and disorder, accidents and neglect. When they finally come upon Mrs. Jellyby, they find her a diminutive, plump, amiable woman with handsome eyes, that "had a curious habit of seeming to look a long way off . . . as if they could see nothing nearer than Africa." She had "very good hair but was too much occupied with her African duties to brush it." We learn that Mrs. Jellyby is a woman devoted to Christian philanthropic projects. Her current passion is Africa, cultivating coffee and Christianizing the natives of Borrioboola-Gha on the left bank of the Niger and establishing there a settlement of two hundred families. Every room in her house is covered with litter — "not only untidy but very dirty." But Mrs. Jellyby comports herself through it all with "a sweet smile."

She introduces herself to the three young people who are to be her guests for supper and the night, saying, "You find me, my dears, as usual very busy; but that you will excuse. The African project at present employs my whole time. It involves me in correspondence with public bodies and with private individuals anxious for the welfare of their species all over the country.... It involves the devotion of all my energies, such as they are; but that is nothing, so that it succeeds; and I am more confident of success every day."

Dinner is served. Esther reports, "We had a fine cod-fish, a piece of roast beef, a dish of cutlets, and a pudding; an excellent dinner, if it had had any cooking to speak of, but it was almost raw. All through dinner — which was long, in consequence of such accidents as the dishes of potatoes being mislaid in the coal scuttle, Mrs. Jellyby preserved the evenness of her disposition. She told us a great deal that was interesting about Borrioboola-Gha and the natives, and received so many letters that we saw four envelopes in the gravy at once.... She was full of business and undoubtedly was, as she had told us, devoted to the cause."[2]

Dickens titled his comedic chapter on Mrs. Jellyby and the African mission in Borrioboola-Gha "Telescopic Philanthropy." It would be a lot funnier if the conditions were not so often repeated in the Christian community. But unhappily it happens frequently: the practice of resurrection, the very heart of the church's life, is squandered into disembodied causes and projects in far-off Borrioboola-Gha by men and women who give neither time nor attention nor touch to what is going on in their home and workplace. These men and women, the considerable progeny of Mrs. Jellyby, are totally absorbed in making plans, gathering support, and whipping up enthusiasm for what is dramatic, romantic, challenging gospel work — and far away. Too far away for personal, hands-on involvement. Meanwhile they are far too busy to engage in the glorious practice of resurrection in caring for their own children and keeping the household clean in the tedium of the ordinary.

2. Charles Dickens, *Bleak House* (New York: New American Library, 1964), pp. 49-61.

\*     \*     \*

Household and workplace immerse us in specific details in which we have specific relationships and duties, whether it is picking up a screwdriver to tighten a door hinge or answering a question of child or spouse or fellow worker regarding the time of day. What takes place in home and workplace cannot be generalized. There is nothing abstract about any of it. Everything has a name. Everyone has a name. Everything is within touching distance. And everything and everyone is always in a working context in relation to virtually everything and everyone else. No one thing or person in either home or workplace is a piece of art in a museum to be contemplated apart from everything else.

Ernest Hemingway has a character in a novel speak for him when he writes, "I was always embarrassed by the words sacred, glorious, and sacrifice, and the expression in vain. Abstract words such as glory, honor, courage, or hallow were obscene beside the concrete names of villages, the numbers of roads, the names of rivers, the numbers of regiments and dates."[3] Hemingway taught a generation of Americans to be suspicious of "big" words, sticks-and-stones nouns that have no texture, no embodiment in the neighborhood.

And that is what Paul is doing here. As he rounds out the ways that the Holy Spirit is at work making personally present the "boundless riches" of Christ (Eph. 3:8) to us for our participation, it is significant that he ends up insisting that we pay careful attention to what is going on in family and workplace. The *practice* of resurrection begins in household and workplace. And we never graduate to higher ground. The big words are there still, keeping us in prayerful and believing relation with the glories that are extravagantly spread out before us, but *practice* immerses us in named people, specific tasks, the stuff of everyday.

\*     \*     \*

3. Ernest Hemingway, *A Farewell to Arms* (New York: Scribner's, 1957), p. 191.

Paul leads us step by step into a life of participation in the resurrection of Jesus, leads us into maturity, makes us familiar with the details involved in living to the "praise of his glory." He cautions us not to slip back into old assumptions or practices (to "no longer live as the Gentiles live") but to cultivate ready, courteous responsiveness ("do not grieve the Holy Spirit of God") as the Spirit introduces righteousness and holiness into our lives (5:17-32). He goes over the basics of love and worship that provide focal practices for personal relationships and congregational adoration as we make ourselves at home at the church's center, working up an appetite ("be filled with the Spirit!") for receiving all the gifts of God for living to "the praise of his glory" (5:1-20).

We sense a movement upward, inward, Godward. Our anticipation quickens. We find ourselves "singing and making melody to the Lord . . . giving thanks to God the Father at all times and for everything in the name of our Lord Jesus Christ" (5:20). This is getting better and better. We can't wait. What great things there must be just around the corner. We are ready for the next level of glory in the heavenlies. What's next in this Holy Spirit formed life?

Well, get this — *this* is next: "Be subject to one another . . ." (5:21), followed by an immersion in the details of family life and work relationships. If we were expecting something cosmic, this is like a door slammed in our faces.

*       *       *

Does Paul sense that there are seeds of Borrioboola-Gha fantasies lying dormant in all of us, just waiting for favorable conditions to sprout? Has he known people who daydream that it is the work of the Spirit to rescue us from the boredom of domesticities and to relieve us from having to live by the sweat of our brow by giving us a vision of the "work" to be done in Borrioboola-Gha? Is that why before he is done with introducing us to the way the Spirit makes God present and active among us, livable right where we are, he makes sure that our feet are firmly planted on the ground that is most immediate to us, household and workplace? I think so.

## "Wing to wing and oar to oar"

"Be subject to one another out of reverence for Christ" (Eph. 5:21) is the lead sentence on the practice of resurrection in household and workplace. It is followed by naming eight representative "one anothers" that all of us deal with in the course of any ordinary day, six of them in the home, two of them in the workplace.

We do not become mature on our own. Maturity, especially if it is to be to the "measure of the full stature of Christ," can be accomplished only in relationship with others, *named* others, not any of those two hundred families in Borrioboola-Gha whose names we have never heard and wouldn't recognize if we had. Neither can these others be handpicked, people we quite naturally like or admire. We start with those who are there by no choice of our own — parents for a start, then children — and persons to whom we are committed regardless of changing circumstances, "in plenty and in want, in joy and in sorrow, in sickness and in health, as long we both shall live." And again, at this starting place, "all the saints." Church refuses to individualize our identity, refuses to put us in charge of our own growing up, but insists that we are "members of one another" and "subject to one another." Family language (brother and sister, father and mother) is consistently used in the church to give us both responsibility for and intimacy with those who are not blood relations. Jesus gave us our text when he extended his and our family relations exponentially, pointing to his followers and saying, "Here are my mother and my brothers" (Matt. 12:49).

Each of Paul's eight household and workplace designations refers to a role that is more or less culturally defined. A woman who grows up in a Korean Buddhist home has a different experience of how children, husbands and wives, and fathers and mothers live their roles than a woman who grows up in an Italian Catholic home. A young man in inner-city Detroit who has never known a father has a very different experience of family life than someone on a family farm in Kansas with both parents and seven siblings, along with grandparents on a neighboring farm. Workplace roles are experienced in radically different ways on an Israeli kibbutz and in a Chicago meatpacking plant.

The cultural details involved in household and workplace are enormously complex, as most of us already know from experience, some of them excruciatingly painful. There is no lack of experts offering counsel and instruction in marriage relations and child rearing. There is extensive economic analysis and programmatic initiative in matters of leadership management and job satisfaction. There is obviously no lack of concern in either world or church regarding how we fare in our homes and workplaces.

Most people have a home. Most people go to work. But given the wide range of cultures in which home life and work life are formed, how can Paul possibly tell us how to go about the practice of resurrection in our various cultures and settings?

We see right off that beyond a few general considerations, he doesn't. He doesn't give detailed advice or counsel. He doesn't hand out official "Christian" counsel on how to raise our children or get along with our spouses. What he does is replace our understanding of our already culturally defined roles with a Christ-defined role. Every aspect of our family and work life is redefined in relation to Christ rather than to what we have grown up with as wives to husbands, husbands to wives, children to parents, parents to children, slaves to masters, masters to slaves.

The repeated phrase that redefines who we are in all the complexities of household and workplace is "as to the Lord" (nine times), and "in the Lord" (two times) — eleven phrases that link the way we understand our role, not in terms of the culture, but in terms of Christ. A final identification places both slaves and masters as peers under "the same Master," regardless of how they are viewed by the culture. The "same Master" — that is, Christ — rounds out our now reassigned roles from culture to Christ to an even dozen.

Across the board, the way Paul trains us to re-understand ourselves in relation to those we live with and work with is *as* to Christ or *in* the Lord or *under* a common Master. In the practice of resurrection we no longer understand our role by comparing it to some model taken from the culture, but always, without exception, to Christ. The measuring stick for maturity for the Christian is the "measure of the full stature of Christ."

If we are serious about the practice of resurrection, we have to do it in company with the risen Christ. We pay attention to the *ways* that Jesus forgave, loved, touched lepers, received outsiders, prayed for his friends. We know a lot about Jesus' *ways*. Resurrection is not a dogmatic truth that we spend the rest of our lives trying to understand. Resurrection is not a behavior that we can perfect through carefully managed ascetic techniques. Resurrection is a *practice* in which we engage as we "trust and obey, there is no other way," as the Spirit, "God's Empowering Presence," brings the life of the Trinity alive in us, in Jesus' name.

*    *    *

The litany of links (*as . . . just as . . . the same*) to the place of Christ in forming our roles in family and at work anchors us to Paul's exhortation: "Be subject to one another out of reverence for Christ" (Eph. 5:21). Both parts of the sentence, "be subject to one another" and "out of reverence for Christ," are radically countercultural, but only when they are combined. Separated, they lose potency.

"Be subject to one another." Maturity is not analogous to a bodybuilding regimen in which we lift weights to build our muscles to the max, and then periodically stand before a mirror to examine our progress. Maturity is not a solitary state; it is relational. Maturity does not come about by making the most of ourselves by ourselves; it is making the most of personal relationships. We don't do that by becoming stronger than the other, overpowering him or her, dominating either emotionally or physically. We don't impose ourselves. We enter into another person's life sharing both weakness and strength. We *enter* the life of another, but we don't force the entrance. Mutuality is always involved in "be subject."

Americans are not used to this. We are raised in an aggressively competitive culture. We measure ourselves over against one another, be it in educational learning, athletic competition, salary, popularity, fashion, appearance, or performance. Competition is bred into us from the cradle. When we evaluate the people around us as winners and losers, we reflect this.

There are many settings in which this competitive spirit brings out the best in us. But there are just as many, maybe more, when it brings out the worst. And the one setting in which it often brings out the very worst in us is the family. If family members are in competition with one another — husbands and wives, parents and children, brothers and sisters — intimacy is insidiously undermined. We can achieve maturity in families only by being "subject to one another." But it doesn't come easy. Competitive skills are far easier to come by than submission skills. Maturity is an art form. The household is the primary setting in which we acquire it.

The workplace comes in a close second as a setting in which a competitive spirit prolongs immaturity. But the dynamics of competition are more subtle in the workplace, where personal relationships are not as intimate as in the family. Elements of competition in matters of productivity and performance are obviously useful. Still, discernment is required lest competition depersonalize the worker into a function. Almost all work is done with others, and, if it is to be done well, requires courtesies and relational give-and-take. If the worker is identified solely with the work, if the employer functions exclusively in an impersonal role, the workplace becomes an emotional and spiritual wasteland.

And when the competitive spirit enters the church, we end up with a *real* mess.

"Out of reverence for Christ" is the companion phrase to "be subject to one another," and provides the working conditions apart from which "be subject" cannot flourish. Without reverence for Christ, it is highly unlikely that "be subject to one another" will happen in either household or workplace. Without "reverence for Christ," the counsel "be subject" reduces us to doormats.

Reverence: Paul's word is "fear" (*phobos*) — "out of fear of Christ." "Fear of the Lord" is the most common phrase from the Hebrew Scriptures for an appropriate life attitude, our learned response for responding adequately to God's word and God's ways. The stock phrase "fear of the Lord" that he learned from Deuteronomy and Isaiah, Proverbs and the Psalms, he here amends to "fear of Christ."[4]

Most translators dull the sharp edge of Paul's "fear" by paraphrasing it as "reverence," "respect," or "awe." This is understandable as a way to avoid connotations of terror or horror or panic, but they probably sacrifice too much.[5] What is lost is the "fear and trembling" (Kierkegaard) that comes from an encounter with The Holy. God cannot be domesticated; God cannot be reduced to whatever we are cozily comfortable with. A God without holy mystery is not a God to worship on our knees but a cheap idol to be used on demand.

Just as "be subject to one another" is hard to come by in the American world of competitiveness, the "out of reverence [*fear*] of Christ" that supplies the umbilical cord for living submissively is hard to come by in the American culture of irreverence. We may be the proud owners of the most thoroughly irreverent mind-set in human history. Americans as a whole have a minimal sense of The Holy.

Reverential fear, or fearsome reverence, is an attitude or disposition that acknowledges the presence of the Sacred. I stand or kneel or bow before someone or something that is more and better than I am. It begins at the burning bush, as we remove our sandals. It continues and permeates our relations as we recognize and reverence Christ in every man and woman we meet.

Reverence is in some unaccountable way a response to holy mystery. It follows that we will never adequately understand or be able to define what exactly holy is. Holy fear has energy in it. It attracts us to something that is beyond us. We don't "work up" reverence. We cannot "will" reverence. We cannot create reverence. The distinguishing element that brings us to our knees in reverence or silences our chatter is not us or in us.

Reverence opens up in us a capacity to grow, to become more

---

4. I discuss "fear of the Lord" in detail in *Christ Plays in Ten Thousand Places* (Grand Rapids: Eerdmans, 2005), pp. 39-44.

5. Markus Barth, *Ephesians 4–6*, The Anchor Bible, vol. 34A (Garden City, NY: Doubleday, 1974), pp. 608, 662-68.

than we are — to mature. Fear of the Lord opens our spirits, our souls, to become what we are not yet. Lacking it, we are stuck at whatever level of knowledge or behavior or insight that we have reached at the time.

Without a cultivated fear, "out of reverence for Christ," we inevitably develop habits of irreverence and are liable to the pandemic "nothing but" disease. A fetus is nothing but a sack of protoplasm. A horse is nothing but power to pull a plow. A Rembrandt is nothing but daubs of paint on canvas. A child is nothing but a nuisance. A woman is nothing but a pretty face. A meal is nothing but a puddle of vitamins and calories on a plate. A man is nothing but a meal ticket.

Or, in the settings of household and workplace, out of which all the mystery has long ago leaked out, the wife is nothing but "the little woman," the husband is nothing but "my man," the owner is nothing but "the boss," the worker is nothing but "the help." Words without intimacy. Words without human content, only role or function.

Here is a detail I find interesting. In chapter four, as Paul writes about the church as a body of which Christ is the head and of which we are the parts, he describes it anatomically as a "whole body, joined and knit together by every ligament with which it is equipped as each part is working properly, [that] promotes the body's growth in building itself up in love" (Eph. 4:16). A few sentences earlier he had told us that the Holy Spirit brings gifts into our lives "to equip the saints for the work of ministry" (4:12).

The word "equip," *kartartismos*, occurs only here in the New Testament. It is a medical term. The venerable Greek physician Galen used it of setting a dislocated joint. It is derived from the verb *kartartidzo*, which occurs several times in the New Testament in various contexts: to mend or repair nets (Matt. 4:21), to make fit, to become qualified for your task (Luke 6:40), to frame the pre-creation chaos into a working cosmos (Heb. 11:3) — all variations on restoring or creating the condition of wellness or wholeness (*artios*).[6]

---

6. T. K. Abbott, *The Epistles to the Ephesians and to the Colossians: A Critical and Exegetical Commentary* (Edinburgh: T. & T. Clark, 1897), p. 119.

A body is held together by its joints. If what is "joined and knit to-gether by every ligament" (4:16) is "out of joint," or stiff with arthritic stubbornness, or swollen with hubris, the body does not function as intended. Paul names eight major "joints" in the body of Christ, six in the home (wives, husbands, fathers, mothers, children, parents), and two in the workplace (slaves and masters, corresponding to workers and employers in our workplaces). In the body of Christ, it is the joints between family members and fellow workers that keep the body func-tioning, in good repair, "fit" to live "to the praise of his glory." If the joints between family members or workers on the job are not func-tioning, if there is no suppleness in the joints making for easy coordi-nation, the body is not "fit" because the parts do not fit.

$$* \quad * \quad *$$

Of the several relationships that Paul names in household and work-place, it is the marriage of husband and wife that he deals with most extensively. No other relation that we enter into is more complex and difficult and demanding, or more fulfilling and pleasurable and satisfy-ing. Similarities between marriage and church are extensive. Paul makes the most of them as he simultaneously draws us into the ways we understand and participate in both marriage and church.

Marriage and church are both composed of relationships that are a bold assault on the individualism in both society and church — the *sin* of individualism, the sin of wanting to have my own way with God, my own way with my spouse, my own way with my children. If matu-rity, growing up in Christ, insists above all on relationships — relation-ships of trust and adoration with God, relationships of righteousness and love with one another — observing and meditating on what takes place in marriage is an excellent way to acquire the insights and de-velop the habits of heart that parallel what takes place in church.

Robert Frost wrote a poem on marriage with a striking image that has always seemed to me to be as much about church as about marriage. He wrote the poem in celebration of his daughter's mar-riage. The poem observes that the intimacy of marriage provides a

freedom not "chiefly to go where you will" but a different kind of freedom, a "swiftness, not for haste," but rather to live together in graceful,
unforced, rhythmic coordination: "wing to wing and oar to oar."[7]

Intimate relationships within the husband-and-wife "one body"
of marriage are not static but dynamic, in constant, swift, and moving
mutuality: "wing to wing and oar to oar." Intimate relationships within
the head-and-members "one body" of church are not static but dynamic, in constant, swift, and moving mutuality: "wing to wing and
oar to oar."

\*     \*     \*

Paul is obviously interested in marriage as a primary life setting in
which the Holy Spirit brings the love and righteousness, the love and
singing, the ways we talk and the ways we forgive into the practice of
resurrection. He gives thorough attention to it. He knows both how
central and complex it is and how demanding and difficult. Margaret
Miles, in a rigorous discussion that insists on the fundamental ascetic
provided by family and marriage for an embodied, not just a concep-
tual, maturity in Christ, posts the witness of Clement of Alexandria,
who "regarded marriage as a strenuous spiritual discipline; he saw the
celibate life as luxurious by comparison with the demands of life in the
world, the cares of a home, and the responsibilities of raising children."[8]

But Paul, with marriage as background, is even more interested in
church as *the* primary life setting in which the Holy Spirit brings all the
operations of God to maturity in us. Five times in this section (Eph.
5:22-32) Paul pairs church and marriage in various ways, but his last
word is church: "This mystery [marriage] is a profound one, and I am
saying that it refers to Christ and the church" (5:32 RSV). Marriage is a
mystery, how a husband and wife can "be subject to one another out of
reverence for Christ," experiencing marriage as a way to mature in love

7. Robert Frost, "The Master Speed," *The Poetry of Robert Frost* (New York: Holt,
Rinehart and Winston, 1969), p. 300.

8. Margaret Miles, *Practicing Christianity* (New York: Crossroad, 1990), p. 99.

and holiness. But comparatively, church is a greater mystery as a way to maturity in a life of love and holiness — Christ the head and Christians the body, "wing to wing and oar to oar."

## Between

Most of what the church is, we don't see: all the operations of the Trinity in the ways of Father, Son, and Holy Spirit. Neither do we see the "heavenly places" or "the seal of the promised Holy Spirit." And no one has yet succeeded in taking a photograph of "all things under his feet," or the broken down "dividing wall."

At the very same time, though, simultaneous with all this "not seeing," without even trying, without the aid of microscope or telescope, we see a great deal when we look at church. We see men, women, and children being baptized; neighbors whose names we know eating and drinking the body and blood of Christ in the Lord's Supper; friends who three days ago shared a picnic supper at an open-air concert now listening to the reading and preaching of the Scriptures. We see a man praying — we assume he is praying, his head is bowed — who only last week repaired the crumpled fender of my car, and just over there the woman who diagnosed my cancer and arranged for radiation a little over a year ago, playing the organ.

In matters of church, nothing of what we see apart from what we don't see is church. And nothing of what we don't see apart from what we see is church. There is no invisible church. There is no visible church. Invisibility and visibility coinhere in church. There is no church without God, whom "no man has seen . . . at any time" (John 1:18 NAS). There is no church without the "great multitude that no one could count, from every nation, from all tribes and peoples and languages" (Rev. 7:9) that we can see.

Church is a staging ground for what takes place *between* heaven (invisible) and earth (visible).

\*　　\*　　\*

"Between" is a word that I have found to be essential for understanding church. I didn't find it on my own; Martin Buber gave it to me. Buber was a German Jew who spent his life writing and teaching on how to live life whole and holy in the specific conditions posed by the times we live in. He was very much involved in all the visibilities reported in the newspapers of his day: the stuff of politics, economics, and war; Nazi concentration camps and the furnaces that murdered six million of his fellow Jews; the Zionist movement that doggedly worked to find a homeland for displaced and marginalized Jews. Forced to leave Germany, he migrated to Palestine in 1938. He participated in the formation of the new nation of Israel and became a professor at its newly formed university.

I mention all of this — his deep and complex involvement in massive public and social events that radically changed the face of the world we live in — because he wrote a book in which he never said a word about the violently catastrophic events of his time, but, as it turned out, what he wrote had and continues to have everything to do with them. *I and Thou*[9] is a book about the invisible, something that cannot be seen, a relationship, a "between." The book made no headlines at the time he wrote it. For several years it was nearly as invisible as the invisibles about which he wrote.

The seed from which the book grew is God, as God named himself to Moses at the burning bush in Midian over three thousand years ago (Exod. 3:13-14). It became for many, and most certainly for me, a definitive book for recovering a biblical grounding in understanding the nature and significance of God's unseen presence in the middle of everything that goes on around us, an "everything" that at that time in Europe included at its very center the attempted extermination of the Jewish people and their God, followed by an unprecedented acceleration of a depersonalizing technology and communications industry. Enormous energy continues to issue from this book, energy that in the ninety years since its publication has not diminished.

9. Martin Buber, *I and Thou*, trans. Walter Kaufmann (New York: Charles Scribner's Sons, 1970 [first published in 1923 as *Ich und Du*]).

The book grew from a three-word sentence (in Hebrew), *ehyeh asher ehyeh*. When God spoke to Moses at the burning bush in Midian and Moses asked him for his name, the answer he got was not a name. A name is a noun. It identifies and locates, objectifies. What Moses heard from the bush was a verb: "I am. . . . I am just who I am. . . . I am here. . . . I am present." The verb in Hebrew is the basic verb for "to be" (*hayah*) spoken in the first person, "I am," and then repeated, "I am." *I AM WHO I AM.* "I am" — doubled. "*I am*" — most emphatically. I am present. I am Presence. The non-name "name" of God is vocalized in English as *Yahweh*. Buber translates, "I am there as whoever I am there." He then elaborates, "[I am] that which reveals. . . . [I am] that which has being here, nothing more. The eternal source of strength flows, the eternal touch is waiting, the eternal voice sounds, nothing more."[10]

We cannot make an object of God; God is not a thing to be named. We cannot turn God into an idea; God is not a concept to be discussed. We cannot use God for making or doing; God is not a power to be harnessed.

This sounds simple enough — and it is. But none of us finds it much to our liking. We have a long history in wanting to make God into our image and use him for our purposes. Moses, followed by a long succession of Hebrew prophets, did his best to free us from ideas or attitudes or practices that would prevent us from letting God be God for us on God's terms, not ours. Jesus is the final word on God.

But given our stubborn preference for having God on our terms, not God's terms, we need repeated refresher courses on Moses at the bush, on Elijah in the cave, on Isaiah in the temple. Martin Buber is a compelling witness in this extensive Hebrew prophetic tradition. *I and Thou* is a sustained, detailed, energetic recovery of God as God reveals himself: God not as thing or idea or power, but Presence to whom we can only be present.

\*     \*     \*

10. Buber, *I and Thou*, p. 160.

At the core of his book Buber developed a hyphenated vocabulary of three pairs of words: I-It, Them-Us, and I-You. None of these paired pronouns can be split in half and then understood in isolation, separated from its companion word. It can exist only in combination, in hyphenation. The paired words are basic to human relationships, but by extension they inevitably become God relationships.

I-It: This is the relationship that denies and then destroys relationship. I-It turns the other into an object, a thing. An It is a person depersonalized. The other is some *thing* to be experienced or used. The other is there for me to do with as I like. I do not listen to an It. I tell It what I want, what I think of It. I amuse myself with It as a novelty, an experience. I don't converse with an It. There is no mutuality between an I and an It — none. The I-It person does not know reciprocity. "When he says You he means: You, my ability to use!"[11]

Us-Them: the world is divided into two, the children of light and the children of darkness. This is a very convenient way to think about the world because whatever is wrong, it's obviously because of "them." Complexities vanish. Everything is suddenly tidy. There are goats and sheep, and the sheep by the very nature of things will triumph — didn't Jesus say so? Us-Them has always attracted demagogues, and the demagogues have attracted great crowds. This in effect demonizes everyone who doesn't think or feel along the lines of Us. Them can be a nation, religion, race, family, political party, or team.[12]

I-You: this is the basic word in an accurately lived life, a life lived in personal relationship. "I-You can be spoken only with one's whole being. The concentration and fusion into a whole being can never be accomplished by me, can never be accomplished without me. I require a You to become; becoming I, I say You. All actual life is encounter."[13]

There is no humanity without relationship. "In the beginning is

---

11. Buber, *I and Thou*, p. 109.

12. "Us-Them" is a gloss of the translator, Walter Kaufmann, on Buber's basic hyphenations. In his words, "There are many ways of living in a world without a You" (p. 14).

13. Buber, *I and Thou*, p. 62.

the relation."[14] Reciprocity is built into the very nature of all that is. A person "becomes an I through a You."[15]

The hyphens in I-It and Us-Them are marks of separation, isolation, and finally desolation. The hyphen in I-You marks a "between," a dynamic relation of spirit between persons.

I-It turns persons into things so that I can control or use or dismiss or ignore them. It is the basic word that is particularly attractive in buying and selling, but it infiltrates every sector of life. When it infiltrates our congregation, the men and women with whom we worship and work become objectified. Instead of being primarily persons whom we love, whether through natural affection (spouse, children, friends) or by Christ's command ("love your neighbor as yourself"), they gradually become functionalized. Under the pressure of "working for Jesus" or "carrying out the church's mission," we begin to treat our family members and fellow workers more like parts of a machine than parts of a body. We develop a vocabulary that treats men and women and children more like problems to be fixed or as resources to be used than as participants in a holy mystery. We develop an extensive I-It vocabulary to facilitate the depersonalization: "assets and liabilities," "point-man" or "-woman," "dysfunctional," "leadership material," "dead weight." Love, the commanded relation, gives way to considerations of efficiency interpreted by abstractions — plans and programs, goals and visions, evangelism statistics and mission strategies.

Us-Them turns others into the enemy. It is the basic word that demonizes others. It is prominent in military and religious wars, in political conflicts and ideological battles. It abolishes language as a way to tell the truth.

\*       \*       \*

We cannot live in isolation, disconnected, independent. Life is far too complex. The web of living is far too intricate. There is more to us than us.

14. Buber, *I and Thou*, p. 69.
15. Buber, *I and Thou*, p. 80.

Not that we don't try. We try to live with an "It-God," a God whom we can talk about all we want to but whom we never listen to as a You or address as You. We try to live by keeping our distance from others, including God. We try to live indifferently to the entire cosmos that provides the conditions for breathing and eating and drinking. We try to live without a church that keeps us in a place of obedient listening to the God who speaks, nourished by the life of Jesus as he gives himself to us in holy communion, receiving the gifts of his Spirit as he woos us into participation in his love and the community of his love.

Life exists only relationally. Everything is connected. God is God only relationally — Father, Son, and Holy Spirit. God creates only relationally. God exists only relationally. God gives only relationally. Church is a gathering of Christians under the conditions of God's relationality. Ephesians is an immersion in relationality.

We are conceived in an act of relationship, a conception followed by a nine-month apprenticeship of total intimacy in the womb. We are not ourselves by ourselves. We have our origin by means of a relationship between our parents. After coming out of the womb we find it easy going for a couple of years. We have all our needs cared for, food and warmth and affection. We are one with our mother at her breast. We are one with our father, riding on his shoulders. Our siblings entertain us, playing and laughing with us. But it isn't long before we begin to explore the illusions of making it on our own, of getting our own way, of imposing our will on another. The weeds of I-It grow over us. Sin-cracks begin to appear in the intimacies of I-You. Unchecked, the disintegration leaves us without a You. Paul calls it "dead through trespasses and sin" (Eph. 2:1).

It is a strange thing and truly sad: the first casualties among those who have set out on the way to maturity, equipped to "build up the body of Christ" (4:12), are the people closest to us.

*        *        *

The transition is silently insidious. We start out as participants in this rich heritage of church and feel called to something beyond and more

**245**

intense than simply "Christian" — we have *work* to do. We find ourselves in positions of leadership and responsibility for the church, going about making recruits, lining up allies, arguing the opposition into compliance, motivating the lethargic, and signing up participants to insure the success of a project or program designed for "the glory of God." But there is no God in it. Spouses and children recede into the background. God may theoretically take precedence over working companions (the "masters and slaves"). But the God whom we name has been de-godded into an It. Under the despotism of the proliferating It, the I continues to dream that it is in command, administering the programs, casting the visions, bringing in the kingdom.

Martin Buber is relentless. He shows how easy and common it is to treat both people and God as It instead of You. He also shows how awful it is, turning what God created as a human community, intended to be "subject to one another out of reverence for Christ," into a depersonalized wasteland of self-important roles and impersonally efficient functions. No matter how righteous the roles and functions, sacrilege has been committed.

## The Ark and the Tomb

Wayne Roosa, professor of art history at Bethel University in St. Paul, in a brilliant piece of art criticism, calls attention to Israel's Ark of the Covenant as a way of attending to "the Between of relationship."[16] His insights reinforce what is involved in the practice of resurrection.

The Ark, set at the heart of the wilderness Tabernacle, provided a visible focus for the worship of God. It was a rectangular, coffin-like box, 4 feet 2 inches long and 30 inches wide and high, covered with gold. The lid of the Ark was called the Mercy Seat. It was flanked on either end by cherubim with outstretched wings. But the Mercy Seat was

---

16. Wayne Roosa, "A Meditation on the Joint and Its Holy Ornaments," in *Books and Culture, A Christian Review* (Carol Stream, IL, Christianity Today International), January/February 2008, pp. 16-23.

not a seat at all. It was empty space, a void, defined by the angel wings as the presence of the enthroned God, Yahweh. Yahweh: "enthroned upon the cherubim" (Ps. 80:1). Yahweh: God who revealed himself to Moses as Presence, God who delivered his people from Egyptian slavery, God who spoke to his people in thunder from Sinai, God who fed them on quail and manna on their way through the wilderness to Canaan. Inside the Ark were the tablets containing The Ten Words, their charter of salvation.

The focus and function of the Ark was the empty space marked off by the cherubim — nothing to see, nothing to hear, nothing to handle. But it was not an incomplete emptiness, but rather an emptiness that is fullness, "the fullness of him who fills all in all" (Eph. 1:23): "I am that I am; I am here, present to you; and you are present to me." The "I am that I am" at the burning bush is filled out by Jesus in his seven-fold litany in St. John's Gospel of "I am's" that includes "I am the resurrection and the life"[17] — all the ways that Jesus is God *present* to us as a *between*. We cannot see a between; we cannot see a relationship. A relationship is an absence of *It* so that *You* can be given and received. There is plenty in this life to be talked about. There is plenty in this life to do. But when it comes to *living*, relationship is basic. Nothing said or heard, seen or done, but an act of mutuality, reciprocity, a *between*: I and You, You and I. Only participants need apply.

The space between the cherubim is an inaudibility, an invisibility: nothing to be conjured, nothing to be controlled or manipulated. It is a nothingness that holds a fullness. The void is not a vacuum. It is comprised of the most basic rarefied element, air: the Hebrew *ruach*, the Greek *pneuma*, the Latin *spiritus*, the German *Geist*. In English we have different words for it: breath, wind, the invisibility that makes life possible, that quite literally animates, gives life. In English when we speak of the medium of relationship we commonly use the word "spirit." But "spirit" in English has lost touch with its metaphorical root as the air

---

17. The complete list of seven: bread of life (John 6:35), light of the world (8:12), gate for the sheep (10:7), good shepherd (10:14), resurrection and the life (11:25), the way, the truth, and the life (14:6), the true vine (15:1).

we breathe and the wind that blows. We need reminding: spirit/air is the stuff from which words are made as air is formed by throat, larynx, teeth, tongue, lips, and lungs into words. You can't see air. You can't hear air. You can't reach out and touch air. But under certain conditions our senses can uniquely detect some things. When certain changes in atmospheric pressure take place, air moves and we can feel the breeze. We can contract our lungs and blow on our hand and verify the actuality of air. After a rain, if the temperature is right, certain chemical changes release the pungent aroma of ozone in the air. When the wind blows we can see the results in the movement of air that rustles trees, flies kites, and sails boats.

If we still need verification of the reality of the invisible air, all we have to do is hold our breath and quit breathing. Soon enough we will turn blue in the face and know with our entire bodies that there is no living without breathing, without air-ing. Without wind in our lungs we are dead.

Spirit — wind, air, breath — provides our most pervasive metaphor for life. Spirit is the invisibility that gives life to all that is visibility, the internal that animates all that is external, that without which nothing lives.

Spirit inhabits the unseen "Between," the condition in which relations take place, the invisibility that provides for reciprocity. The most characteristic element of our humanity, our capacity for relationship, takes place in the Between as spirit. You can't see a relationship. You can only see or participate in what takes place in the emptiness, the eternal, the unspeakable Depth demarcated by the wings of the cherubim.

Another term for the Between is "mystery." Mystery is beyond our control. An individual cannot create mystery. There is something beyond or other than what we can control or contribute. Paul named the relation between husband and wife a mystery, and then immediately reapplied it to Christ and the church (Eph. 5:32). In order to enter a mystery we have to submit, to be humble before what is other and more than us. The precondition for apprehending mystery is letting go, what the Germans name *Gelassenheit*, the relaxed passivity of receptivity.

248

\*     \*     \*

Spirit is God-in-relationship: relationship within himself as Father, Son, and Holy Spirit in unity, and relationship with us as he gives and we receive God. God is God only relationally. We can know and be with God only relationally. God does not present himself to us as an idea to be pondered. God does not present himself as an experience to be savored. God does not present himself as a power to be used. God presents himself to us only in relationship. If we choose to study God as we would study philosophy or astronomy, or set out to experience God as we would a safari in Africa, or use God to change the world for the better or change ourselves into saints, we will never know the first thing about God. God is only to be received in the mutuality in which he receives us. God does not thingify us, treat us as objects or resources or interesting pieces of humanity put on display in something like a church zoo so that visitors can stroll through and see "what God hath wrought." Neither do we thingify God, depersonalizing him into an idea or force or argument.

> God only reveals himself as I-You.
> We only know God as I-You.
> I only know you as I-You.
> You only know me as I-You.

The empty space in which that relation takes place, marked by the hyphen, is not empty at all, but full of Presence. Presence is not an object to be measured, not an idea to be discussed, not a resource to be used. It is relation, embrace, encounter: *between* I and You. Without an I, there cannot be a You. Without a You, there cannot be an I. Spirit is the unseen *between* where relationship is born and matures.

Take no one for granted, especially in household and workplace where it is easy to take people for granted. Say "You," not "Hey you."

\*     \*     \*

A friend suggested this to me: "Do you think that the empty tomb of the Resurrection is an echo of the empty Mercy Seat of the Ark? That the two angels 'in dazzling clothes' [Luke 24:4] who gave witness to the empty tomb as evidence of resurrection might be an allusion to the two cherubim marking the emptiness that is fullness at the Ark?"

I'd never thought of that before. I'm intrigued. I'm still thinking about it.

**CHAPTER 13**

# The Wiles of the Devil and the Armor of God: Ephesians 6:10-17

*Finally, be strong in the Lord and in the strength of his power. Put on the whole armor of God . . . stand against the wiles of the devil . . . pray in the Spirit. . . . Tychicus will tell you everything.*

EPHESIANS 6:10-11, 18, 21

*The devil's first trick is to convince us that he doesn't exist.*

BAUDELAIRE

Last words: Paul takes his leave, says his goodbyes. The tone is crisp, almost matter-of-fact. Given the seriousness of what is ahead for the Christian church — opposition and persecution, with the attending fallout dangers of discouragement and defection and martyrdom — the language is remarkably free of anything suggesting anxiety or panic. He doesn't raise his voice. There is no adrenaline-infused rhetoric like the kind used by military leaders — Scottish highlanders with bagpipes, the fife-and-drum corps of the American Revolution, army and navy bands — to rouse their troops for battle. Nothing like the locker-room pep talks that whip up enthusiasm to "give it your all!"

Baron Friedrich von Hugel, one of our wisest masters in guiding us into a persevering, lifelong obedience in following Jesus, often said that nothing is ever accomplished in a stampede: "stampedes and panics are of no earthly use."[1] Undisciplined energy is useless, or worse than useless. When the tactics of fear are used in Christian communities to motivate a life of trust in God and love of neighbor, habits of maturity never have a chance to develop. When the church reduces its preaching and teaching to punchy slogans and clichés, it abandons the richly nuanced intricacies that bring all the parts of our lives into a supple and grace-filled wholeness. Christians who let themselves be seduced into taking promised shortcuts of instant gratification that bypass the way of the Cross eventually find that the so-called gratifications turn into addictions, incapacitating them for mature relationships in household, workplace, and congregation.

Paul's last words steady us in the conditions and along the way upon which he has been leading us. There is nothing new to be said on the subject. But a succinct reminder is useful. His reminder consists of five items: affirming a stance of steadfastness, accurately naming the "enemy," maintaining a practiced readiness in the basics of living a life of "glory," and praying, mostly praying. A personal reference to Tychicus is a finishing touch.

## "Stand firm"

First of all, "stand." Paul repeats the word four times: "that you may be able to *stand*" (Eph. 6:11), "that you may be able to with*stand*," (v. 13), "having done everything, to *stand* firm" (v. 13), and "*stand* therefore" (v. 14). Steady now. Stand your ground. Stay on your feet. Don't let yourself get distracted. Don't check out every new offering or advertisement or program that comes down the pike. Stand firm.

Stand firm in this place of blessing that we now inhabit. What can we hope to add to the blessings of God that have been lavished on us?

1. Baron Friedrich von Hugel, *Selected Letters 1896-1924*, ed. Bernard Holland (New York: E. P. Dutton, 1933), p. 147.

Do we realize how unique this is and how refreshing it is to simply be blessed? And by *God* no less? In a world that confronts us with demands, criticism, misunderstanding, mistrust, manipulation, rivalry, getting and spending, lies and seductions, is there anything like this — sheer, unqualified blessing? Stand still and take it in.

Stand firm in the church that God has given us, this gift of a place and community where we have ready access to the revelation in the Scriptures and Jesus and companions in praise and suffering. We have a long way yet to go to adequately assimilate this revelation. This is a *living* word — keep listening. And continue to embrace this church with its profound gift of hospitality, where over and over and over again we are invited to the Table to eat and drink our Lord's life in the company of his friends. We are not used to this. To shopkeepers we are customers, to our physicians and counselors we are problems to be fixed. To the unscrupulous we are victims to be exploited. Otherwise, we are strangers to be avoided. Happily, there are many exceptions, but the protective, individualized, standoffish indifference that is widely cultivated in our society saps our spirits and leaves us lessened. Do you realize how rare this clear revelation and this standing hospitality of church are? Don't take this gift for granted. Make the most of it.

Stand firm in the Spirit. Spirit is God in relationship: by means of Spirit our spirits enter the relationship with God and with one another. God is Presence: by his Spirit our spirits are present to the Presence. Don't settle for anything secondhand, hand-me-downs. We are immersed in a world of gifts, Spirit-gifts. Our lives are made up of gifts, gifts given and received. A gift is always reciprocal — without receiving there is no gift, without giving there is no gift. A gift withheld is no gift. And until it is received a gift doesn't really become a gift. Grace is another word for this comprehensive and continuous interchange between all the operations of the Trinity in us, which we then practice with one another — the practice of resurrection.

But habits of sin corrode our capacity for living a relational life. Old sin-habits are daily reinforced by a world that wants to keep God at the margins and other people either walled out or on a leash, under our control. It is hard to get out of this swiftly moving stream so polluted by the dead fish of depersonalization. Remember the outreached hand that you grabbed? You were pulled out of the river choking and sputtering. You found your footing on solid ground and began breathing the clean air of spirit, of Spirit. It took you a while to find out what was going on: to receive rather than to possess; to give rather than to get; to look a person in the face and learn his or her name rather than treat people as non-persons — which is so much less trouble!

You found that you needed a lot of help. You still do. And here it is: this community of men and women you have joined in order to practice a relational life, a Spirited gift-life of receiving and giving, through worship and prayer and compassion. You have noticed by this time that many of them are not very good at it. That's not such a bad thing; otherwise you would be intimidated. But where else are you going to find companions who are willing to give it a try? Take your stand with these people in this Trinitarian constituted company.

*　　*　　*

The message to the Ephesians is a solid orientation for the entire Christian church in the conditions created by God in Christ through the Spirit for a life of growing to maturity in Christ. This is a dependable place to stand. This is solid ground. Conditions here are favorable to growing up to the "measure of the full stature of Christ." Stand firm.

We live in an advertisement culture in which new products are continuously presented to us. This is a culture of built-in obsolescence. Nothing is designed to last. In order to keep the economy healthy we are conditioned to respond to the latest as the best: a new car, the latest fashion in clothes, the breakthrough model of computer, the newly published best-selling novel, the just-discovered miracle diet. We have no sooner bought or tried one thing than we are off to the next. Quickly bored, we are easily diverted from whatever we have just purchased or the book that we have not quite finished or the church we joined two months ago. Highly skilled and lavishly budgeted attention-getters target us tirelessly. Every "latest" is overtaken by another "latest" in dizzying succession.

When this novelty mentality seeps into the church, we start looking for the latest in God, the latest in worship, the latest in teaching, the best preacher in town. Church shopping is epidemic in America. When religion as novelty spreads, maturity thins out. The well-established and much-verified fact is that following Jesus is not a consumer activity. Prayer is not a technique that can be learned as a skill; it can only be entered as a person-in-relation. Love cannot be improved with jewelry or an exotic cruise; it requires submission and sacrifice and reverence.

Paul has warned us that we are perpetuating our adolescence when we indulge in spiritual novelties: "We must no longer be children, tossed to and fro and blown about by every wind of doctrine. . . . *we must grow up*" (Eph. 4:14-15). Brace yourself. Keep your footing. Stand firm.

## "The wiles of the devil"

As followers of Jesus we live in a hostile country. We find ourselves, like Moses, aliens "in a strange land" (Exod. 18:3 KJV). But it is not always easy to locate or name the enemy. Paul acknowledges this: "our struggle is not against enemies of blood and flesh" (Eph. 6:12). So what are these bloodless, fleshless enemies? Ghosts? Not quite.

Paul hasn't said much about these unseen enemies so far. He used the terms "all rule and authority and power and dominion" (Eph. 1:21) in contrast to Jesus ruling in "the heavenly places" (1:20). He mentioned, almost as an aside, "the ruler of the power of the air" (2:2). He spoke of "the hostility between us" that was broken down by Jesus "through the cross" (2:14, 16). He warned against making "room for the devil" (4:27). He used the phrase "the days are evil" to account for the times in which we live (5:16).

Mostly, though, Paul has been giving us a thorough exposition of the centrality and overwhelming presence of God in this world, who created church as a way of providing witness and representation to his presence and called us to live "wing to wing and oar to oar" with him

— in who he is and what he does. In his last words to the Ephesians Paul is more pointed, more explicit, and more expansive about enemies. We are up "against the wiles of the devil . . . against the rulers, against the authorities, against the cosmic powers of this present darkness, against the spiritual forces of evil in the heavenly places" (6:11-12).

We have a long history as a people of God confronted and endangered by enemies. People who hate God express their enmity against God's people. The story of God's people Israel is peppered with named enemies, armored and armed with swords and javelins and chariots — Egypt most prominently. Psalm 83 provides a colorful and extensive litany of people who are *against* the people of God: "the tents of Edom" and the Ishmaelites, Moab and the Hagrites, Gebal and Ammon and Amalek, Philistia "with the inhabitants of Tyre," Assyria, "the children of Lot," Midian, Sisera and Jabin, Oreb and Zeeb, Zebah and Zalmunna (Ps. 83:6-11). Each of those names sparks the memory of war and violence.

But Paul's list of enemies is different in nature: rulers, authorities, cosmic powers, spiritual forces of evil (6:12). There are no names here that evoke stories. What are we dealing with? *Who* are we dealing with? "Evil" *(ponerias)*, the last word in Paul's list, is a variant of the same word used in the final petition in the Lord's Prayer, "deliver us from the evil one [*ponerou*]." What are we watching out for? What do we need deliverance from? We need deliverance from evil that doesn't look like evil, evil that we are not likely to recognize as evil.

There are a lot of things in this world that people do that are wrong and that *look* wrong. Paul has mentioned some of them: fornication, theft, hardness of heart, licentiousness, impurity, lusts, falsehood, evil talk, bitterness, anger, wrangling, slander, malice. He doesn't explain why they are wrong, he doesn't warn us about them, he simply tells us not to do them. They are easily identified. "No" is a complete sentence. The stone tablet commandments in the Mosaic Law name ten of them. Our ancestors posted seven "deadly" sins to provide clear signposts to guide our moral behavior. We more or less know where we stand in regard to these wrongs, these sins. When we commit these sins we can confess and repent, be absolved and forgiven. It is not simple and there are often complications and ramifications, but it is all out in the open. We have parents to guide us, pastors and priests to instruct and pray for us, laws to protect us from one another, punishments to deter criminal behavior, and a huge and complex justice establishment to keep wrongdoing under control: police and the military, judges and lawyers, security guards and surveillance systems, jail cells and prison bars.

There is no huge mystery about sins, most of them anyway. They can be named and dealt with appropriately. Not everything, of course, is black and white, but by and large we know what we are dealing with.

But there is far more that is wrong with the world than the sum total of what we name as sin and sins. There is evil that is impossible to pin on an individual or even a group of individuals. There is evil that rarely looks like evil. This evil has nothing to do with cartoon caricatures of pitchfork-wielding demons or sulphur-breathing dragons. A few years before writing this letter, Paul had warned the Corinthian Christians, two hundred miles west across the Aegean Sea from the Ephesians, not to be deceived by evil that has every appearance of being good. And not merely good but dazzlingly good: "Even Satan disguises himself as an angel of light" (2 Cor. 11:14).

Now with the Ephesians Paul prefaces his list of the enemies that we can't see or touch (not "blood and flesh") with the heading "wiles of the devil" (Eph. 6:11). Paul used the same word in 4:14, where it is translated "deceitful *scheming.*" The devil's *wiles;* deceitful *scheming.* There are enemies — enemies of God, enemies of the church, enemies of the people of God, enemies of every man, woman, and child that is following Jesus — enemies out there that you can't see, that don't have a form you can recognize and name as evil. Paul is calling us to be alert to the evil that, in fact, looks like the good.

There is a clue to the way evil enters surreptitiously into our lives in the word *wiles.* The *wiles* of the devil. The word in Greek is *methodias:* the methods, the *ways* that the devil does things. You can't see a method, a way — you see only what it accomplishes. If it efficiently brings about what you want, it is readily embraced. The evil is hidden within the way itself. If the end product is something we count as good, we are indifferent to the way. If the way we get people to buy something we want succeeds and they buy it, we don't notice that the way was a lie (propaganda). If the way we get someone to do something benefits society, we don't notice that the way is manipulative and depersonalizing. The evil of the way is concealed in the benefits of the achieved goal.

Compare this with Jesus, who tells us, "I am the way, the truth, and the life" (John 14:6). Jesus doesn't trick us into anything, doesn't scheme to get us to follow him. It is all one: way, truth, life. It is all of an organic whole: way and truth and life — all visible, personal, out in the open, *revealed*. Not so with the devil, where everything is abstract, impersonal, disguised as good — evil concealed in a method that you can't see.

*　　*　　*

The four items in Paul's listing, often summarized using the KJV translation "principalities and powers," are this kind of evil: evil that doesn't look like evil, evil that is disguised as light, evil that has all the appearance of good but silently and invisibly destroys people's lives. We don't know exactly what the "powers" consist of, their essence. We recognize the evil only through its functions — dehumanizing, death-dealing, alienating. Where do we look for this faceless, bloodless, difficult-to-detect evil?

Markus Barth articulates the consensus of the church when he directs us to look for the principalities and powers in "those institutions and structures by which earthly matters and invisible realms are administered."[2] Because of the anonymity they provide to the people who work in them and the opportunities they offer to exercise impersonal power, institutions provide a ready breeding ground for evil. It is not as if the institutions are evil in themselves, but they provide a cover for the "spiritual forces of evil." Human complicity is involved here

---

2. Markus Barth, *Ephesians 1–3*, The Anchor Bible, vol. 34 (Garden City, NY: Doubleday, 1974), p. 174.

and there but rarely everywhere, yet it is dispersed throughout the structure long before its cumulative effects are eventually, if ever, recognized as evil. The larger the institution and the more public relations care is taken to maintain its reputation for good (running the country, making money, administering justice, organizing religion, caring for the sick, etc.), the more hidden the evil and the more difficult to detect and do something about it.

The scholar in the Christian church who has given the most searching thought and analysis to the way institutions provide an anonymous home base for this kind of evil is Jacques Ellul, a French sociologist.[3] Most of the people, sometimes all, involved in these institutions have no idea of the accumulation and dispersion of evil going on in their workplace. How could they? The evil is masked by what is good. Ellul's many books give us a comprehensive study of the powers and the way the powers insidiously make themselves at home in institutions established for good and then use the institution as a cover for evil. Because of the good intentions at the foundation of the institution and the ongoing benefits that society experiences from them, the evil goes mostly undetected — at least until Ellul and some like-minded others come on the scene.

Ellul is a good detective. He pays especially close attention to ways in which money, language, and technology, all good things in themselves, without anyone noticing can become evil when institutionalized in businesses, governments, the media, schools, churches, and other social, political, and cultural structures. The basic good of money is idolized into the god Mammon; the basic good of language is debased into the lies of propaganda; the basic good of technology is depersonalized into a world of non-relationship.

William Stringfellow, a lawyer who got his start working with the poor in a mission in East Harlem, picked up on Ellul's insights and developed them in the American context: "there is unleashed

---

3. Ellul's earliest of many books and basic to all that followed is *The Presence of the Kingdom*, trans. Olive Wyon (Colorado Springs: Helmers and Howard, 1989 [first published as *Presence au Monde Moderne* in 1948 by Editions Roulet]).

among the principalities in this society a ruthless, self-proliferating, all-consuming institutional process which assaults, dispirits, defeats, and destroys human life."[4]

## "The whole armor of God"

So — the world is dangerous. We are in peril of our lives. This life of practicing resurrection is seriously threatened. Growing up in Christ is under attack. Who and where is the enemy? We find ourselves slogging through a quagmire of the devil's wiles, his hard-to-detect deceit. What do we do? The obvious responses fall into one of two categories: we sink into a quicksand of paranoia, live in panic, never sure of where the evil is coming from or how it will show itself, doing everything we can to keep the evil at a distance; or we join forces with demagogues, moralists, and defenders of purity, we vilify, mount crusades, define ourselves by what we are against, and live lives of negative spirituality. There are, of course, a great many who don't join up with either side but get along as best they can in a kind of flaccid complacency, inoffensive Laodicean lukewarmness.

But there is another way: to live neither on the defensive nor on the offensive, but to take our stand as Christians, acting and believing out of who we are in Christ, neither in panic before the enemy nor in a crusade against it. This is the way Paul lays out in Ephesians. We are called to realize and cultivate our unique identity as men and women living under the lordship of Christ in the household of God that is the church; we are witnesses to a unique and revealed way of life in the practice of resurrection — resurrection not as an abstract doctrine or "truth," not as a strategy or program, but as personally incarnate in Jesus and now in us.

Paul gives us a representative sampling of what this life consists of — six items: truth, righteousness, peace, faith, salvation, and word

---

4. William Stringfellow, *An Ethic for Christians and Other Aliens in a Strange Land* (Waco, TX: Word Books, 1973), p. 93.

of God. In contrast to "the wiles of the devil" none of these six items is a way to *do* anything. They do not add up to a plan or program. None of them can be done on our own, autonomously. They are gifts and can be maintained as gifts only in acts of giving. They can exist only by becoming incarnate in human beings with other human beings in acts of living — *being*. None is impersonal. We don't look up the meaning of these words in a dictionary. They are not spiritual skills that we perfect. We have a whole book of stories that give flesh-and-blood content to these six terms in the lives of Abraham, Isaac, Jacob, Joseph, Moses, Joshua, Samuel and David, Elijah and Elisha, Isaiah and Amos, Jeremiah and Habakkuk, Ezra and Nehemiah, Mary and Elizabeth, John the Baptist and Simeon, Peter and James and John, Paul and Barnabas. Putting them all together, we find the six words incarnate in Jesus, who is "the way, the truth, and the life" (John 14:6), who gave "his life as a ransom for many" (Matt. 20:28 RSV).

\*     \*     \*

By linking each of these terms with an item of military ordinance, Paul reinforces our sense of danger. This is entirely biblical. The Revelation of John is our most comprehensive picture of the apocalyptic dimensions in which we are involved — in which *God* is involved! — in dealing with sin and evil: the enmity set between the serpent and the woman (Gen. 3:15), and the war that broke out in heaven (Rev. 12:7). The labeling of each of the six aspects of the practice of resurrection with an item of armor helps us realize that this life in Christ is not made up of passive qualities; rather, each one forms a field of participation in Christ's work of redemption. The words are not job descriptions from which we improvise a strategy and then implement the best we can. We *are* the weapons. *Who we are* takes precedence over what we do.

Jacques Ellul insists that this resurrection life must be lived in this world, but at the same time he insists that the Christian "must not act in exactly the same way as everyone else. He has a part to play in this world which no one else can possibly fulfill." This function is defined in three ways (I am abbreviating and paraphrasing Ellul):

1. You are the salt of the earth (Matt 5:13).
2. You are the light of the world (Matt. 5:14).
3. I send you forth as sheep in the midst of wolves (Matt. 10:16).

*Salt of the earth* is a precise reference to Leviticus 2:13, where we are told that salt is a sign of the covenant between God and Israel. What Jesus is saying, then, is that the Christian is a visible sign of the new covenant in Jesus Christ. So it is essential that Christians should really *be* this sign, allow this covenant to be seen by others. Otherwise, how will the others know where they and the world are going?

*The light of the world* eliminates darkness, separates life from death, gives meaning and direction to history. This is supplied by the presence of the church. The Christian is a witness to the salvation of which he or she is representative.

*Like sheep in the midst of wolves.* Jesus Christ is the Lamb of God who takes away the sins of the world. But all Christians are treated like their Master. They are sheep not because their action or sacrifice has a purifying effect on the world. "In the world everyone wants to be a 'wolf,' and no one is called to play the part of a 'sheep.' Yet the world cannot *live* without this living witness of sacrifice. That is why Christians should be very careful not to be 'wolves' — that is, people who try to dominate others."[5]

Marva Dawn continues to carry on this prophetic penetration of contemporary American culture (including our church culture) in a torrent of lectures, sermons, and books. She is one of our most invaluable and discerning witnesses in exposing the "wiles of the devil." She is especially useful and timely in elaborating Ellul's interpretation of Jesus' "sheep," and then demonstrating what she names as "the tabernacling of God and a theology of weakness."[6]

✳   ✳   ✳

---

5. Ellul, *The Presence of the Kingdom*, pp. 8-11.
6. Marva J. Dawn, *Powers, Weakness, and the Tabernacling of God* (Grand Rapids: Eerdmans, 2001), pp. 35-71.

The six military metaphors in Ephesians 6:10-20 — belt, breastplate, shoes, shield, helmet, sword — sharpen the sense of danger, heighten the apocalyptic urgency involved in the battle between light and darkness, God and the Evil One. This is serious war, war in heaven. The hosts of Yahweh and every last "Christian soldier" are called into battle. The metaphors make sure that we never for a moment forget that it is a *battle*, requiring our full participation.

But Paul's metaphors at the same time make sure that we do not interpret them as exterior to us, something we can put on and take off, something we can do or not do. G. K. Chesterton accurately observed that Christians, in relation to all that is wrong around us, are either crustaceans or vertebrates. Crustaceans have their skeletons on the outside; vertebrates have their skeletons on the inside. Crustaceans are solid on the outside, soft on the inside. Vertebrates are soft and vulnerable on the outside, solid on the inside. It is not difficult to recognize which is the higher form of life, Christian crustacean or Christian vertebrate. The armor of God is the embodiment, the internalization of the life of the Trinity — truth, righteousness, peace, faith, salvation, word of God — Christ in us, the hope of glory.

Armor is redefined in terms of who we are, not in what we do. And who are we? To start with, like the Lamb of God and the "sheep of his pasture" (which is us) we are non-domineering, non-combative. In the practice of resurrection the metaphors are totally de-militarized. The practice of resurrection is a thoroughly pacifist, but never passive, way of life. Violence, whether verbal or physical, is inadmissible. It is also, given the "whole counsel of God" (Acts 20:27 RSV), unthinkable. But far too many of us drag our feet for a long time on this. In a culture that romanticizes war and promotes it as a "crusade against evil," it is not easy to hear the clear word of God on this. Foot-dragging clearly is *not* standing against the "forces of evil."

The "armor of God" has nothing to do with killing or overcoming the opposition by force. If the weapons that we are given don't make us card-carrying pacifists, they at least post a severe prohibition against using combative language. With the armor of God internalized, we will not deepen our paranoia by either cowering in fear or demonizing the opposition. The six "weapons" are not weapons in any exterior sense. The practice of resurrection is a thoroughly non-violent way of life, neither defensive nor combative. Jesus did not use the "wiles of the devil" to defeat the devil. Neither can we. Evil cannot be overcome by calling in the intimidating principalities and powers as allies.

*　　*　　*

A major hurdle to get across before putting on the armor of God against "the wiles of the devil" — and having put it on, *keeping* it on — is that it often looks as if we are failing to gain ground, let alone post an outright victory. At the end of the day we look back and can't see that the weapons of truth, righteousness, peace, faith, salvation, and the word of God have made a particle of difference. If this keeps up for months or even years, we may lose patience and take up a weapon or two that does seem to make a difference. Propaganda, for instance, often gets results a lot quicker than truth or the word of God. Money makes things happen far more effectively than righteousness and salvation ever have. Technology is far more efficient in matters of communication and organization than patient love. Violence forces change right before our eyes while peace and praise and faith appear to be mere fantasy words born of wishful thinking.

At such times it is required that we re-enter God's revelation in our Scriptures and in Jesus and read contemplatively, that is, in a patient, slow, *listening* way, to what is going on and has been going on since the beginning of creation.

It is particularly useful to listen in a fresh way to the witness of wise men and women who have unflinchingly spent their lives immersed in the seemingly intractable complexities and difficulties of working to give visibility to the presence of the kingdom of God in "this present darkness" (Eph. 6:12).

Martin Buber bears the witness of wisdom. All through the inexorable secularizing of Europe and the horrible atrocities of the Holocaust, he maintained a faithful witness that kept the hope of his Hebrew ancestors present and articulate throughout the twentieth century and beyond: "True victories happen slowly and imperceptibly, but they have far-reaching effects. In the limelight, our faith that God is the Lord of history may sometimes appear ridiculous; but there is something secret in history that confirms our faith."[7]

And Herbert Butterfield, professor of modern history at Cambridge University, carefully studied and wrote of the ways the Christian faith gave presence to God's ways in our history. In the context of observing that the church has never been able to subdue the demons of violence and corruption and decadence in a head-on fight, he gives this blunt counsel: "Let us take the devil by the rear, and surprise him with a dose of those gentler virtues that will be poison to him. At least when the world is in extremities, the doctrine of love becomes the ultimate measure of our conduct."[8]

On American soil, Dorothy Day spent her life generously providing food and shelter to the poor. The terrible poverty that ravaged our country in the Great Depression galvanized her into a life of advocacy for the down-and-out in New York City. Her life and writings spawned Hospitality Houses in cities all over the country. Her journalism — rooted in firsthand participation on the streets and ghettos and slums and reported in the weekly paper she founded, *The Catholic Worker* — maintained a nonviolent, compassionate, intelligent, and courageous Christian witness through the worst of times. She worked her entire life in poverty and obscurity, actively opposed by government and much of public opinion, but through it all maintained a stubbornly practiced resurrection life among "the least of these my brethren" (Matt. 25:40).

## "Pray in the Spirit at all times"

The counsel to "put on the whole armor of God" and stand against the "forces of evil" is brought to a conclusion in a comprehensive admoni-

---

7. Martin Buber, *I and Thou*, trans. Walter Kaufmann (New York: Charles Scribner's Sons, 1970 [first published in 1923 as *Ich und Du*]), pp. 238-39.

8. Herbert Butterfield, *International Conflict in the Twentieth Century* (New York: Harper and Brothers, 1960), p. 98.

tion to pray. "Pray," along with its synonym, "supplication," is used as either a noun or a verb six times here.

Overall, Ephesians is a revelation of church as God's gift that provides us with conditions for growing up to maturity in Christ, who is the head of the church. The message opens with prayer that bursts off the page like an artesian spring (Eph. 1:1-23). Then the prayer goes underground, prayers like a subterranean river deep within the church keeping the aquifers filled. Midway, the waters again come briefly to the surface (3:14-21). But all through the letter we are aware that all the nouns and verbs, all the syntax and all the parts of speech, have been watered by artesian springs of prayer. This message that guides us in growing up in Christ in the company of church develops in a community of prayer. "All that the epistle has to say about faith and life is wrapped up in the form of prayer. It actually is said to God and to the Ephesians at the same time in solemn, dignified, devoted prayer."[9]

Now as the message moves to a conclusion, prayer surfaces again: "Pray in the Spirit at all times" (6:18). Prayer is not just "saying prayers," although it is also that. As we grow into maturity, prayer is the language that increasingly underlies and suffuses all of our language. Paul wrote to the Romans that when we pray, however spontaneously and briefly — "Abba! Father!" for instance — the Spirit of God is in that prayer (Rom. 8:15-16). And even when we don't know how to pray, and even when we don't know we *are* praying, the Spirit within us is praying, "with sighs too deep for words" (Rom. 8:26).

Not all prayers are conscious. Not all prayers can be identified as prayers. Prayer is the language underlying and sometimes surfacing in all our language as we grow up in Christ. Most of us pray a good deal more than we are aware that we are praying. It's not that prayer does not involve attentiveness and alertness to God; it's only that it doesn't require a learned skill. Trying harder doesn't help.

We are entering into a world of language in which the text is Scripture and church is the language school. But it does not always,

9. Markus Barth, *The Broken Wall* (Chicago: Judson Press, 1959), p. 29.

maybe even mostly, sound or appear or feel "religious." Prayer is the language most congruent with practicing resurrection. As in learning any language, keeping company with those who are using it provides the most congenial companionship for becoming proficient. Unself-consciously we acquire fluency in our mother tongue long before we enter a school, simply by being talked to and talking with our parents and siblings and the neighborhood children. When we keep company with Moses and his stories, David and his psalms, the preaching of Isaiah, our Lord himself in his parables and prayers, pastors and priests who lead us in the church's common worship, singing hymns with Wesley and Watts, we are praying and learning to pray even when we aren't aware of it.

\*     \*     \*

Prayer and "supplication for all the saints" (Eph. 6:18) keeps prayer from fuzzy generalities and excessive preoccupation with oneself. Not that generalities and self are inappropriate in prayer, but particular, named relationships keep us focused on the everyday ways that we practice resurrection: responsible and involved, acting in love, "tenderhearted, forgiving one another" (4:32). We are in a community, these baptized men and women, "the saints" whose names we know, brothers and sisters in Christ. Human relationships require alert and persevering maintenance. Begin with these saints, the people that in Christ you have most in common with, and *then* move outwards. That many of them don't behave or look the way we think saints should is no concern of ours. They are saints by virtue of the way God looks on and treats them. It is always easier to pray for people we don't know and don't have to deal with than for those in our own congregation and home. But we are not God's schoolmarms assigned to keep order, set standards, and enforce compliance. Our assignment is to practice resurrection with them. And prayer is the most personal and gospel way to do that.

\*     \*     \*

And then, twice, "pray also for me" (Eph. 6:19-20). Paul is no more self-sufficient than are the Ephesians. Paul is not at all reluctant to ask others for help. Many of us would much prefer to be in a position to only help others, to pray for them instead of asking them to pray for us. Asking for help is an admission that we are not adequate for the task at hand. Asking for help reveals weakness. It also exposes a failure to achieve the ideal, "I can do all things through [Christ] who strengthens me" (Phil. 4:13). But my sense is that Paul's "I can . . ." most probably is more like "we can. . . ." "Pray also for me. . . . Pray that I may. . . ."

Asking for prayer keeps us all on the same level. When we ask for prayer we are companions in the pilgrim life of church.

Asking for prayer also keeps prayer immediate, relationally personal, local, and honest. Of all forms of language, prayer is most vulnerable to cliché. A cliché is a word or phrase that can be literally both accurate and true, but the personal, relational meaning has leaked out. This is a huge irony. The language of prayer is the most personal, intimate way of speaking and listening to God and with our neighbors that we have, but also in some ways the most demanding, for it requires us to be present, attentive, *there*. When the words of prayer are removed from the personal (whether with God or with another person), there is no prayer. A cliché prayer is no prayer. The words mask a void. But this is less likely to take place when we expose our needs to others and ask, "Pray also for me."

\*      \*      \*

A good friend of mine was leaving his congregation for several months on a sabbatical. He had been the organizing pastor of these people, and relationships were very close, intricately intimate after nine years together. But the nine years had also been an intense and demanding nine years. The sabbatical would renew his strength. There was an elderly woman in the congregation who prayed with him each Sunday before worship and continued her prayers for him behind the scenes through the week. She would often send prayerful notes to him. On his last Sunday, after worship, as he prepared to leave for a ten-day retreat at a Benedictine monastery that would launch his sabbatical, she gave him a note that included this:

"Pastor, if you can't read this because of all the other things you need to do, that is fine. It just wasn't fine for me not to tell you that Sunday was a good day. Your sermon was really appropriate and you took the time to help everyone make the bridge between the first sermon and its follow-up. I didn't hear much of it because I was concentrating very hard on praying for you. I just wanted you to make it through the hour in a way that you could look back on and feel good about — and you did make it and I hope you feel good about it. I think everyone else does. Your candid remarks about how you were feeling were a genuine part of your endearment to everyone. We don't ever need to wonder what you were REALLY feeling — we know.

"Now, my son, go with God as He loves you and speaks to you alone or with the Benedictine brothers or with your beautiful family. I am expecting more than one life-changing experience throughout the next months. I am eager to meet the new Hans. We will all be praying for you, your family, and this church. God will be with all of us, all the way. My love. . . ."

Several months after his return, she died. Part of his remembrance of her in what he wrote in the church newsletter, remembering her to the congregation, was this excerpt from her letter, which he set in the context of Paul's "Pray also for me."

Every time we ask someone, "Pray also for me," the church becomes stronger and more mature. We grow.

## "Tychicus will tell you everything"

There is only one personal name in the Ephesian letter: Tychicus. It interests me that Tychicus is first mentioned in Acts in connection with Ephesus (Acts 20:4). Some years before he wrote this letter to the Ephesians, Paul had preached in Ephesus. His sermon set off a riot in the city. Paul and seven of his companions, one of whom was Tychicus, cleared out. They headed back across the Aegean Sea to Macedonia and eventually on to Jerusalem. Now, at the end of his life, Paul is a prisoner in Rome. Having written this Ephesian letter, probably his last, Paul sends it to Ephesus by the hand of Tychicus, who had shared that earlier Ephesian adventure.

It wasn't the first time that Tychicus had been sent by Paul to represent him; he is also cited in three other letters (Col. 4:7; 2 Tim. 4:12; and Tit. 3:12). We know nothing else about Tychicus, but his name here provides a personal touch, keeping us aware that what Paul has written comes out of years of living in communities of actual named men and women who are being formed by the Spirit into church congregations, who are worshiping and giving witness to this gospel life, this "kingdom of Christ" (Eph. 5:5) life, in named towns and cities in the first-century Roman empire.

One of the striking features of Paul's letters is the number of personal names that appear on the pages — eighty of them. Some of those eighty, like the name Tychicus, are repeated in more than one letter. Each of those eighty names links the message of the gospel to a particular man or woman growing up in Christ, practicing resurrection while working for a living, raising a family, dealing with whatever political and economic conditions impinged on his or her life. Every word written on these pages has been *lived* — not just written or preached or taught or discussed, but lived in real-world conditions with all the factors of those conditions at play.

Church is the gift of a community of Christians in which we rehearse and orient ourselves in the practice of resurrection. It is never an abstraction, never anonymous, never a problem to be fixed, never a romantic ideal to be fantasized. The rehearsal and orientation take place in various ways but never apart from conversations between God, who reveals himself in Jesus, and named men and women, Tychicus for a start.

"Tychicus will tell you everything." Paul intends his message to the Ephesians to be delivered and received in the context in which it was written, conversationally: "everything" that is going on with Paul, everything that is going on with the congregation in Rome, the ways in which political events in Rome are impinging on the congregation of believers, perhaps gossip and greetings from acquaintances and friends, stories of the journey.

There is more to the church than sermons and sacraments, theology and liturgy, Bible studies and prayer meetings, committee minutes and mission statements. There are names, meals, small talk, births, deaths. There is *us*. Conversation is the form that language takes when the persons of the Trinity and the persons of the congregation are in the same room. The "everything" that Tychicus will have to say to the Ephesians is no insignificant part of what it means to be the church. And you and I *are* Tychicus.

# APPENDIX

## *Some Writers on the Practice of Resurrection*

"The only sadness — not to be a saint" (Leon Bloy). This phrase has haunted me for most of my adult life. What the man who wrote it meant, I think, is that given the generous extravagance that is the gospel, the rich life that comes from following Jesus, and the companions available to us on the journey, to *not* embrace and enter into all this is such a waste. When we squander life on anything less than the God revealed in Jesus and made present in the Spirit, we miss out on life itself, resurrection life, the life of Jesus. When we segregate life into secular and sacred, we confine the so-called sacred into what happens on Sundays and in heaven. And when we do that, we are crippled, prevented from enjoying the glory of God that pulsates in the so-called secular. This accounts for the considerable sadness that lies like a blanket of smog over our world. But "saint" and "the holy" don't sell well in the American market. They are niche items.

Ephesians is a resurrection document. It trains us in understanding ourselves as saints, not saints in the sense of haloed exceptions to garden-variety Christians, but simply Christians who realize that Jesus' resurrection places us in a position to live robustly in the world of The Holy, growing up in Christ, practicing resurrection. The message of resurrection predominates throughout the letter, leaving no room for living as if, in the words of Markus Barth, "the Gospel were only for the next world, while the hard realities of greed, cheating, and impurity are all that is left for the present world."[1]

The Christian life was never intended to be a conventional, cautious, careful, tiptoeing-through-the-tulips way of life, avoiding moral mud puddles, staying out of trouble, and hopefully accumulating enough marks for good behavior to insure us a happy hereafter. And the church was never intended to be a subculture specializing in holiness, sanctification, or perfection. The Holy is not a specialist activity.

*　　*　　*

Voices keep arriving in every generation, waking us up to the life that has been provided for us — right here, right now, this resurrection life — echoing Paul's imperative to the Ephesians:

> Wake up from your sleep,
> Climb out of your coffins;
> Christ will show you the light!
>
> (5:14 *The Message*)

These voices are not the loudest voices. They are not the in-your-face voices. They are not after our vote. They are not trying to sell us anything. They don't promise solutions to our problems. They are not even trying to tell us anything new. They are simply witnesses to the practice of resurrection, to what is involved in growing up "to the measure of the full stature of Jesus Christ." Despite their non-assertive obscurity, there are more of them around than you might think. Their voices are often drowned out by the prevailing adolescent clamor and traffic noise that fill the air with sounds of "the only sadness." But an attentive ear, trained in listening for these witnesses in the practice of resurrection, will have no trouble picking them out. Here are seven writers who have confirmed for me so much of what is involved in

---

1. Markus Barth, *The Broken Wall* (Chicago: Judson Press, 1959), p. 60.

growing up in Christ, and over many years continue to be faithful companions in the practice of resurrection.

## Dante, *The Divine Comedy*

One of the persistent difficulties in becoming mature in Christ is thinking small. Most of us — all of us? — keep trying to fit the life of Christ into our lives. We resolve to "make room" for God. But more often than not we end up with a lot of religious clutter. Instead of becoming large, we find ourselves feeling claustrophobic. Dante's great poem — many believe he is our greatest Christian poet — brings us into a quite unimaginably large and comprehensive world of God and church, sin and salvation, the country I live in and the neighbors I have, hell and heaven. Nothing is left out; everything and everyone are included: politics and business, war and family, the famous and the ordinary — everything has to do with God, everyone has to do with everyone. We can't cramp God into our small lives. Dante fits us into the largeness of God, where we have room to grow up. It is also significant that Dante chose to use everyday, colloquial language to write his penetrating, soul-searching, society-discerning poem. He deliberately chose a diction in continuity with the street language of Jesus. The cultural elite of his day were mightily offended that he wrote in the language of blacksmiths and donkey drivers. This greatest and most cosmic of Christian poems places the practice of resurrection in the language in which we practice it. (There are many excellent translations. I grew up on the translation of Dorothy Sayers [New York: Basic Books, 1962].)

## Charles Williams, *The Descent of the Dove: A Short History of the Holy Spirit in the Church*

When I started reading Williams I was a sectarian Christian, "related" only to a small coterie of people who lived and thought and prayed like me. When I finished, I was part of a congregation centuries deep and continents wide. I started with a spirituality that was almost totally subjective; then I found myself in something large — creational and incarnational. It is not uncommon in the world of "church" to find oneself in tiresome conversations that turn into competitive arguments of the "true" church or the "best" church. Church gets narrowed down to matters of taste and preference as if church came in one of several models, like cars that you could choose by color and horsepower and gas mileage. Or church gets trivialized by polemics, children arguing and sometimes fighting with their friends over whose dad is biggest and strongest. Or church gets flattened into a one-generational, one-dimensional amnesiac incapable of awareness or interest in anything previous to the minutes of the last meeting.

Williams has no time for any of that. He is interested in what God the Holy Spirit has been doing in and through the church for two thousand years. Men and women, of course, are necessarily involved, but it is the Holy Spirit that keeps the whole operation together, keeps all these saints and sinners in a comprehensive and coherent body of Christ. (New York: Oxford University Press, 1939)

## Kathleen Norris, *The Quotidian Mysteries: Laundry, Liturgy, and "Women's Work"*

The devil specializes in providing anyone who will give him the time of day — he takes special delight in targeting Christians — with technicolor, wide-screen versions of what it means to live a full life. Lots of drama, adventure, glamour and size — most of all, Size. He tried it, most famously, on Jesus: "... all the kingdoms of the world and their splendor" (Matt. 4:8). Failing with Jesus, he has gone on to work his illusions on Jesus' followers. He has considerable more success with us. Meanwhile, we have a considerable number of witnesses in every generation who counter the devil's grandiosity and keep our ears close to the ground, our eyes on who or what is right before us, following Jesus in our own Galilees, practicing resurrection in our kitchens and backyards. Kathleen Norris, a poet in North Dakota, is a brilliant contemporary witness in this cultivation of mature simplicity in American life. (New York: Paulist Press, 1998)

## Frederick Buechner, *The Sacred Journey;*
## *Now and Then; Telling Secrets*

There is a shyness inherent in holiness that does not welcome direct attention. So how does one write or talk about a holy life without in the very process distorting or falsifying what you set out to render? Frederick Buechner has found a way. He is best known for his fiction that takes flawed and confused men and women and traces in them lines of grace that converge in a robust overflow of life, contagious and believable. But these three thin books of memoirs give it to us straight: honest, unpretentious accounts using the material of his own life — "listening to his life" is his way of putting it — as a Holy Spirit work in progress. All of us in some way or another, when we give our assent, are in the business of holy living, the practice of resurrection. But holy living must never be confused with niceness. A holy life isn't a matter of men and women being polite with God; it is a matter of humans who accept and enter into God's work of shaping a holy life out of the unlikely materials of our sin and ignorance, our ambition and waywardness — also our loves and aspirations and nobilities — but never smoothing over our rough edges. Holiness is not polish. Buechner has exquisitely provided the testimony and stories that make the holy life accessible and attractive. (San Francisco: Harper & Row, 1982; San Francisco: HarperSanFrancisco, 1991; San Francisco: HarperSanFrancisco, 1991)

## C. S. Lewis, *Till We Have Faces*

There are no shortcuts in growing up. The path to maturity is long and arduous. Hurry is no virtue. There is no secret formula squirreled away that will make it easier or quicker. But stories help. By means of story we are immersed in the intricate complexities of persons and places, sacrifice and trouble, failure and achievement, laughter and tears, to say nothing of the intricate simplicity of Father, Son, and Holy Spirit that word by word, day by day, gives form and beauty — the Genesis *good,* and *very good!* — to it all. But we must stay in the story as it is being told, give our consent, and not impatiently or angrily go off and improvise our own. The biblical story is our most comprehensive story for doing this. Other storytellers step in from time to time to help us find ourselves in the story. C. S. Lewis is one of our great storytellers. His Narnia Chronicles and Space Trilogy baptized our imaginations so that we could get a better grasp of what is involved in living the Christian life in our time and place. The last novel he wrote, *Till We Have Faces*, he thought was his best. I agree. But it is also the most difficult, the most demanding. The root of the difficulty is that it is about the most demanding of human tasks, becoming mature, growing up to the measure of the stature of Jesus Christ. (New York: Harcourt, Brace, 1957)

## Baron Friedrich von Hugel, *Letters from Baron Friedrich von Hugel to a Niece*

A layman, von Hugel was a spiritual director of great wisdom in the early decades of the twentieth century. He lived on a private income and gave a lifetime of attention to the life of the Spirit and to the spiritual lives of his contemporaries. There is a kind of German ponderousness in the way he writes, but I find him to be the most sane, balanced, and wise mind/spirit of my acquaintance. By sinking himself into the deeply lived truth of the centuries, he provided a mature center for many others in his counsel and writings. He was absolutely impervious to the fads and fashions in both culture and church that swirled around him like flies. Most of his spiritual direction was given in handwritten personal letters in any of several languages. So as we read them, we are always in touch with the actual stuff of life being lived out in an actual, named person. No great generalizations. No pompous "wisdom" from on high. As I read von Hugel, I am constantly aware that I am in the presence of a man who is primarily interested in *living* the Christian faith and living it well, not merely talking about it, not just arguing over it. (Chicago: H. Regnery, 1955)

## John Henry Newman, *Apologia Pro Vita Sua*

The brightest mind of nineteenth-century England was also a person of astonishing humility. By giving up just a little integrity, he could have been the most honored and lauded Christian of the century; as it was, he was mocked, vilified, and slighted — and hardly seemed to have noticed. Newman taught me never to expect applause or reward from either church or world for a life lived in pursuit of God.

Newman's life (1801-1890) spanned the nineteenth century, a century in which the Christian church was being assaulted from all sides. Many were convinced that it was a sinking ship. There was much panic, skepticism, and hand-wringing — and also considerable ho-hum complacency. Through it all, Newman kept his head. He made it his business to understand the church in its entirety, early and contemporary, inside and out, and to write what he understood so that others could understand it. His century was a century not unlike our own: many outsiders condescendingly dismissed the church as irrelevant; many insiders were muddled and uncertain about what it meant to be the church. Newman wrote in extraordinarily clean and accurate prose on what the church is and what it means to be in it. But what stands the test of time is not only what he wrote, but that he lived what he wrote — his life *(vita sua)*. (London: J. M. Dent and Sons; New York: E. P. Dutton, 1955)

\*　　　\*　　　\*

Newman wrote letters, sermons, histories, poems, theology, and novels — all of them expressing in one way or another the practice of resurrection. I want him to have the last word in this book — this prayer that he wrote, which is still sung as a hymn by the worshiping church.

> Lead, kindly Light, amid th' encircling gloom,
> Lead Thou me on;
> The night is dark, and I am far from home;
> Lead Thou me on:

Keep Thou my feet; I do not ask to see
The distant scene — one step enough for me.

I was not ever thus, nor prayed that Thou
Shouldst lead me on;
I loved to choose and see my path; but now
Lead Thou me on.
I loved the garish day, and, spite of fears,
Pride ruled my will: remember not past years.

So long Thy power hath blest me, sure it still
Will lead me on,
O'er moor and fen, o'er crag and torrent, till
The night is gone;
And with the morn those angel faces smile,
Which I have loved long since, and lost awhile.

Amen.

# Index of Names and Subjects

Blake, William, 12
*Bleak House* (Dickens), 227-29
"Blessed," 57-58
Blessing: Covenant blessing, 120; God "blessed," 57-58; Paul's introductory 201-word prayer, 53-68, 69-70, 147-48; prayer language of, 71-76
Bloy, Leon, 272
Boundaries, 59-60
Browning, Robert, 149-50
Bruner, F. Dale, 200
Buber, Martin, 241-46, 264-65
Buechner, Frederick, 53, 276
Butterfield, Herbert, 265

Calling: and the Bible, 33-34; and the church *(ekklesia)*, 170; living, 176-78; and paracletic life, 175-76; responding to, 32-34, 169-70; and vocation, 170
Chan, Simon, 119
Chesterton, G. K., 263
"Chose" (God's chosen), 58-59
Church: Americanization, 23-24, 118-19, 220, 255; as "a serious house on serious earth," 113-18; and baptism, 125-26; the building, 114-15, 127-28; the call and *ekklesia*, 170; and Christ (pairing of), 24-29, 131, 148-54, 237-38; and commodification of worship, 23-24, 220, 255; as context in which we grow up in Christ, 11, 113-18; dangers of participation in life of, 190-92; falling attendance, 115-16; as gift, 168-69; "glory in," 148-54; God-revealing vocabulary and prayer-saturated syntax, 163-65; God's creation of/presence in, 167-68; and God's manifold wisdom, 138, 141-46; and Holy Spirit, 11-12, 24-29; hospitality in, 127-28; as human/divine, 148-54; and inscape, 140-42, 146; as invisible/visible, 128, 163-64, 240-46; and love, 216, 220-21; and marriage, 238-40; metaphors, 20-24, 28, 35, 127-30, 134, 237-38; mis-

understandings, 13-14, 17, 20-24, 118-19, 123, 163-64; ontological, 118-27, 137, 142; and paracletic language, 171-76; Paul on what is happening in, 117-18; and people who do not measure up to "the full stature of Christ," 181-82; and the practice of resurrection, 12-14; preconditions of, 121; and prehistory of people of God in Israel, 130-31; recognizing the miracle of, 24-29; and relationship, 220-21, 238-40; and shadow work, 143-46; and "spirituality," 115-16, 151, 168; to "stand firm" in, 253; and worship, 220-22. *See also* Congregation
"Church Going" (Larkin), 115-17
Clement of Alexandria, 239
Colossae and Paul's letter to, 16
Common worship, 36-38, 217
Competition, 234-35
Congregation: "all the saints," 77; the Americanization of, 23-24; and "call," 170; and community, 134-37; Holy Spirit and formation of, 24-29; miracle of, 24-29; people who do not measure up to "the full stature of Christ," 181-82
Corinth and Paul's letter to, 16, 18, 47
Covenant blessing, 120
Creation: Genesis work week, 99-101, 102-3, 104; God's work of, 99-101; and grace, 102-3; preconditions of, 121

Dante Alighieri, 274
Dawn, Marva, 262
Day, Dorothy, 265
Demetrius, 15
Deometry, 177-78
Descent of the Dove, 25-26
"Destine," 59-61
Dickens, Charles, 227-29
Dickinson, Emily, 27
Didactic language (teaching), 171-72

# Index of Scripture References

**289**